LSAT Prep 2022-2023
3 LSAT Practice Tests and Review Book
[8th Edition]

Joshua Rueda

Written and edited by TPB Publishing.

TPB Publishing is not associated with or endorsed by any official testing organization. TPB Publishing is a publisher of unofficial educational products. All test and organization names are trademarks of their respective owners. Content in this book is included for utilitarian purposes only and does not constitute an endorsement by TPB Publishing of any particular point of view.

Interested in buying more than 10 copies of our product? Contact us about bulk discounts:
bulkorders@studyguideteam.com

ISBN 13: 9781637755501
ISBN 10: 1637755503

FREE Test Taking Tips Video/DVD Offer

To better serve you, we created videos covering test taking tips that we want to give you for FREE. **These videos cover world-class tips that will help you succeed on your test.**

We just ask that you send us feedback about this product. Please let us know what you thought about it—whether good, bad, or indifferent.

To get your **FREE videos**, you can use the QR code below or email freevideos@studyguideteam.com with "Free Videos" in the subject line and the following information in the body of the email:

   a. The title of your product

   b. Your product rating on a scale of 1-5, with 5 being the highest

   c. Your feedback about the product

If you have any questions or concerns, please don't hesitate to contact us at info@studyguideteam.com.

Thank you!

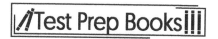

Table of Contents

//Test Prep Books

Quick Overview

As you draw closer to taking your exam, effective preparation becomes more and more important. Thankfully, you have this study guide to help you get ready. Use this guide to help keep your studying on track and refer to it often.

This study guide contains several key sections that will help you be successful on your exam. The guide contains tips for what you should do the night before and the day of the test. Also included are test-taking tips. Knowing the right information is not always enough. Many well-prepared test takers struggle with exams. These tips will help equip you to accurately read, assess, and answer test questions.

A large part of the guide is devoted to showing you what content to expect on the exam and to helping you better understand that content. In this guide are practice test questions so that you can see how well you have grasped the content. Then, answer explanations are provided so that you can understand why you missed certain questions.

Don't try to cram the night before you take your exam. This is not a wise strategy for a few reasons. First, your retention of the information will be low. Your time would be better used by reviewing information you already know rather than trying to learn a lot of new information. Second, you will likely become stressed as you try to gain a large amount of knowledge in a short amount of time. Third, you will be depriving yourself of sleep. So be sure to go to bed at a reasonable time the night before. Being well-rested helps you focus and remain calm.

Be sure to eat a substantial breakfast the morning of the exam. If you are taking the exam in the afternoon, be sure to have a good lunch as well. Being hungry is distracting and can make it difficult to focus. You have hopefully spent lots of time preparing for the exam. Don't let an empty stomach get in the way of success!

When travelling to the testing center, leave earlier than needed. That way, you have a buffer in case you experience any delays. This will help you remain calm and will keep you from missing your appointment time at the testing center.

Be sure to pace yourself during the exam. Don't try to rush through the exam. There is no need to risk performing poorly on the exam just so you can leave the testing center early. Allow yourself to use all of the allotted time if needed.

Remain positive while taking the exam even if you feel like you are performing poorly. Thinking about the content you should have mastered will not help you perform better on the exam.

Once the exam is complete, take some time to relax. Even if you feel that you need to take the exam again, you will be well served by some down time before you begin studying again. It's often easier to convince yourself to study if you know that it will come with a reward!

Test-Taking Strategies

1. Predicting the Answer

When you feel confident in your preparation for a multiple-choice test, try predicting the answer before reading the answer choices. This is especially useful on questions that test objective factual knowledge. By predicting the answer before reading the available choices, you eliminate the possibility that you will be distracted or led astray by an incorrect answer choice. You will feel more confident in your selection if you read the question, predict the answer, and then find your prediction among the answer choices. After using this strategy, be sure to still read all of the answer choices carefully and completely. If you feel unprepared, you should not attempt to predict the answers. This would be a waste of time and an opportunity for your mind to wander in the wrong direction.

2. Reading the Whole Question

Too often, test takers scan a multiple-choice question, recognize a few familiar words, and immediately jump to the answer choices. Test authors are aware of this common impatience, and they will sometimes prey upon it. For instance, a test author might subtly turn the question into a negative, or he or she might redirect the focus of the question right at the end. The only way to avoid falling into these traps is to read the entirety of the question carefully before reading the answer choices.

3. Looking for Wrong Answers

Long and complicated multiple-choice questions can be intimidating. One way to simplify a difficult multiple-choice question is to eliminate all of the answer choices that are clearly wrong. In most sets of answers, there will be at least one selection that can be dismissed right away. If the test is administered on paper, the test taker could draw a line through it to indicate that it may be ignored; otherwise, the test taker will have to perform this operation mentally or on scratch paper. In either case, once the obviously incorrect answers have been eliminated, the remaining choices may be considered. Sometimes identifying the clearly wrong answers will give the test taker some information about the correct answer. For instance, if one of the remaining answer choices is a direct opposite of one of the eliminated answer choices, it may well be the correct answer. The opposite of obviously wrong is obviously right! Of course, this is not always the case. Some answers are obviously incorrect simply because they are irrelevant to the question being asked. Still, identifying and eliminating some incorrect answer choices is a good way to simplify a multiple-choice question.

4. Don't Overanalyze

Anxious test takers often overanalyze questions. When you are nervous, your brain will often run wild, causing you to make associations and discover clues that don't actually exist. If you feel that this may be a problem for you, do whatever you can to slow down during the test. Try taking a deep breath or counting to ten. As you read and consider the question, restrict yourself to the particular words used by the author. Avoid thought tangents about what the author *really* meant, or what he or she was *trying* to say. The only things that matter on a multiple-choice test are the words that are actually in the question. You must avoid reading too much into a multiple-choice question, or supposing that the writer meant something other than what he or she wrote.

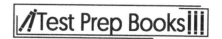

5. No Need for Panic

It is wise to learn as many strategies as possible before taking a multiple-choice test, but it is likely that you will come across a few questions for which you simply don't know the answer. In this situation, avoid panicking. Because most multiple-choice tests include dozens of questions, the relative value of a single wrong answer is small. As much as possible, you should compartmentalize each question on a multiple-choice test. In other words, you should not allow your feelings about one question to affect your success on the others. When you find a question that you either don't understand or don't know how to answer, just take a deep breath and do your best. Read the entire question slowly and carefully. Try rephrasing the question a couple of different ways. Then, read all of the answer choices carefully. After eliminating obviously wrong answers, make a selection and move on to the next question.

6. Confusing Answer Choices

When working on a difficult multiple-choice question, there may be a tendency to focus on the answer choices that are the easiest to understand. Many people, whether consciously or not, gravitate to the answer choices that require the least concentration, knowledge, and memory. This is a mistake. When you come across an answer choice that is confusing, you should give it extra attention. A question might be confusing because you do not know the subject matter to which it refers. If this is the case, don't eliminate the answer before you have affirmatively settled on another. When you come across an answer choice of this type, set it aside as you look at the remaining choices. If you can confidently assert that one of the other choices is correct, you can leave the confusing answer aside. Otherwise, you will need to take a moment to try to better understand the confusing answer choice. Rephrasing is one way to tease out the sense of a confusing answer choice.

7. Your First Instinct

Many people struggle with multiple-choice tests because they overthink the questions. If you have studied sufficiently for the test, you should be prepared to trust your first instinct once you have carefully and completely read the question and all of the answer choices. There is a great deal of research suggesting that the mind can come to the correct conclusion very quickly once it has obtained all of the relevant information. At times, it may seem to you as if your intuition is working faster even than your reasoning mind. This may in fact be true. The knowledge you obtain while studying may be retrieved from your subconscious before you have a chance to work out the associations that support it. Verify your instinct by working out the reasons that it should be trusted.

8. Key Words

Many test takers struggle with multiple-choice questions because they have poor reading comprehension skills. Quickly reading and understanding a multiple-choice question requires a mixture of skill and experience. To help with this, try jotting down a few key words and phrases on a piece of scrap paper. Doing this concentrates the process of reading and forces the mind to weigh the relative importance of the question's parts. In selecting words and phrases to write down, the test taker thinks about the question more deeply and carefully. This is especially true for multiple-choice questions that are preceded by a long prompt.

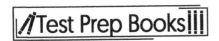

9. Subtle Negatives

One of the oldest tricks in the multiple-choice test writer's book is to subtly reverse the meaning of a question with a word like *not* or *except*. If you are not paying attention to each word in the question, you can easily be led astray by this trick. For instance, a common question format is, "Which of the following is...?" Obviously, if the question instead is, "Which of the following is not...?," then the answer will be quite different. Even worse, the test makers are aware of the potential for this mistake and will include one answer choice that would be correct if the question were not negated or reversed. A test taker who misses the reversal will find what he or she believes to be a correct answer and will be so confident that he or she will fail to reread the question and discover the original error. The only way to avoid this is to practice a wide variety of multiple-choice questions and to pay close attention to each and every word.

10. Reading Every Answer Choice

It may seem obvious, but you should always read every one of the answer choices! Too many test takers fall into the habit of scanning the question and assuming that they understand the question because they recognize a few key words. From there, they pick the first answer choice that answers the question they believe they have read. Test takers who read all of the answer choices might discover that one of the latter answer choices is actually *more* correct. Moreover, reading all of the answer choices can remind you of facts related to the question that can help you arrive at the correct answer. Sometimes, a misstatement or incorrect detail in one of the latter answer choices will trigger your memory of the subject and will enable you to find the right answer. Failing to read all of the answer choices is like not reading all of the items on a restaurant menu: you might miss out on the perfect choice.

11. Spot the Hedges

One of the keys to success on multiple-choice tests is paying close attention to every word. This is never truer than with words like almost, most, some, and sometimes. These words are called "hedges" because they indicate that a statement is not totally true or not true in every place and time. An absolute statement will contain no hedges, but in many subjects, the answers are not always straightforward or absolute. There are always exceptions to the rules in these subjects. For this reason, you should favor those multiple-choice questions that contain hedging language. The presence of qualifying words indicates that the author is taking special care with their words, which is certainly important when composing the right answer. After all, there are many ways to be wrong, but there is only one way to be right! For this reason, it is wise to avoid answers that are absolute when taking a multiple-choice test. An absolute answer is one that says things are either all one way or all another. They often include words like *every*, *always*, *best*, and *never*. If you are taking a multiple-choice test in a subject that doesn't lend itself to absolute answers, be on your guard if you see any of these words.

12. Long Answers

In many subject areas, the answers are not simple. As already mentioned, the right answer often requires hedges. Another common feature of the answers to a complex or subjective question are qualifying clauses, which are groups of words that subtly modify the meaning of the sentence. If the question or answer choice describes a rule to which there are exceptions or the subject matter is complicated, ambiguous, or confusing, the correct answer will require many words in order to be expressed clearly and accurately. In essence, you should not be deterred by answer choices that seem excessively long. Oftentimes, the author of the text will not be able to write the correct answer without

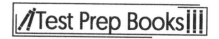

offering some qualifications and modifications. Your job is to read the answer choices thoroughly and completely and to select the one that most accurately and precisely answers the question.

13. Restating to Understand

Sometimes, a question on a multiple-choice test is difficult not because of what it asks but because of how it is written. If this is the case, restate the question or answer choice in different words. This process serves a couple of important purposes. First, it forces you to concentrate on the core of the question. In order to rephrase the question accurately, you have to understand it well. Rephrasing the question will concentrate your mind on the key words and ideas. Second, it will present the information to your mind in a fresh way. This process may trigger your memory and render some useful scrap of information picked up while studying.

14. True Statements

Sometimes an answer choice will be true in itself, but it does not answer the question. This is one of the main reasons why it is essential to read the question carefully and completely before proceeding to the answer choices. Too often, test takers skip ahead to the answer choices and look for true statements. Having found one of these, they are content to select it without reference to the question above. Obviously, this provides an easy way for test makers to play tricks. The savvy test taker will always read the entire question before turning to the answer choices. Then, having settled on a correct answer choice, he or she will refer to the original question and ensure that the selected answer is relevant. The mistake of choosing a correct-but-irrelevant answer choice is especially common on questions related to specific pieces of objective knowledge. A prepared test taker will have a wealth of factual knowledge at their disposal, and should not be careless in its application.

15. No Patterns

One of the more dangerous ideas that circulates about multiple-choice tests is that the correct answers tend to fall into patterns. These erroneous ideas range from a belief that B and C are the most common right answers, to the idea that an unprepared test-taker should answer "A-B-A-C-A-D-A-B-A." It cannot be emphasized enough that pattern-seeking of this type is exactly the WRONG way to approach a multiple-choice test. To begin with, it is highly unlikely that the test maker will plot the correct answers according to some predetermined pattern. The questions are scrambled and delivered in a random order. Furthermore, even if the test maker was following a pattern in the assignation of correct answers, there is no reason why the test taker would know which pattern he or she was using. Any attempt to discern a pattern in the answer choices is a waste of time and a distraction from the real work of taking the test. A test taker would be much better served by extra preparation before the test than by reliance on a pattern in the answers.

FREE Videos/DVD OFFER

Doing well on your exam requires both knowing the test content and understanding how to use that knowledge to do well on the test. We offer completely FREE test taking tip videos. **These videos cover world-class tips that you can use to succeed on your test.**

To get your **FREE videos**, you can use the QR code below or email freevideos@studyguideteam.com with "Free Videos" in the subject line and the following information in the body of the email:

> a. The title of your product
>
> b. Your product rating on a scale of 1-5, with 5 being the highest
>
> c. Your feedback about the product

If you have any questions or concerns, please don't hesitate to contact us at info@studyguideteam.com.

Thanks again!

Introduction to the LSAT

Function of the Test

The **Law School Admission Test** (LSAT) is a standardized test used as part of the admissions process for law schools in the United States, Canada, and certain other countries. Students' scores are rarely used for any purpose other than law school admission. Although there are unaccredited law schools that do not require the LSAT, and although the American Bar Association has recently loosened its previous requirement that all students seeking admission take the test, it remains true that the vast majority of students admitted to law school take the LSAT as part of the admissions process. Schools typically use an index in which the students' undergraduate GPA and LSAT scores are combined in order to analyze candidates' scores.

In 2015-16, 105,883 students took the LSAT. This total was up 4.1 percent from the previous year, but down substantially from the approximately 150,000 students who took the test in the mid-2000's. The number of students taking the exam is divided roughly evenly between the four annual testing dates.

Test Administration

The LSAT will be administered eight times during the 2021-2022 testing year. Hundreds of testing locations are available nationwide and around the world. It is also provided in an online format through June 2022.

The base fee for taking the test is $200, with additional fees for students requesting late registration, a test center change, hand scoring of their exam, or other services. If a student wishes to take a standalone LSAT writing test, the cost is $15.

The Law School Admission Council (LSAC) permits students to take the LSAT no more than three times in a single testing year and no more than five times in a five-year time period including the current and five past testing years. The LSAT can be taken a total of seven times in a student's lifetime. This is a new policy as of September 2019; therefore, tests taken previously to September 2019 will not count against these limits. LSAC does evaluate requests for exceptions based on extenuating circumstances on a case-by-case basis. LSAC also offers accommodations for test takers with documented disabilities and/or a history of previous accommodations on certain standardized postsecondary admissions tests.

Test Format

The LSAT is comprised of five thirty-five minute multiple-choice sections: a Reading Comprehension section, an Analytical Reasoning section, two Logical Reasoning sections, and an unscored or "variable" section used to test material for future exams. Test takers are not told which of the five sections they receive is the one that won't be scored.

The LSAT is currently offered in digital format and is taken on electronic tablets provided by the testing center. Students choose their answers by tapping on their selected answer choice on the screen. The new format allows for highlighting and flagging through the use of a touchscreen. Scratch paper and a pen will be provided for test takers to make notes during the test. Test takers may also use their own pencil and eraser during the test. The Digital LSAT has multiple-choice exam sections with similar structure and content to the traditional pen and paper exam.

Through June 2022, the LSAT is also being administered online and proctored remotely. Test takers will need a private room, computer, and equipment that meets LSAC requirements in order to take the exam online. Requirements can be found on the LSAC website (https://support.proctoru.com/hc/en-us/articles/115011772748-Equipment-Requirements).

The LSAT Writing test is not completed on the same day as the other sections but is completed on the test taker's own electronic device online using a secure testing platform at a time and place convenient to the test taker. The LSAT writing still uses a decision-prompt structure similar to that from the previous LSAT writing exams. Test takers are still given thirty-five minutes to complete their sample. The writing test is not scored, but copies of the sample produced are provided to all schools to which the student applies.

Scoring

The LSAT is scored based on the total number of questions answered correctly. There is no penalty for guessing or incorrect answers, and no section of the test is weighted more or less than any other. That raw score is then scaled to the standard LSAT score from 120 to 180 to account for differences in difficulty between test forms.

There is no set passing score, but admission to a given law school is typically very dependent on LSAT score. For instance, the typical LSAT score for a student admitted to a moderately competitive law school might be 145 or 150, while the most competitive schools typically admit students with LSAT scores of 165 or higher.

Recent/Future Developments

Beginning in July 2019, the LSAT transitioned to the Digital LSAT. All test takers in the United States will begin taking the Digital LSAT starting in September 2019. Changes were also made to the test-taking limit policy in September 2019.

Due to preventative measures related to COVID-19, the LSAT is also administered online and proctored remotely through June 2022.

Study Prep Plan for the LSAT Exam

1   **Schedule -** Use one of our study schedules below or come up with one of your own.

2   **Relax -** Test anxiety can hurt even the best students. There are many ways to reduce stress. Find the one that works best for you.

3   **Execute -** Once you have a good plan in place, be sure to stick to it.

One Week Study Schedule

Day 1	Logical Reasoning
Day 2	Common Question Types
Day 3	The Less Common Question Types
Day 4	Analytical Reasoning
Day 5	Reading Comprehension
Day 6	LSAT Practice Test #1
Day 7	Take Your Exam!

Two Week Study Schedule

Day 1	Logical Reasoning	Day 8	Basic Types of Analytical Reasoning Problems
Day 2	Irrelevant Information, Similar Language...	Day 9	Reading Comprehension
Day 3	Conditional Statements	Day 10	The Organization or Structure
Day 4	Common Question Types	Day 11	The Application of Information...
Day 5	New Information	Day 12	LSAT Practice Test #1
Day 6	The Less Common Question Types	Day 13	LSAT Practice Test #2
Day 7	Analytical Reasoning	Day 14	Take Your Exam!

One Month Study Schedule						
Day 1	Logical Reasoning	Day 11	Paradoxes	Day 21	The Purpose of Words or Phrases as Used in Context
Day 2	Tricks & Fallacies	Day 12	Parallel Reasoning	Day 22	The Organization or Structure
Day 3	Irrelevant Information, Similar Language, and Parallel Reasoning	Day 13	The Less Common Question Types	Day 23	Information or Ideas that can be Inferred
Day 4	Hasty Generalizations	Day 14	Must Be True & Deductions	Day 24	Principles that Function in the Selection
Day 5	Conditions	Day 15	Argument Proceeds By	Day 25	The Impact of New Information on Claims or Arguments in the Selection
Day 6	Reasonableness	Day 16	Analytical Reasoning	Day 26	LSAT Practice Test #1
Day 7	Common Question Types	Day 17	Reading the Setup	Day 27	Answer Explanations #1
Day 8	Inference	Day 18	Rule Busters	Day 28	LSAT Practice Test #2
Day 9	Assumptions	Day 19	Ordering Problems	Day 29	Answer Explanations #2
Day 10	New Information (Most Strengthens or Weakens Questions)	Day 20	Reading Comprehension	Day 30	Take Your Exam!

Logical Reasoning

The **Logical Reasoning** section consists of two, thirty-five-minute sections, each with between twenty-four and twenty-six questions. Every question contains its own argument and a question. The **argument** is sometimes referred to as a stimulus or question stem. For the purposes of this guide, it will be called the argument.

As with all of the other sections, there is no penalty for wrong answers; therefore, all questions should be answered. Complete the section in the allotted time, as opposed to completing it in a time crunch. The questions contain significantly less verbiage than the Reading Comprehension section and range from two to twelve lines of text.

Logical Reasoning is the single most important 20factor in determining the test taker's score. The test includes two of these sections and accounts for half of the final score. To achieve a high score on the LSAT, the test taker must perform well on Logical Reasoning.

Logical Reasoning is more heavily weighted because this section requires test takers to use their fledgling lawyer skills to analyze arguments. The Law School Admission Council does not mean arguments in the colloquial sense. For example, these arguments do not focus on the most prolific player in baseball or the best performance by a male lead in a movie. Instead, arguments are broken down into their basic elements—premises and conclusions.

Premises are the why, and **conclusions** are the what. Stated differently, premises are the evidence or facts supporting why the conclusion is logical and valid. The questions do not require evaluation of the factual accuracy of the arguments; instead, the questions evaluate the test taker's ability to assess an argument's logical strength. For example, John eats all red food. Apples are red. Therefore, John eats apples. This argument is logically sound, despite having no factual basis in reality. In the Logical Reasoning section, logic is imperative. Below is an example of a practice argument.

> Julie is an American track athlete. She's the star of the number one collegiate team in the country. Her times are consistently at the top of national rankings. Julie is extremely likely to represent the United States at the upcoming Olympics.

In this example, the conclusion, or the *what*, is that she will likely be on the American Olympic team. The author supports this conclusion with two premises. First, Julie is the star of an elite track team. Second, she runs some of the best times of the country. This is the *why* behind the conclusion. The following builds off this basic argument:

> Julie is an American track athlete. She's the star of the number one collegiate team in the country. Her times are consistently at the top of national rankings. Julie is extremely likely to represent the United States at the upcoming Olympics. Julie will continue to develop after the Olympic trials. She will be a frontrunner for the gold. Julie is likely to become a world-famous track star.

These additions to the argument make the conclusion different. Now, the conclusion is that Julie is likely to become a world-famous track star. The previous conclusion, Julie will likely be on the Olympic team, functions as a **sub-conclusion** in this argument. Like conclusions, premises must adequately support sub-conclusions. However, sub-conclusions function like premises, since sub-conclusions also support the overall conclusion.

Tips

Test day will be stressful; however, a well-reasoned and well-practiced test-day strategy will alleviate some of this stress and result in a higher final score. Coupling a proven strategy with attentive completion of practice questions will result in the greatest success. Applying a test-day strategy during practice time will make it second nature on the day of the test.

As with the Reading Comprehension section, it is strongly advised that the argument is read before the question. Skipping to the question is often more distracting and confusing than starting with the argument. The Logical Reasoning section is designed for completion within the allotted time; however, confusion could waste valuable time here, and that time might be critical to complete questions appearing later in the test. Remain consistent and practice the same strategy for all questions throughout the section. Do not arbitrarily alter the practiced strategy. Practicing the same approach will make it an engrained part of the test-day strategy and saves valuable time when assessing each question. Although the Logical Reasoning section is not intended to be a time crunch, efficient time management is still paramount.

Another suggestion for a successful test-day strategy is to *always* answer every question. The LSAT does not deduct for wrong answers; however, if time is close to running out, quickly select a guess answer for any unread questions and return to the question last read and continue taking the test. In addition, choose a letter to designate as the guess answer and be consistent. This keeps you from just choosing an answer that *looks* correct. When you just have time to guess and not actually read the questions and answer choices, make sure it's a true guess.

A similar strategy is to identify any areas of weakness. The twenty-four to twenty-six questions per section will mostly be comprised of predictable formulaic prompts. The different types of questions, including the most commonly tested questions, are discussed below. Start with the first question and work through to the end; however, if a question is difficult or confusing, skip it and return to it later. Circle questions in the test booklet and complete these last. If guessing or speed answering becomes necessary due to time, it is much more effective to guess on questions for which answers are likely unknown even if given more time. Additionally, saving the more difficult questions for last will save time. Nevertheless, it is strongly recommended that a strategy be followed when deciding which questions to skip. This strategy should not result in scouring the booklet for favorite questions and skipping over the rest. This method will prove counterproductive, since the time expended will almost certainly exceed any benefits accrued.

When reading the answer choices, always start with the first option. If it is obviously incorrect, then cross it out and remove it from consideration. If it is plausibly correct, then leave it and make a mental note of its logical strength. Use the first possible correct answer as a benchmark to evaluate the other choices relatively. If an answer choice is less strong, then strike it from consideration. A stronger answer choice should replace the benchmark until all of the choices have been reviewed. Once completed, the last remaining benchmark is the final answer.

Of the five answer choices, one or two should be easy to identify as incorrect even on the most difficult questions. Immediately remove these from consideration. Physically cross out the answer choices deemed incorrect to eliminate them.

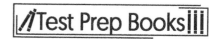

Be wary of answer choices containing information not included elsewhere in the question or prompt. The purpose of Logical Reasoning is to evaluate an argument's logical strength, rather than extrapolating it or exploring other applications. The vast majority of correct answers will not include any new information.

Similarly, the test developers will include answer choices that are exact opposites. These choices will directly contradict each other. For these questions, one of the two is likely the correct answer. Although this is not always the case, these answer choices should be given high priority. Evaluate the opposite answer choices first, and then use the best one as the benchmark for the other choices, as discussed above. Additionally, if a guess must be made to answer the question, quickly look to see if the answer choices include two opposites. If so, select one of the two as the guess answer.

Tricks & Fallacies

It is important to remember that the Law School Admission Council's job is to produce an exam of some predetermined difficulty. Naturally, this means that some questions will be more difficult than others. But it also means that answer choices will be intentionally misleading. The following contains some of the most common tricks that appear on every test. A table summarizing the tricks and logical fallacies is included at the end of this discussion.

Red Herring

A **red herring** is a logical fallacy in which irrelevant information is introduced to alter the argument's trajectory. Red herrings are the irrelevant information used to fallaciously and slyly divert the argument into an unrelated topic. This fallacy is common in thriller movies or television shows in which the audience is led to believe that a character is the villain or mastermind, while the true villain remains a secret. In terms of the Logical Reasoning section, red herrings will attempt to distract the reader with irrelevant information in either the question or answer choice. A red herring is sometimes referred to as a **straw man**, since this fallacy attacks a different argument than the one presented. Consider the following example of a red herring:

> The government must immediately issue tax cuts to strengthen the economy. A strong middle class is the backbone of a fully functional economy, and tax cuts will increase the discretionary spending necessary to support the middle class. After all, it's extremely important for our society to be open-minded and to limit racial discord.

On its face, the argument looks fine. The conclusion is obvious—the government needs to pass tax cuts to strengthen the economy. This is based on the premise that the cuts will increase discretionary spending, which will strengthen the middle class, and the economy will be stronger. However, the last sentence is a red herring. The argument does not address how a society should be open-minded and avoid racism; it holds no connection with the main thrust of the argument. In this scenario, look out for answer choices that address the red herring rather than the essential argument.

Red herrings will be extremely common in the answer choices. The test makers know that test takers are aware of sound logic and flawed reasoning, but they also know that test takers are working quickly to identify key words and phrases. As a result, the test makers will include many red herrings in the answer choices.

Extreme Language

The test makers commonly write appealing answer choices but take the language to such an unjustified extreme that it is rendered incorrect. The **extreme language** usually will take the argument too far.

An example of an argument appealing to the extreme is:

> Weight lifting breaks down muscles and rebuilds them. If one just kept exercising and never stopped, their body would deteriorate and eventually fall apart.

This argument is clearly illogical. The author correctly describes what weight lifting does to the body, but then takes the argument to an unjustified extreme. If someone continually lifted weights, their body would not deteriorate and fall apart due to the weights breaking down muscle. The weightlifter may eventually die from a heart attack or dehydration, but it would not be because of how weight lifting rebuilds muscle.

An example question is:

> All political analysts are eager to declare a winner on Election Day since the first report garners the most credit. This leads to some analysts jumping the gun and predicting outcomes inaccurately. The best analysts wait until they analyze all of the data and information before issuing predictive statements. The worst analysts prioritize speed over accuracy. Smith's Newswire employs many analysts who prioritize accuracy over speed; therefore, Smith's Newswire rarely wins the race to publish the results, but often provides the best coverage.

Given the statement above, which of the following must be true?
a. Smith's Newswire covers Election Day better than all of its competitors.
b. The author of the passage dislikes all news coverage.
c. The best analysts never break election results.
d. The worst analysts never report accurate information.
e. The author probably favors Smith's Newswire's approach.

Practice some of the tips mentioned earlier in this discussion. Start at the top, use the possible answers as benchmarks, and immediately dismiss the one or two wacky choices. Pay particular attention to how some of the choice's wording leads the argument into unjustified and unsupportable extremes.

Choice *A* seems possible. After all, Smith's Newswire does employ what the author describes as the defining characteristic of the best analysts. Additionally, Smith Newswire often provides the best coverage. However, it seems unclear whether Smith's coverage is better than *all* of their competition.

Choice *B* is clearly incorrect, and it should be eliminated from consideration. The passage directly pertains to news coverage, notes a common mistake in the field, and offers a description of the best coverage. The author is clearly interested in news coverage and very likely enjoys it. Furthermore, the word *all* is so extreme and patently false that the choice can be quickly eliminated. If nothing else, the author likes Smith's coverage so it's impossible to say he does not like news coverage. It can also be inferred that the author enjoys the news coverage that he describes as the best.

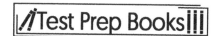

Choice *C* is also clearly incorrect and can be eliminated. The author says that the best analysts wait until they analyze all of the data and information before issuing predictive statements. The answer choice uses extreme language and says the best analysts never *break* the news. This is illogical. Waiting for all of the information before making predictions does not rule out the possibility of *some* of the best analysts receiving the information early and processing it first, allowing them to break news.

Choice *D* is clearly not the correct answer. The author describes the worst analysts as prioritizing speed over accuracy. This is not the same as saying that the worst analysts *never* report inaccurate information. It is clearly possible for someone to prioritize speed over accuracy and provide *some* accurate information.

Choice *E* is a great choice. The author describes what he believes to be the best analysts and states that Smith's employs some of the best analysts. Furthermore, the author explicitly says Smith's often has the best coverage. It seems clear he favors their approach. Use Choice *A* as the benchmark to evaluate the relative strength of Choice *E*; Choice *E* seems much stronger. Choice *E*'s language is less strong, so it only needs to be *probable* that he favors a news coverage strategy and organization. Choice *A* says that Smith's employs news analysts with the best characteristics, but it takes the extreme too far. The argument does not support the claim that Smith's bests *all* of their competition. There is no mention of other elite news organizations. In fact, the author uses limiting language while describing how Smith's *often* has the best coverage. This implies that some organization is providing better content during the other times. It is certainly possible for there to be *some* organization that reports news better than Smith's. Therefore, the correct answer is Choice *E*.

Irrelevant Information, Similar Language, and Parallel Reasoning

The test developers will usually include **irrelevant information** among the answer choices. Such choices can be persuasive but are actually unconnected to the argument's logic or context. **Similar language** will also be seen throughout the Logical Reasoning section. Answer choices will often have similar language, such as the exact same words or phrases, to trick the test taker into selecting it. Similarly, **parallel reasoning** will be used by the test makers to make otherwise illogical answer choices seem more credible by mimicking the argument's structure.

These three tricks will often be deployed simultaneously in the same group of answer choices to maximize confusion and difficulty. An argument that is similar to the previous argument, but with some alterations, is the following:

> All political analysts are eager to declare a winner during elections since the first report garners the most credit. This leads to some analysts jumping the gun and predicting outcomes inaccurately. The best analysts wait until they analyze all of the data and information before issuing predictive statements. The worst analysts prioritize speed over accuracy. Smith's Newswire employs many analysts who prioritize accuracy over speed; therefore, Smith's Newswire is a top-rated newsgathering organization.

Which of the following, if true, would most *strengthen* the argument?

a. Historically, news organizations always waited to verify information and sources, and the change is due to the advent of the Internet.

b. Jumping the gun is the worst mistake any analyst could make.

c. Smith's competition, Johnson's Newswire, prioritizes speed over accuracy, and it is the winner of the most awards and accolades for both speed and content.

d. Smith's competition, Johnson's Newswire, prioritizes accuracy over speed, and it is the winner of the most awards and accolades for both speed and content.

e. The worst sports analysts prioritize speed over accuracy when announcing trades and other roster moves.

In this type of question, break down the argument before determining how it could be strengthened. The argument is: the best analysts wait until they analyze all of the available information. Conversely, the worst analysts prioritize speed over accuracy. Smith's Newswire employs many analysts who prioritize accuracy over speed. Therefore, the conclusion is that Smith's is a top-rated newsgathering organization.

An answer that strengthens this argument in some way is the correct answer. Review the answer choices.

Choice *A* is an example of an irrelevant piece of information. This answer choice discusses the history of newsgathering and attributes industry changes to the Internet. The author does not touch on how this situation came into being, and the argument does not concern itself with why it has happened. Whether the Internet caused some analysts to become worse due to the importance of speed is irrelevant to the argument's point—the best news organizations carefully consider all of the information before jumping to conclusions. Additionally, the answer choice is tricky since it reaffirms what people believe to be true, which is that the Internet and related technological development has altered the media landscape. It is extremely important to ignore external knowledge on test day. As previously discussed, if an answer choice requires additional information or unjustified inferences to be logical, it is usually incorrect.

Choice *B* uses similar language as the argument but takes it to an unjustified extreme. The argument uses the same phrase *jumping the gun* and also discusses worst practices. Do not be fooled by such similar language. The argument never addresses whether focusing on speedy reporting is the worst possible mistake. Whether it is the worst type of mistake is irrelevant.

Choice *C* and Choice *D* use opposite language. As previously discussed, pay close attention to these answer choices. One is not always the correct answer, but it is more likely to be correct than the standard choice. Choice *C* is saying that a competitor consistently wins awards for speed and content while prioritizing speed over accuracy. This directly contradicts the argument's conclusion that accuracy leads to better newsgathering. Choice *D* strengthens the argument by introducing an example of an award-winning news organization that follows the author's preferred priorities. Choice *D* is a very strong answer.

Choice *E* deploys parallel reasoning by making the same argument for what constitutes poor newsgathering, but in the sports field. Although it could be connected to the argument with additional premises, those are missing in the available information. Here, the connection is too tenuous to strengthen the argument.

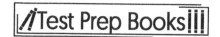

Therefore, Choice *D* is the correct answer. Often times, especially with the *strengthen* or *weaken* questions, there will be multiple answers that impact the argument in the same way but to different degrees. Be careful to always follow the instructions and choose the best of the good answers.

Appeals to Authority Fallacy

Arguing from authority occurs when an author uses an expert to justify his argument. Whether the appeal is fallacious depends on the status, authority, or expertise of the cited authority. If the authority cannot reasonably be relied upon, then the author is committing a logical fallacy.

Always keep in mind that **appealing to authority** can be valid or invalid argumentation. It all depends on the authority's credibility. The test developers will often include appeal to authority as a choice in questions involving flawed reasoning. Sometimes the author will appeal to a fully credible authority in an otherwise extremely flawed argument. Be careful of answer choices stating something the author actually does but does not do it in the way prescribed by the answer.

How is the credibility of a cited authority evaluated? Even on the more difficult questions, it should always be apparent whether the author is justifiable in their reliance on the authority. Indicators are listed below:

- Whatever expertise is stated in the field. The required qualifications will depend on the field, such as a PhD in chemistry or two decades experience as a senior bricklayer.

- Whether the claim being asserted by the qualified authority is actually within their field of expertise.

- Whether the majority of other similarly qualified experts agree, or if there is open disagreement on the subject.

- Whether the author is biased in some manner. On the test, bias will present itself by some obvious conflict.

- Whether the claimed field of expertise is legitimate.

- Whether the authority is identified. The author will sometimes preface the argument with phrases like, *experts say, a book stated, a documentary reported*, and *they say*. The unidentified authority is almost always a sign of fallacious argumentation.

Always ask yourself these questions when an argument cites an authority. They will help you determine if the authority is reliable and relevant to the argument at hand. If the authority can be trusted, this may lend weight to one of the answer choices. If, however, the authority is in question, this can divert you to a better option. Here's an example of a flawed argument from authority:

> Bill Gates is the preeminent mathematical and computer genius of his era. Bill Gates believes in our government making huge economic investments in the research of renewable energy. The government should obviously follow this advice.

The argument relates the genius of Bill Gates in math and computers. The author is hoping the inference is that math and computer genius translates to expertise in government fiscal and energy policy. The argument offers no support as to why the expertise would be applicable to this seemingly unrelated field. This is flawed reasoning. Although Bill Gates is an authority on computers, it does not mean that the government should follow his thoughts in an unrelated field.

Hasty Generalizations

A **hasty generalization** involves an argument relying on insufficient statistical data or inaccurately generalizing. One common generalization occurs when a group of individuals under observation have some quality or attribute that is asserted to be universal or true for a much larger number of people than actually documented. Here's an example of a hasty generalization:

> A man smokes a lot of cigarettes, but so did his grandfather. The grandfather smoked nearly two packs per day since his World War II service until he died at ninety years of age. Continuing to smoke cigarettes will clearly not impact the grandson's long-term health.

This argument is a hasty generalization because it assumes that one person's addiction and lack of consequences will naturally be reflected in a different individual. There is no reasonable justification for such extrapolation. It is common knowledge that any smoking is detrimental to everyone's health. The fact that the man's grandfather smoked two packs per day and lived a long life has no logical connection with the grandson engaging in similar behavior. The hasty generalization doesn't take into account other reasons behind the grandfather's longevity. Nor does the author offer evidence that might support the idea that the man would share a similar lifetime if he smokes. It might be different if the author stated that the man's family shares some genetic trait rendering them immune to the effects of tar and chemicals on the lungs. If this were in the argument, we would assume it as truth, like everything else in the Logical Reasoning section, and find the generalization to be valid rather than hasty. Of course, this is not the case in our example.

COMMON LOGICAL FALLACIES

Fallacy	Summary	Example
Red Herring	A red herring is a logical fallacy in which irrelevant information is introduced to alter the argument's trajectory and divert the argument into an unrelated topic.	The government must immediately issue tax cuts to strengthen the economy. A strong middle class is the backbone of a fully functional economy, and tax cuts will increase the discretionary spending necessary to support the middle class. After all, it's extremely important for our society to be open-minded and limit racial discord.
Extreme Language	Extreme arguments will take the language to such an unjustified extreme, or push it so far, that the extremeness will render the argument incorrect.	Weight lifting breaks down muscles and rebuilds them. If one just kept exercising and never stopped, their body would deteriorate and eventually fall apart.
Irrelevancy	Although usually persuasive, irrelevant information is unconnected to the argument's logic or context.	Argument only discusses the balance of speed and accuracy and does not mention history. Answer Choice: Historically, news organizations always waited to verify information and sources, and the change is due to the advent of the Internet.
Similar Language	Answer choices deceptively bear similar language, like the exact same words or phrases, as the argument.	Argument: This leads to some analysts jumping the gun and predicting outcomes inaccurately. Answer Choice: Jumping the gun is the worst mistake any analyst could make.
Parallel Reasoning	Parallel reasoning will make otherwise illogical answer choices seem more credible by mimicking the argument's structure.	Argument only involves news analysts prioritizing speed and accuracy. Answer Choice: The worst sports analysts prioritize speed over accuracy when announcing trades and other roster moves.
Appeal to Authority	Arguing from authority occurs when an author uses an expert to justify his argument, which is illogical if the supposed authority lacks the required status or expertise.	Bill Gates is the pre-imminent mathematical and computer genius of his era. Bill Gates believes in our government making huge economic investments in the research of renewable energy. The government should obviously follow this advice.
Hasty Generalizations	A hasty generalization involves an argument relying on insufficient statistical data or inaccurately generalizing.	I smoke a lot of cigarettes but so did my grandpa. He smoked nearly two packs per day from his World War II service until he died at ninety years of age. Continuing to smoke cigarettes will clearly not impact my long-term health.
Confusing Correlation with Causation	Arguments confuse correlation with causation by saying that one event caused another just because they occurred at the same time.	Jacob adopted a puppy last week. I saw him on Monday and he's lost fifty pounds since last summer. He looks really good. Adopting a puppy must be the secret to weight loss.

Confusing Correlation with Causation

In LSAT, **correlation** means that two events occur at the same time; however, **causation** indicates that one event caused a separate event. It is a common logical fallacy for correlation to be confused with causation. Arguments confuse correlation with causation by stating that one event caused another just because they occurred at the same time.

When evaluating whether an argument's reasoning is confusing the terms causation and correlation, always identify the actual cause of the event. Is there another more likely or reasonable event that could have been the true cause? If there is no causation, then there is a logical error. Also, be mindful of the events' timing and relationship to each other. If the author is drawing undue attention to the fact that the events occurred close in time, then check for this fallacy. However, remain aware that it is always possible for events occurring at the same time to be the cause.

Below is an example of an argument confusing correlation with causation:

> Jacob adopted a puppy two months ago. I saw him on Monday, and he's lost fifty pounds since summer. He looks really good. Adopting a puppy must be the secret to his weight loss.

In this argument, the author is saying that he saw Jacob with a new puppy, and Jacob looked good; therefore, adopting the puppy caused Jacob to look better. This is clearly illogical. Jacob could have been on a serious juice cleanse. He could have started running or lifting weights. Although the events (adopting the puppy and losing weight) occurred at the same time, it does not necessarily mean that one caused the other.

This is often a judgment decision. The argument must justify the assumption of causation in some meaningful way. For example, in the sample argument it would not be fallacious if the author stated that Jacob adopted the puppy a while ago, and they often run together. This would not be a logical flaw since starting to exercise with a new dog could reasonably cause the weight loss and improved looks.

Basic Concepts

The Logical Reasoning section contains a vast variety of arguments and question types. The next section is devoted to learning the nuances of each type. This section addresses basic concepts with wide applications. Mastering these concepts is important regardless of question type.

Conditions

There are two types of conditions—necessary conditions and sufficient conditions. It is extremely important to understand their applications, especially in reference to each other.

A **necessary condition** is a requirement that needs to be satisfied in order for another condition to be met. For example, in a theoretical state of affairs, X is a condition that must be satisfied before Y is obtained. Simply stated, a necessary condition is a defining characteristic such that some result, event, or circumstance cannot be achieved without it.

A **sufficient condition** is something that if satisfied, the condition is met without satisfying other conditions. For example, in a theoretical state of affairs, X is a condition that when met, satisfies X itself. Simply stated, a sufficient condition automatically satisfies the requirements by itself. A sufficient condition is enough to bring about an outcome by itself, but it is not necessarily the only condition that can do so. For example, a forest fire has many possible sufficient conditions. Lightning could strike a tree and set it ablaze. A careless hiker could toss a lit cigarette into unnoticed brush. An explosion at a nearby manufacturing plant could spread to the nearby forest. Any of these scenarios are sufficient conditions for a forest fire, while an uncontained fire is the only necessary requirement. In this example, the fire acts as a necessary and sufficient condition. An example is:

> All practicing attorneys are college graduates.

Since a person cannot be a practicing attorney without being a college graduate, being a college graduate is a necessary condition to be a practicing attorney. However, this is not also a sufficient condition. Being a college graduate is not sufficient to be a lawyer. There are many college graduates who are not practicing attorneys. Earning an undergraduate degree does not automatically achieve the

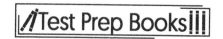

outcome of being a practicing attorney. It is merely a necessary requirement for the condition to be satisfied. Therefore, the statement is a necessary condition and *not a* sufficient condition.

Below are some practice problems working with sufficient and necessary conditions.

Statement	True	False
Being a mammal is a sufficient condition for being a dog.		
Being a mammal is a necessary condition for being a dog.		
Being a woman is a sufficient condition for being pregnant.		
Having legs is a sufficient condition to walk.		
Having available oxygen in the Earth's atmosphere is a necessary condition to sustain human life.		
Being male is a necessary condition to be a bachelor.		
Having been married is a sufficient condition to being a widow.		

The answers are respectively: False, True, False, False, True, True, False. Remember, any condition that automatically results in an event or result occurring without satisfying any additional conditions is a sufficient condition. Any condition that is a requirement for an event or result to occur is a necessary condition. Conditions can also be both necessary and sufficient if there's only one way for a condition to be met and that one condition automatically satisfies it.

Conditional Statements

This concept builds off the discussion directly above. **Conditional statements** are also known by how they most often appear: as *If/Then* statements. If X occurs, then Y will result, occur, or otherwise happen. An example is:

> If it is snowing, then Maria wears boots to work.

The first clause (If) is called the **hypothesis**, while the second clause (Then) is known as the **conclusion**. Snowing is a sufficient condition to Maria wearing boots. If it snows, then she will always wear the boots. However, it is not a necessary condition. An addition to this example is:

> If Maria is wearing her boots to work, then it is snowing.

Since this is the opposite of the first example, it is known as the **converse**. Switching the clauses does not preserve the logical strength of the original statement.

Think of how the cumulative property (4 + 2 = 2 + 4) does not apply to subtraction (4 − 2 ≠ 2 − 4).

This statement is illogical; wearing boots does not impact the weather or serve as an automatic signal for snow. There could be a number of reasons why Maria wears boots to work. The boots could be stylish and match her outfit. It could be raining. Her work shoes could be in need of a repair. Wearing boots is neither a necessary nor sufficient condition for it to be snowing. The converse of a valid original conditional statement may or may not be true.

An **inverse** of the original statement occurs when both clauses are negated. The inverse of the original statement is:

> If it is not snowing, then Maria will not wear boots to work.

Similar to the converse, the inverse is also illogical. As discussed, there could be many reasons why Maria does not wear boots to work. Even if it is not snowing does not mean that she won't be wearing her boots.

Invert the converse to see how that impacts the statement:

> If Maria is not wearing her boots to work, then it is not snowing.

This is called the **contrapositive** of the statement, and the contrapositive of a conditional statement is *always* true. This is extremely important. If X, then Y is always equal to Not Y, then not X.

To be clear, *true* as it is applied on the Logical Reasoning portion of the exam is utilized here. There could certainly be scenarios where it is indeed snowing, but Maria isn't wearing her boots. However, for purposes of this exam, remember that the contrapositive of an original conditional statement is always true. Logical Reasoning questions bear a much greater resemblance to the theoretical logic found in an undergraduate philosophy class than to real life happenings.

The factual accuracy of arguments, statements, or answer choices does not apply here. This is not a fact-based exam. It is an evaluation of the test taker's ability to think logically within the confines provided by the test makers.

Reasonableness

Although different from conditions and If/Then Statements, **reasonableness** is another important foundational concept. Evaluating an argument for reasonableness entails evaluating the evidence presented by the author to justify their conclusions. Everything contained in the argument should be considered, but remember to ignore outside biases, judgments, and knowledge. For the purposes of this test, the test taker is a one-person jury at a criminal trial using a standard of reasonableness under the circumstances presented by the argument.

These arguments are encountered on a daily basis through social media, entertainment, and cable news. An example is:

> Although many believe it to be a natural occurrence, some believe that the red tide that occurs in Florida each year may actually be a result of human sewage and agricultural runoff. However, it is arguable that both natural and human factors contribute to this annual phenomenon. On one hand, the red tide has been occurring every year since the time of explorers like Cabeza de Vaca in the 1500's. On the other hand, the red tide seems to be getting worse each year, and scientists from the Florida Fish & Wildlife Conservation say the bacteria found inside the tide feed off of nutrients found in fertilizer runoff.

The author's conclusion is that both natural phenomena and human activity contribute to the red tide that happens annually in Florida. The author backs this information up by historical data to prove the natural occurrence of the red tide, and then again with scientific data to back up the human contribution to the red tide. Both of these statements are examples of the premises in the argument.

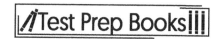

Evaluating the strength of the logical connection between the premises and conclusion is how reasonableness is determined. Another example is:

> The local railroad is a disaster. Tickets are exorbitantly priced, bathrooms leak, and the floor is sticky.

The author is clearly unhappy with the railroad service. They cite three examples of why they believe the railroad to be a disaster. An argument more familiar to everyday life is:

> Alexandra said the movie she just saw was amazing. We should go see it tonight.

Although not immediately apparent, this is an argument. The author is making the argument that they should go see the movie. This conclusion is based on the premise that Alexandra said the movie was amazing. There's an inferred note that Alexandra is knowledgeable on the subject, and she's credible enough to prompt her friends to go see the movie. This seems like a reasonable argument. A less reasonable argument is:

> Alexandra is a film student, and she's written the perfect romantic comedy script. We should put our life savings toward its production as an investment in our future.

The author's conclusion is that they should invest their life savings into the production of a movie, and it is justified by referencing Alexandra's credibility and current work. However, the premises are entirely too weak to support the conclusion. Alexandra is only a film *student*, and the script is seemingly her first work. This is not enough evidence to justify investing one's life savings in the film's success.

Causality

Causality is simply cause and effect. Event A causes Effect B to come into existence. Determining the strength of the relationship between the cause and effect will make evaluating the argument much easier. The more the events are directly related, the greater the causality.

Be wary of language that implies that there is direct causation when none actually exists. This trick usually involves correlation, which is a separate concept. **Correlating events** simply occur at the same time. One event does not cause or affect the other. Here's an example:

> Jeffrey Johnston is having the best year of his career. He hit twice as many home runs as last year and increased his batting average by one hundred points. He clearly must have wanted to earn more money in the offseason.

The author is unreasonably identifying an athlete's desire to enhance his value as the cause of his career year. It's illogical to say that some intangible increase in motivation is the reason why a player doubled his productivity. There could be any number of reasons why Jeffrey Johnston is playing much better. Maybe he was a young player who was still developing? Maybe a new coach fixed his batting swing? Maybe he is finally healthy for the first time in his career? There are a number of explanations as to why he improved. There is not enough evidence to suggest that desiring more money caused the spike in production.

An addition of more information to the argument is:

> Jeffrey Johnston is having the best year of his career. He hit twice as many home runs as last year and increased his batting average by one hundred points. He clearly must have wanted to earn more money in the offseason. After all, he spent the whole offseason talking about how he

increased his training regimen to put himself in a better position to earn more money as a free agent.

This argument adds more justification for attributing the desire for more money to the player's successful career year. This argument states that Jeffrey Johnston publicly discussed working harder to get a bigger contract. However, a strong causation is still not established. Some other causal agent could have been a much bigger reason for the bump in productivity. Another addition to the argument is:

> Jeffrey Johnston is having the best year of his career. He hit twice as many home runs as last year and increased his batting average by one hundred points. He clearly must have wanted to earn more money in the offseason. After all, he spent the whole offseason talking about how he increased his training regimen to put himself in a better position to earn more money as a free agent. Not to mention, he tattooed dollar signs on his forearms and painted his bat green.

The author has now included Jeffrey's tattoo and custom bat as evidence of his complete focus on money. This is the strongest causation since it has the most evidence directly related to the conclusion. According to the argument, Jeffrey knew he was a free agent before the season, he made public comments about working hard for better compensation, and he illustrated his mindset on his forearm and baseball bat. It seems likely that a desire for more money caused Jeffrey's career year.

Presumably, every test taker is taking the LSAT to gain admission into law school and become a lawyer. Lawyers question everything, and the Logical Reasoning section emphasizes this point. Do not mistake this intellectual exercise for introducing personal experiences or external information into the argument. The questions should remain in the context provided by the argument, but everything within that context must be questioned.

As a final note on causality, be wary of a conclusion that is indirectly completed by unrelated evidence. The test developers will write arguments that present facts about a subject and then offer an unrelated conclusion. There is typically a gap in logic between the premises and conclusion. This usually presents itself as an argument with a missing premise. The following is an example of an argument with a missing premise:

> Premise: Christina found a strange-looking creature that has eight legs.
>
> Conclusion: The creature is not an insect.

For the example above, we should add a second premise between the first premise and conclusion that would connect the two facts, thus making the argument valid. The following would be the new argument:

> Premise: Christina found a strange-looking creature that has eight legs.
>
> Premise: Insects have exactly six legs.
>
> Conclusion: The creature is not an insect.

Note how the second premise fills in the gap from the first premise to the conclusion. While you likely know from general knowledge that insects have six legs, that fact must be stated to make the conclusion valid. If an added premise allows us to arrive at a conclusion with certainty, then it is probably a deductive argument.

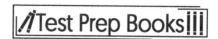

Dealing with the Unknown and Incomplete Arguments

LSAT arguments commonly contain a variety of flaws. Besides those described previously, one of the most common flaws is the unknown element or incomplete argument. An argument will fail to include a premise or the evidence necessary to link the rest of the statement to the conclusion. Sometimes the argument will include too little or too general evidence. Other illogical arguments could also leave out the conclusion and bait the subconscious into implicitly inferring one. Missing links, disconnected information, and irrelevant facts are the norm, not the exception.

Test developers assume that test takers will naturally fill the logic gap with common sense. For example: *Increased expenditures are often trumpeted as a solution to national problems.* The LSAC preys on the test taker's subconscious. Always make sure the argument supplies all of the argument's elements. An example is:

> In the United States, over 50 million people would be medically classified as obese. Americans rank as the world's thirty-second country in terms of obesity-related deaths. Clearly, Americans are not devoting enough revenue to health initiatives.

This argument does not make logical sense. Taking the author at their word, as one must during the Logical Reasoning section, the United States has quite the health problem. However, the argument fails to connect how paying for more health initiatives impacts the obesity epidemic. Obesity could be a cultural phenomenon. The argument makes no mention of *how* spending more money would increase health and wellness. The argument is missing a premise, such as *America spends the least on measures to fight obesity proven to be effective in countries where they have been implemented.* Without this link, there is no logical causality between the health crisis and government spending.

Let's look at another example:

> Geoffrey loves art. He frequently visits local museums and showings. Geoffrey is a millionaire.

This argument is dealing with an unknown that leaves the argument incomplete. The author states that Geoffrey is wealthy and loves art. There is no mention of how one has to do with the other. Many people have some hobby or interest unrelated to their career. Geoffrey could work as a banker, lawyer, entrepreneur, or professional baseball player. The argument does not present any ascertainable conclusion. Two facts about Geoffrey are known. Incomplete arguments with unknown elements will sometimes ask for the test taker to identify the assumption. In this case, a strong answer choice might read: *Geoffrey's passion for art led to a successful and lucrative career as a collector.* Or maybe the argument will ask the test taker to supply the author's conclusion, such as: *Geoffrey loves art. He frequently visits local museums and showings. Geoffrey's passion for art led to a successful and lucrative career as a collector.*

A correct answer could be a conclusion such as, *it is certainly true what they say, that following one's passion will always pay off financially in the end.* When working through the dozens of arguments included in each of the two Logical Reasoning sections, always be mindful of missing information and avoid filling in any logic gaps. Identifying the missing part is often the key to answering some questions.

Common Question Types

The test writers at LSAC will ask a host of questions in a variety of ways. Fortunately, some of the question types are more common than others. This section explores the eight most common question types, and the last section will discuss the other less likely possibilities.

Main Point Questions

Main Point or **Primary Purpose** questions are some of the most common questions on the Logical Reasoning section of the LSAT. No matter which of the three ways it is worded, these questions ask the same basic thing—what is the author's conclusion? These questions are also described as Primary Purpose questions. There is minimal difference between the two. For Main Point questions, identify what the author is trying to express. For Primary Purpose questions, identify what the author is trying to accomplish through voicing the conclusion. Either way, the test taker must identify the overall conclusion. Although not explicitly categorized as Main Point questions, consider any questions that ask for the author's conclusion among this type.

Although there is some difficult iteration of these types of questions, students generally find Main Point or Primary Purpose questions to be some of the easiest questions in this section. This is largely due to the difficulty in writing an argument so complex it defies understanding in less than half of a page. These questions are also extremely straightforward and easy to understand.

Here are some ways Main Point questions will be phrased:

- Which of the following is the main point of the passage?
- What is the argument's primary purpose?
- Which of the following most accurately represents the author's conclusion?
- What is the conclusion set forth by the author?

An argument that features a Main Point question is:

> Scientist: A recent peer-reviewed study sent waves of excitement across the medical community. The study found that a niche vaccine had a possible application to Elephant Pox. Experts in the field previously believed a vaccine to be impossible due to the structure of the virus. Dr. George Smith has been credited with the discovery. Because of the Elephant Pox viruses' similarities with another class of viruses, this study should have far-reaching implications for the field.

Which of the following is the main point of the passage?
> a. Dr. George Smith is a hero.
> b. Peer-reviewed studies cannot be trusted.
> c. The study is extremely important and could possibly lead to the development of more vaccines.
> d. A recent peer-reviewed study sent waves of excitement across the medical community.
> e. The breakthrough will revolutionize the field.

Remember to identify the author's conclusion. It should be the overall idea. If these remarks were overheard at a dinner party, what might the listener convey when mentioning the encounter to a friend? The choices are:

Choice *A* is clearly not the main point of the passage. Dr. George Smith's name appears once in a six-line argument. The argument merely mentions he was credited with the discovery and does not dwell on his role. This answer choice can quickly be eliminated.

Choice *B* is clearly incorrect. Not only does the author fail to discuss the credibility of peer-reviewed studies, but he would also probably disagree with this statement in its entirety. It can also be quickly eliminated.

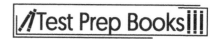

Choice *C* is easily the best answer so far. The author describes the study as *sending waves of excitement across the medical community*. In addition, the author mentions that the vaccine might have far-reaching applications. Choice *C* appears to be the correct answer and should be used as a benchmark.

Choice *D* is tricky since its language is similar to the argument. In fact, it is a restatement of the author's first statement. The test maker is attempting to fool the test taker into believing this is the conclusion since many LSAT Legal Reasoning arguments list the conclusion as the first sentence. Do not fall for it. The main point is not that a new development sent waves of excitement across the medical community. The author goes into more specifics than general excitement and mentions possible ramifications. Choice *C* remains a more accurate summary of the author's main point.

Choice *E* takes the author's conclusion to an unjustified extreme. The author uses cautious language when describing possible developments, such as *should* have far-reaching implications. Although the author might agree that the discovery could revolutionize the field, he would not go so far as to say that it *would* revolutionize it.

Inference

Inference questions ask the test taker to infer something from the passage, which usually requires that a logic gap be filled with an implied assertion. An author implies something when it is suggested without being directly stated. Inference questions are generally more difficult than the Main Point questions since they require reading between the lines.

Here are some examples of how inference questions will appear on the test:

- The author would most likely concur with which one of the following?
- The author would be least likely to agree with which one of the following?
- Which one of the following can be properly inferred from the argument?
- The argument most strongly supports which of the following assertions?

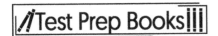

Note that the table below does not include every possible inference. Almost any statement or sentence could allow for dozens of inferences. On the Logical Reasoning section, identifying the author's inferences will be invaluable, especially for inference-related questions.

INFERENCE PRACTICE	
Statement	**Inferences**
George is the best baker in Black Acre and owns his own bakery shop on Main Street.	George is a baker. George is better than every other baker in Black Acre. George owns a bakery shop. There is at least one business on Main Street.
Joel works nights but manages to listen to every New York Yankees game on his radio.	Joel works at night. Joel is a Yankees fan. Joel owns a radio. Joel listens to every Yankees game. Joel is capable of listening to the radio while at work.

A typical inference question is:

> Thomas Jefferson is deservedly lauded for his devotion to liberty and commitment to equality, especially in his drafts of the Declaration of Independence. However, he still adhered to and followed horrid societal racism and discrimination, such as owning slaves. Jefferson also fathered at least one documented child with a woman he owned. Furthermore, Jefferson often wrote of the biological inferiority of African peoples and used this to justify their enslavement. Even Thomas Jefferson could not overcome the racism of his time.

The author would most likely agree that:
a. Thomas Jefferson is a racist.
b. Current historians believe that Jefferson's practice of slavery negated his role in the American Revolution.
c. It is not unusual for people to overcome the racism of their time.
d. Thomas Jefferson was insincere when writing the Declaration of Independence.
e. It is difficult to overcome societal contexts, such as racism.

Choice *A* seems appealing. The author is certainly critical of Jefferson's personal practice of slavery. The author mentions that Jefferson fathered a child with a slave and argued for the inferiority of Africans. However, the author also concludes with *racism of his time*. This language feels like an appeal to context. For now, keep this choice as an option.

Choice *B* is clearly incorrect. Although the author touches on the apparent contradiction between Jefferson's role in the American Revolution and the practice of slavery, he makes no substantive comparisons and does not evaluate them relatively. The argument does not support something so

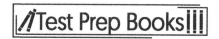

strong as negating Jefferson's role as a Founding Father. The answer choice would be more appealing if it used less extreme language, such as *clouded* instead of *negated*.

Choice *C* is also clearly wrong. The author starts the last sentence with *even Thomas Jefferson*, which implies that Jefferson would be someone more likely to overcome societal racism than just anybody. The author also discusses how Jefferson is *deservedly lauded for his devotion to liberty and commitment to equality*. The author is implying that if Jefferson fell into societal discriminatory pitfalls, then it happens to just about everyone. This answer choice is the reverse of the author's point. Be careful of answer choices expressed as a double negative, such as *not unusual*.

Choice *D* is not supported by the argument. Despite the author's discussion of Jefferson's discriminatory practices, he never discusses sincerity. It is certainly possible to lead a contradictory life while being sincere. Whether someone is sincere is a subjective state of mind. This argument only touches on Jefferson's accomplishments and disappointments and not on how he viewed his own work.

Choice *E* is a strong choice. It is the direct opposite of Choice *C*, which means it should strongly be considered. As discussed while evaluating the other answer choices, the author definitely believes that Jefferson is a complicated historical figure. The argument is devoted to showing the irony of America's greatest idealist practicing one of America's most heinous acts. The last sentence of the argument— *Even Thomas Jefferson could not overcome the racism of his time*—expresses the author's belief that if Thomas Jefferson could practice racism, then anyone could. The author would strongly agree with this answer choice.

Therefore, Choice *E* is the correct answer since there is more evidence that the author would support it more strongly than Choice *A*.

Assumptions

This type of question is frequently tested. Underlying **Assumption** questions ask the test taker to identify the argument's assumption. Think of assumptions as unwritten premises. Although they never explicitly appear in the argument, the author is relying on it to defend the argument, just like a premise. Assumptions are the most important part of an argument that will never appear in an argument.

An argument in the abstract is: The author concludes Z based on W and X premises. But the W and X premises actually depend on the unmentioned assumption of Y. Therefore, what the author is really saying is that X, W, and Y make Z correct, but Y is assumed.

People assume all of the time. Assumptions and inferences allow the human mind to process the constant flow of information. Many assumptions underlie even the most basic arguments. However, in the world of Legal Reasoning arguments, assumptions must be avoided. An argument must be fully presented to be valid; relying on an assumption is considered weak. The test requires that test takers identify these underlying assumptions. One example is:

> Peyton Manning is the most over-rated quarterback of all time. He lost more big games than anyone else. Plus, he allegedly assaulted his female trainer in college. Peyton clearly shouldn't make the Hall of Fame.

The author certainly relies on a lot of assumptions. A few assumptions are:

- Peyton Manning plays quarterback.

- He is considered to be a great quarterback by at least some people.

- He played in many big games.

- Allegations and past settlements without any admission of guilt from over a decade ago can be relied upon as evidence against Hall of Fame acceptance.

- The Hall of Fame voters factor in off-the-field incidents, even if true.

- The best players should make the Hall of Fame.

- Losing big games negates, at least in part, the achievement of making it to those big games

- Peyton Manning is retired, and people will vote on whether he makes the Hall of Fame at some point in the future.

The author is relying on all of these assumptions. Some are clearly more important to his argument than others. In fact, disproving a necessary assumption can destroy a premise and possibly an entire conclusion. For example, what if the Hall of Fame did not factor in any of the off-the-field incidents? Then the alleged assault no longer factors into the argument. Even worse, what if making the big games actually was more important than losing those games in the eyes of the Hall of Fame voters? Then the whole conclusion falls apart and is no longer justified if that premise is disproven.

Assumption questions test this exact point by asking the test taker to identify which assumption the argument relies upon. If the author is making numerous assumptions, then the most important assumption must be chosen.

If the author truly relies on an assumption, then the argument will completely fall apart if the assumption isn't true. **Negating** a necessary assumption will *always* make the argument fall apart. This is a universal rule of logic and should be the first thing done in testing answer choices.

Here are some ways that underlying assumptions will appear as questions:

- Which of the following is a hidden assumption that the author makes to advance his argument?
- Which assumption, if true, would support the argument's conclusion (make it more logical)?
- The strength of the argument depends on which of the following?
- Upon which of the following assumptions does the author rely?
- Which assumption does the argument presuppose?

An example is:

Frank Underwood is a terrible president. The man is a typical spend, spend, spend liberal. His employment program would exponentially increase the annual deficit and pile on the national debt. Not to mention, Underwood is also on the verge of starting a war with Russia.

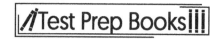

Upon which of the following assumptions does the author's argument most rely?
  a. Frank Underwood is a terrible president.
  b. The United States cannot afford Frank Underwood's policy plans without spending more than the country raises in revenue.
  c. No spend, spend, spend liberal has ever succeeded as president.
  d. Starting a war with Russia is beneficial to the United States.
  e. Past presidents held drastically different policies and beliefs than the ones held by Underwood.

Use the negation rule to find the correct answer in the choices below.

Choice A is not an assumption—it is the author's conclusion. This type of restatement will never be the correct answer, but test it anyway. After negating the choice, what remains is: *Frank Underwood is a fantastic president.* Does this make the argument fall apart? No, it just becomes the new conclusion. The argument is certainly worse since it does not seem reasonable for someone to praise a president for being a spend, spend, spend liberal or raising the national debt; however, the argument still makes *logical* sense. Eliminate this choice.

Choice B is certainly an assumption. It underlies the premises that the country cannot afford Underwood's economic plans. When reversed to: *The United States can afford Frank Underwood's policy plans without spending more than the country raises in revenue.* This largely destroys the argument. If the United States can afford his plans, then the annual deficit and national debt won't increase; therefore, Underwood being a terrible president would only be based on the final premise. The argument is much weaker without the two sentences involving the financials. Keep it as a benchmark while working through the remaining choices.

Choice C is largely irrelevant. The author is not necessarily claiming that all loose-pocket liberals make for bad presidents. His argument specifically pertains to Underwood. Negate it— *Some spend, spend, spend liberals have succeeded as president.* This does not destroy the argument. Some other candidate could have succeeded as president. However, the author is pointing out that those policies would be disastrous considering the rising budget and debt. The author is not making an appeal to historical precedent. Although not a terrible choice, it is certainly weaker than *Choice B*. Eliminate this choice.

Choice D is definitely not an assumption made by the author. The author is assuming that a war with Russia is disastrous. Negate it anyway—*Starting a war with Russia is not beneficial for the United States.* This does not destroy the argument; it makes it stronger. Eliminate this choice.

Choice E is not integral to the argument. Whether past presidents held the same policies as Underwood is largely irrelevant. After reversing the choice, it reads: *Past presidents held the same policies and beliefs as the ones held by Underwood.* This makes the argument odd, like in the discussion of *Choice A*. The author's argument remains logically intact. He could mean that Underwood is continuing the same terrible policies. The argument is not broken, so it cannot be the answer. Eliminate this choice.

New Information (Most Strengthens or Weakens Questions)

Another common question type asks the test taker to analyze or reconsider the argument after providing **new information**. The proposed new information will appear in the answer choices. The new information will either strengthen or weaken the argument. These questions come in three varieties. In one, the question will simply ask the test taker to choose a statement that, if true, strengthens or weakens the argument. In another, the question will ask what *most* strengthens or weakens. The third variety is the trickiest and will ask what statement is the only one that does *not* strengthen or weaken.

This is how these questions are phrased:

- Which of the following statements, if true, strengthens (weakens) the argument?
- Which one of the following, if true, *most* strengthens (weakens) the argument?
- Each of the following, if true, weakens (strengthens) the argument, EXCEPT:

The first and third type of questions can be answered by finding the answer choice that goes in the opposite direction. For there to be a statement that strengthens or weakens an argument, the others necessarily must do the opposite. This is especially true for the questions with *except*. Although this analysis makes those questions much easier, the test taker should always check the answer with the argument.

For the second type, or the *most* questions, the answer choices could weaken, strengthen, or be completely irrelevant. All of the five answer choices could go in the same direction. For example, in a most weakens question, all five answer choices could weaken that argument. Or, three could be weakening choices, one a strengthening choice, and the other an irrelevant choice. Or, it could be some other combination. No matter what, the goal is to concentrate on the *most* part of the question. Weigh competing choices relative to each other, and always choose the one that does the *most*.

Follow these two preliminary steps when solving new information questions. Remember, practicing these skills will make them second nature. First, determine if it is something that weakens or strengthens. Second, determine the *most* strengthening or weakening answer. Always keep a lookout for the *except* variety because the test makers always include deceiving and tricky choices. Finally, as with the Logical Reasoning section in general, but particularly important for these question types, if the question says *if true*, then assume that it is true. No matter how ridiculous it seems or how strongly it generates disagreements, if it says true, then it is true.

Below are examples of the three different types:

Strengthens

Countries that favor rehabilitation over retribution for crimes involving substance abuse, such as minor possession, have much lower rates of recidivism. Once countries commit to providing drug and alcohol rehabilitation, people who enter the criminal justice system are much less likely to return. Rehabilitation has been proven over and over again to cause crime rates to drop. The United States imprisons more drug parents who struggle with addiction and alcoholics than any other country in the world. The United States would greatly benefit by reconsidering its use of rehabilitation.

Which of the following statements, if true, strengthens the argument?
a. Fewer substance abusers live in the countries that have succeeded with increased rehabilitation.
b. The United States holds the second most prisoners in the world.
c. Rehabilitation is much cheaper than imprisonment.
d. Rehabilitation is much more expensive than imprisonment.
e. The United States currently favors retribution over rehabilitation more than any other country.

Since the answer wants the one answer choice that strengthens the argument, the other four answer choices will either weaken the argument or be irrelevant altogether.

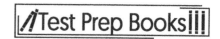

Choice *A* is irrelevant. The argument does not say how a larger number of substance abusers impact the success of rehabilitation. According to the argument's logic, it does not matter how many substance abusers live in the countries that have succeeded in rehabilitation.

Choice *B* is also irrelevant. Like Choice *A*, the argument makes no mention as to whether an increased number of inmates would impact the effectiveness of transitioning to rehabilitation. Do not be tricked into selecting an answer just because two of the choices touch on the same irrelevant point.

Choice *C* is deceptive but irrelevant for the purposes of strengthening the argument. Rehabilitation's lower cost seems to be quite the benefit. However, the argument does not argue that rehabilitation would be cost-effective, or how these financial savings would make rehabilitation more appealing. It's making the argument that rehabilitation is better than retribution since it reduces recidivism, which lowers crime rates overall. It does not matter whether it is cheaper for purposes of this argument.

Choice *D* is also irrelevant for the same reasons as Choice *C*. In addition, even if it were relevant, it would weaken the argument. In this situation, pay special attention to the two *opposite* answer choices; however, one of them does not happen to be correct for this question.

Choice *E* strengthens the argument. If the United States currently uses an extreme amount of retribution and less rehabilitation than the rest of the world, then the benefits of a transition to rehabilitation would be enormous. The argument states that increased rehabilitation lowers crime rates. If the United States does not currently use any rehabilitation, then it would be in line for the biggest drop in crime rates. This is the correct answer since it is the only one that strengthens the argument.

Most Weakens

Reading is the most important factor in academic achievement. Anyone who starts reading at a young age and continues reading throughout their schooling scores better on all levels of standardized tests. Mandatory reading requirements should be enforced in all grade levels from kindergarten through sixth grade.

Which one of the following, if true, most weakens the argument?
   a. Some states already mandate required reading in their schools.
   b. Anyone forced to read will actually read less overall.
   c. The top 1 percent of LSAT scorers reported reading as their number one hobby.
   d. Young readers usually stop reading for fun after graduating college.
   e. Affluent students read more than their less wealthy peers.

This is a most weakens question, so it is possible for more than one answer choice to weaken the argument. The one that weakens the argument the *most* should be selected.

Choice *A* is irrelevant. It does not weaken the argument to say that some schools have already started what the author believes to be the most effective solution. Eliminate this choice.

Choice *B* definitely weakens the argument. The author's conclusion is that mandatory reading requirements should be enforced in early schooling. This will presumably increase reading, which is the most important factor in academic achievement according to the argument. If it is true that anyone forced to read would actually read less overall, then the argument makes no sense. If the goal is to increase reading and forcing reading decreases overall reading, then it makes no sense to make it a mandatory part of the curriculum. This certainly seems very forceful; however, review the other answers before making a choice. Look for the statement that would undermine the argument.

Choice *C* actually strengthens the argument. It proves one of the argument's premises that reading boosts standardized test performance. This is clearly incorrect and should be eliminated.

Choice *D* is irrelevant. The author wants to increase reading through mandatory requirements in order to increase academic achievement. If people stop reading after graduating college, it does not impact the argument.

Choice *E* is also irrelevant. It adds another factor that could be the reason for increased academic performance. It's saying that wealth directly contributes to increased reading, and therefore better performance. This choice is offering a competing theory. However, we need to evaluate it relative to our other option. Choice *B* totally destroys the logic's argument, while Choice *E* alters the discussion. Choice *B* is the better of the two.

Except Type

Football should be banned until the end of high school. Until completing puberty, at approximately sixteen years of age, the brain is still developing. High impact sports, such as football, are simply too damaging to developing brains. The risk of permanent injury is simply too great.

Each of the following, if true, strengthens the argument, EXCEPT:
 a. Studies have shown that people who suffer concussions before puberty are three times as likely to drop out of high school.
 b. The earlier in life someone suffers a concussion, the more concussions he or she will suffer throughout their life disproportionately increases.
 c. The camaraderie and work ethic learned in youth football is invaluable.
 d. Football cannot be made safe at the youth level.
 e. Young athletes wishing to play college or professional football will not have more opportunities if they start playing young.

This an exception question. Notice that the wrong answer will always go in the opposite direction indicated in the question. The question states that the four remaining answers will strengthen the argument. In this instance, look for what weakens the argument.

Choice *A* strengthens the argument. This supports the argument's conclusion that the risk of permanent injury is too great to allow young people to play football. This statement says that people who suffer concussions before puberty are more likely to drop out of high school. It further justifies the author's desire to prohibit youth football.

Choice *B* strengthens the argument. If people suffer more concussions after suffering the first injury before puberty, then it further supports the prohibition.

Choice *C* weakens the argument. The choice attributes *invaluable* skills to youth football, which means that the risk might not be too great. If the skills learned could outweigh the risk, then it would not be reasonable to prohibit the sport at the youth level. This seems like the right choice; however, make sure that the remaining answer choices strengthen the argument.

Choice *D* strengthens the argument. If football cannot be made safe at the youth level, then a ban is the only solution. If there are no ways to reduce the harm, then it must be eliminated.

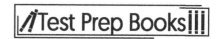

Choice *E* strengthens the argument. A reasonable suggestion is that the possibility of a college scholarship or professional career could outweigh the risk. This answer choice shuts down that potential counterargument. It definitely does not weaken the argument.

Therefore, Choice *C* is correct since it is the only answer choice that weakens the argument.

Paradoxes

Paradox questions provide a half-formed argument. Technically, the passages are not arguments since they generally do not provide a conclusion. Paradox arguments provide a series of facts without drawing a conclusion out of those facts. The facts will be at odds with each other in some way, and the question will require a resolution. The correct answer choice will provide some explanation, which generally comes from outside the framework set up in the argument. This outside information is an **inference**.

Here are some examples of how paradox questions will appear on the test:

- Which of the following statements, if true, would resolve the discrepancy?
- Which of the following statements, if true, would resolve the apparent paradox?
- Which of the following best explains the situation in the argument above?

An example of a paradox question is:

> In 2015, a country's unemployment rate rose above 10 percent for the first time in two decades. However, the Gross Domestic Product—the broadest quantitative measure of a country's cumulative economic activity—rose 25 percent. The country's investors and debt holders are extremely pleased with these developments.

Which of the following, if true, would explain the paradox?
a. The country's economy is falling apart.
b. The economic conditions of 2015 benefited the wealthy much more relative to the lower classes.
c. GDP does not accurately reflect economic realities.
d. The investors are wrong.
e. Automation has rendered many jobs obsolete and boosted productively overall.

Choice *A* does not explain the apparent paradox. If the country's economy were falling apart, it would explain the recent rise in unemployment; however, the country's GDP also increased, which does not indicate a disastrous economy. The correct answer will explain why the typical economic indicators are going in the opposite directions. Eliminate this choice.

Choice *B* is tricky since it plays into a line of thinking in popular discourse. If wealth is consolidated in a few hands, then the economy could improve overall even with rising unemployment. This is an adequate explanation, but it requires an assumption about the context. For now, keep this choice as an option.

Choice *C* partially explains the paradox. If GDP does not accurately reflect economic realities, then it is irrelevant and leaves high unemployment as the only economic indicator. However, the argument's last sentence indicates that the country's investors and debt holders are pleased with the developments. Presumably, investors and debt holders would want the country's economy to improve overall so their investments are worth more, and debts can be repaid. Dismissing GDP as unreliable does not explain the paradox within the framework of this question. Choice *C* is not as strong as Choice *B* and must be eliminated.

Choice *D* does not explain the paradox. The investors could surely be wrong, but it does not explain why GDP and unemployment offer conflicting economic news. Eliminate this choice.

Choice *E* looks very promising. Increased automation could explain why unemployment has increased since robots or machines could have replaced human labor, and that same automation could be more productive than its human counterparts and lead to GDP growth. Does this explain the paradox? Yes, it does. Automation is the outside factor responsible for the conflicting economic indicators. Choice *E* is stronger than Choice *A* since it provides a more complete explanation. Therefore, Choice *E* is the correct answer.

Note that the correct answer merely needs to be the best explanation provided in the choices. It is not necessarily the best possible explanation imaginable. Focus on selecting the best explanation provided as an option.

Flawed Reasoning

Flawed Reasoning questions include unsound reasoning. Some flaw will be present, and the test taker will be asked to identify what is illogical. The difficulty of these questions depends on the subtlety of the flaw. Some flaws will be obvious, while others will go unnoticed by 90 percent of test takers until they read the question prompt.

As previously discussed, *read the argument before the question*. This is one of the few cases where it is beneficial to read the question first. However, continue to read all of the arguments before the questions. This strategy will work better for the other questions, and the flawed reasoning can be quickly reread if the flaw was not immediately apparent. In the interest of time management, keep a consistent flow.

Authors will make a variety of logical errors. Common examples include: relying on an unreasonable assumption, extrapolating information from sample sizes, mistaking correlation with causation, wrongly assuming the continuation of current conditions, incorrect measurement, and inapplicable analogies, etc. Look for anything illogical when asked to describe the flaw in reasoning or some similarly phrased question.

The answer choices in flawed reasoning questions tend to be trickier than the average questions. Be careful of red herrings and tricks in the answers. Some of the answer choices could involve things in the author's logic that are actually logically sound and use valid reasoning. Other answer choices will list a logical error that the author did not make in the particular argument.

Here are some examples of flawed reasoning questions:

- The argument above is most vulnerable to criticism on the grounds that:
- What is a flaw in the argument's reasoning?
- What mistake does the author commit in their reasoning?

An example of a Flawed Reasoning question is:

> Hector went fishing in the morning, the time when fish are most active, and still didn't catch anything while he was there. Therefore, Hector must be a bad fisherman.

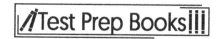

What is the flaw in the argument's reasoning?
  a. The author assumes Hector has never had success fishing.
  b. The author is not a marine biologist, and doesn't understand fish behavior.
  c. Hector is really a champion fisherman.
  d. The author doesn't take into account external and environmental factors that might have contributed to Hector not getting a bite.
  e. Fish aren't smart creatures.

Choice *A* presents a very plausible answer. The author's logic is flawed in thinking that just because Hector didn't catch any fish that morning, he is not good at fishing. Let's keep this option open.

Choice *B* is irrelevant and misleading. While this could be true about fish, we must take statements in the LSAT questions as fact. Choice *B* doesn't address Hector's proficiency at fishing at all. Eliminate it.

Choice *C* is also misleading. While if this were true it would certainly put a kink in the author's reasoning, this still doesn't address the logic used in coming up with the conclusion that Hector is a bad fisherman. Additionally, no previous mention of Hector's credentials is even mentioned. Eliminate this option completely. Remember, we don't want to necessarily prove the author wrong here; we just want to discover the flaw in the author's reasoning. Ask yourself why the argument is flawed and what factors did the author take or not take into account to make their conclusion.

Choice *D* gives a very complete synopsis of the argument's flaw in reasoning. The author immediately concludes that just because Hector didn't catch any fish he is a bad fisherman. There can be many factors in Hector's failure to catch a fish: perhaps there weren't any more fish in the water where he was fishing; maybe the climate played a big factor in the fish not biting; or there could have been a predator in the area that scared the fish away. The fact that there are more factors at play than Hector's skill eliminates the conclusion that Hector himself is a bad fisherman. Thus, Choice *D* is the correct answer.

Choice *E* is irrelevant information and has nothing to do with Hector as a fisherman.

Again, for flawed reasoning questions, take care to examine how the conclusion is wrong. Look for the answer that best explains this. Your goal is to find the holes in the author's reasoning and choose the answer that best fills these holes.

Parallel Reasoning

Parallel Reasoning questions are also extremely common on the Logical Reasoning portion of the LSAT. Expect at least two of them on each of the sections. A parallel reasoning question provides a concise argument, usually no more than two or three lines, and then the question asks which of the five answer choice arguments displays parallel reasoning. The parallel is also sometimes flawed reasoning. In practical terms, this all means that parallel reasoning questions will necessarily take more time since they require analyzing six arguments—the argument and five answer choices.

The structure of a parallel reasoning question requires a slightly different strategy. First, break the argument into its corresponding parts: *premises*, *sub-conclusions*, and *conclusion*. Then, identify all assumptions or flaws. Some of the questions will specifically ask that the parallels in flawed argumentation be identified. Second, quickly assess the answer choices; the choice should be obvious. Third, break down the premises and conclusions of each answer choice to find the right match.

If the argument or answer choices are confusing, move on. As previously discussed, parallel reasoning questions take more time than the average question. While studying for the exam and practice questions, pay attention to how quickly the parallel reasoning questions can be completed and calculate a personal accuracy rate. If this is the question type that takes the longest or is the most trouble, be ready to move on to the next question. Always read the argument, question, and answer choices, but if nothing clicks immediately, then mark it and move on. This decision increases in importance depending on the confidence the test taker has over parallel reasoning questions. The preliminary sweep of the choices should have resulted in the elimination of a couple of choices. Therefore, if one question needs to be answered with a guess, it still increases the chance of guessing correctly.

Here are some examples of how parallel reasoning questions will appear on the test:

- Which of the following arguments is most similar to the reasoning in the politician's argument?
- Which of the following most closely parallels the scientist's argument?
- The flawed reasoning in which of the following arguments is most similar to the baseball coach's argument?

An example of a problem asking the test taker to identify parallel flaws is:

Jockeys are clearly world-class athletes. The best jockeys stand somewhere between four-feet-eleven inches tall and five-feet-six inches tall. Therefore, jockeys make for excellent basketball players.

The flawed reasoning in which of the following arguments most mirrors the flawed reasoning presented in the argument above:
a. For years, countries have backed their currency in gold. This will never change.
b. Leopards' spots help them blend into their native bush. Polar bears' camouflage would be greatly benefited if they had leopard spots.
c. Gymnasts are clearly excellent athletes. The best gymnasts are less than five feet tall. Unlike other sports, professional gymnasts' minimum age requirement is sixteen instead of eighteen. Therefore, gymnasts' prime professional years occur during their teenage years.
d. Jack is the smartest eighth-grader at his middle school. Jack could complete college-level coursework.
e. Tuck's Bar & Grill closed its doors for good on Wednesday. One week later, the nearby Lucy's Laundromat also shut down for good. Tuck's closing must have turned away a lot of customers who did their laundry at Lucy's while drinking at Tuck's Bar & Grill.

First, break down the argument. The author's conclusion is that jockeys make for excellent basketball players. The only provided justification is that jockeys are world-class athletes. There is definitely an insufficient amount of evidence to support why a jockey's skill set would be applicable to a completely different sport. Furthermore, the author's only other premise seems to directly contradict the author's conclusion. The argument is an unreasonable application of facts to an unrelated situation. Now that the types of flaws have been identified, look at the answer choices.

Choice *A* makes an unjustified assumption to appeal to the continuation of a trend. Why would countries not change their economic policies if there were good reason? Why would countries continue doing X because they had always done X? An unjustified assumption of continued trends is certainly illogical, but the argument's author does not claim a situation will continue unchanged.

Choice *B* is an unreasonable application of facts to an unrelated situation. This looks very promising. Look at the argument contained in Choice *B*: *Leopards' spots provide excellent camouflage in the bush. The otherwise distinct pattern blends right into the foliage and vegetation. But then the author says this*

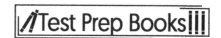

camouflage would retain its excellent cover if applied to polar bears. This does not make logical sense. The author has not justified what makes a leopard's spots universally strong camouflage. It does not make sense why the spots would be useful to a different animal that lives in a different environment. Spots would not make for good camouflage on the Arctic tundra, or floating on ice at sea, etc.

Compare Choice B's flawed reasoning with the argument. Choice B unreasonably applies leopards' spots to the unrelated context of a polar bear. The argument seems to do the same by claiming that jockeys are excellent athletes because they are short; therefore, they would be great basketball players. Both discuss some attribute that works well in one context and then illogically apply it in a different context where the attribute would actually be detrimental. This feels correct but continue reviewing the other choices in case there is a better parallel.

Choice C is intentionally structured in a deceiving way. Be careful of the structural similarities this answer shares with the argument. This answer choice is written with the same structure and uses some of the same exact wording. The test makers often do this to catch test takers who rush through the question.

Despite the seeming similarities, Choice C is clearly incorrect. The answer choice is much more logical than the argument. This choice claims that gymnasts' prime professional years occur during their teenage years. The answer choice justifies this claim by pointing to the lower age requirements and benefit of diminutive size. This answer choice is much more logically sound than the author's jockey argument. Eliminate this choice.

Choice D is also flawed but incorrect. This choice makes an unreasonable and unjustified leap by stating that Jack could complete college work based on his superlative performance in eighth grade. If the choice added examples of other young savants or showed similarities in coursework, then this would be more logically defensible. Although definitely illogical, the author's argument does not share a similar flaw. The argument does not unjustifiably extrapolate an attributes quality; it changes the context of that attribute (leopards' spots). Eliminate this choice.

Choice E is also incorrect. This answer choice illustrates the fallacy of confusing correlation with causation. This is another common fallacy used by the test makers in the arguments and answer choices. Confusing correlation with causation will occur in the same way as this answer choice—two events will occur at the same time (**correlation**) and the argument will say that one event caused the other in some way (**causation**).

Here, the answer choice is claiming that the closing of Tuck's Bar & Grill caused Lucy's Laundromat to permanently shut its doors. This is justified partially by confusing correlation with causation. Although these events happened within one week of one another in close proximity, this does not automatically mean that they are related events. The answer choice additionally asserts that people simultaneously drinking at Tuck's and doing laundry supported Lucy's business. This is an unreasonable assertion of cause for the slowdown of Lucy's business. Eliminate this choice.

Therefore, Choice B is the correct answer, since it best parallels the flawed reasoning presented in the argument.

The Less Common Question Types

The vast majority of the twenty-four to twenty-six questions in each of the two Logical Reasoning sections will be the types described above. However, the Law School Admission Council may add deceptive questions of a different variety. The rest of this discussion focuses on the less common question types on the test.

Not all of these **less common question types** will be on the test. However, it would not be a Law School Admissions Test if a couple were not added. Just as this discussion focused on the most commonly tested types of questions, the test taker should focus on studying the more common questions. Do not fret about being unprepared for the wildcard questions. Spend time on what is guaranteed to be applicable.

The following consists of a brief introduction to the more uncommon questions. Although it is not necessary to master all of these question types, it is best to be prepared for anything. A table summarizing these lesser known questions will follow this final discussion.

Passage Completion

These questions will leave the argument's last sentence blank, and the questions will ask the test taker to choose the statement that best completes the passage. Aside from fitting within the argument's logic and structure, the right answer will also fit stylistically. The tone and voice should fit with the rest of the author's argument. Typically, two or three of the choices will not make sense within the context of the argument and the remaining incorrect choices will not fit the structure or style.

Here are some examples of how **passage completion** questions will appear on the test:

- Which of the following best completes the passage?
- Which of the following statements best completes the last sentence according to the author's argument?

An example of a passage completion question is:

The United States suffered more combat casualties in the Civil War than it suffered in World War I and World War II combined. In fact, more Americans died in the Civil War than in all of America's other wars and conflicts combined. Every war or conflict besides the Civil War involved at least one foreign country or territory. The United States suffered such astronomical casualty rates because _____.

THE COMMON QUESTIONS

Question	Phrasing	Task
Main Point	• Which of the following is the main point of the passage? • What is the argument's primary purpose? • Which of the following most accurately represents the author's conclusion? • What is the conclusion set forth by the author?.	Select the answer that best identified the conclusion or purpose behind the argument.
Inference	• The author would most likely concur with which one of the following? • The author would be likely to agree with which one of the following? • Which one of the following can be properly inferred from the argument? • The argument most strongly supports which of the following assertions?	Fill the logic gap or identify an implied premise asserted by the author.
Assumptions	• Which of the following is a hidden assumption relied upon by the author to advance their argument? • Which assumption, if true, would support the argument's conclusion? • The strength of the argument depends on which of the following? • Upon which of the following assumptions does the author rely upon? • Which assumption does the argument presuppose?	Identify what implicit premise the author is relying upon to justify their conclusion.
New Information	• Which of the following statements, if true, strengthens (weakens) the argument? • Which one of the following, if true, offers the most strengthens (weakens) the argument? • Each of the following, if true, weakens (strengthens) the argument, EXCEPT:	Determine what the question is asking. Are you looking for some movement one direction, the strongest movement in a certain direction, or the one choice that is unlike the others?
Paradoxes	• Which of the following statements, if true, would resolve the discrepancy? • Which of the following statements, if true, would resolve the apparent paradox? • Which of the following best explains the situation in the argument above?	The provided facts will be at odds with each other in some way, and the correct answer will resolve or explain it in some way.
Flawed Reasoning	• The argument above is most vulnerable to criticism on the grounds that: • What is a flaw in the argument's reasoning? • What mistake does the author commit in his reasoning?	Identify the flaw actually present in the author's reasoning.
Parallel Reasoning & Flaws	• Which of the following arguments is most similar to the reasoning in the politician's argument? • Which of the following most closely parallels the scientist's argument? • The flawed reasoning in which of the following arguments is most similar to the baseball coach's argument?	The answer choices will all be arguments. Select the one most similar to the argument in style, structure, and logic or lack thereof.

Which of the following most logically completes the passage?

    a. The Civil War involved little understood developments in weapons.
    b. The United States lost the Civil War.
    c. The United States has limited experience in foreign conflicts.
    d. The Civil War was the bloodiest war in American history.
    e. The Civil War casualty number accounts for soldiers on both sides.

Choice *A* is misleading since it is technically true in real life. Deaths were high during the American Civil War due to developments in weapons outpacing military strategy. Therefore, Union and Confederate soldiers, wielding the early forbearers of modern guns, ran directly at each other as if they still were using muskets and bayonets. Unfortunately, this goes unmentioned in the argument; therefore, it does not exist in this question's universe. The correct selection is limited to what logically completes the passage. It would not be logical for the conclusion to introduce fresh and unrelated support. Eliminate this choice.

Choice *B* is incorrect in real life and irrelevant to the argument. Eliminate this choice.

Choice *C* makes a relative claim that's unaddressed by the argument. It could be possible that Civil War combat casualties were more than all other wars combined because there were not many other wars, but the argument does not reflect this. In fact, the argument mentions America's participation in both world wars. Eliminate this choice.

Choice *D* is true according to the argument, which states that the Civil War resulted in the most combat casualties in American history. It was definitely bloody. However, *Choice D* does not logically complete the argument: *The United States suffered such astronomical casualty rates since the Civil War was the bloodiest war in American history.* The second half of the sentence merely restates the first half. It makes no logical sense. Eliminate this choice.

Choice *E* logically completes the argument. The argument is clearly leading toward mentioning that combat casualties were the highest in the Civil War since it is the country's only civil war. Americans fought on both sides, so combat casualties would obviously be higher. This is directly related and logically completes the argument.

Must Be True & Deductions

These questions are basically the same as the inference questions discussed at length previously. Both **"must be true"** and inference questions ask the test taker to deduce or extrapolate from the argument. The questions will be phrased like, *Based on the passage, which one of the following must be true?* or *Which one of the following statements can be deduced from the passage?*

Here are some examples of must be true and deduction questions:

- Which one of the following statements can be deduced from the passage?
- Based on the passage, which one of the following must be true?

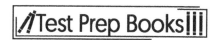

An example of a "must be true" question is:

Denzel Washington is a lizard. All lizards are phenomenal swimmers.

If the statements above are correct, what must be true?
a. Denzel Washington is a lizard.
b. Denzel Washington is neither a lizard nor a phenomenal swimmer.
c. Denzel Washington is a Komodo dragon.
d. Denzel Washington is a phenomenal swimmer.
e. Denzel Washington won the Olympic gold in swimming.

Choice *A* restates the first sentence of the argument. Eliminate this choice.

Choice *B* directly contradicts the argument. There is no way this can be true since the question explicitly states that those statements are correct.

Choice *C* is irrelevant to the argument. The argument does not discuss different species of lizards and how a person could be classified as such.

Choice *D* is the correct choice. If all lizards are phenomenal swimmers and Denzel Washington is a lizard, then it follows that Denzel Washington is a phenomenal swimmer. Do not be put off by arguments that depart from reality. Stick within the argument's framework, resist applying real-world information, and assume everything is true whenever told that it is true.

Choice *E* is irrelevant to the argument. The argument makes no mention of any lizards' swimming accomplishments or accolades.

Point at Issue

Point at Issue arguments will present statements or arguments from two different speakers or perspectives. The question will then ask the test taker to identify the point of contention or how the two conflicting views could be reconciled. Although typically brief, the test makers will pack superfluous and extraneous language and details into the statements. Ignore these distractions and break down the arguments into their main point, using the same method as used for Main Point type of questions. The main points will conflict over some point or detail, which will be the correct answer.

Here are some examples of point at issue questions:

- Jack and Jill disagree on which of the following statements?
- Jack and Jill would most likely agree on which of the following statements?
- What is the main point of dispute in the two arguments?

Practice with this Point at Issue question:

> Scientist: The amount of carbon released into the atmosphere increases every year leading to temperatures at all-time highs. World weather patterns are clearly in flux and climate change is readily apparent. Some tropical rainforest species are going extinct before they can even be discovered. Climate change is causing this modern mass extinction. America needs to assume a leadership position in the global policy discussion regarding climate change.
>
> Politician: World weather patterns are clearly in flux, climate change is readily apparent, and extinctions are now more common. But there's no need to reconsider or reconfigure our energy policy. The Earth's climate has changed throughout its history.

What is the main point of dispute between the scientist and politician?
  a. Whether mass extinctions are of legitimate concern.
  b. Whether climate change is caused by increased carbon emissions.
  c. Whether weather patterns are clearly in flux and climate change is readily apparent.
  d. Whether America needs to take the lead on climate change.
  e. Whether humans can cause or impact climate change.

Choice A is a strong answer choice. The two would likely disagree as to whether mass extinctions are of legitimate concern. The scientist's argument describes the event as modern mass extinction, while the politician just notes that extinctions are more common. The scientist is clearly much more concerned. However, the politician does not explicitly say that the issue is not of legitimate concern. He could consider it concerning and reasonably believe there is nothing to be done. Choice A is not perfect but keep it for now.

Choice B is also fairly strong. The scientist explicitly states that increased carbon emissions are to blame for climate change. Similar to Choice A, the politician does not mention carbon. He could also believe that carbon is causing climate change, but it is a natural process, and nothing can be done about it. This answer is nearly the same as Choice A. Eliminate this choice.

Choice C is incorrect on its face. Both arguments use this same exact language in describing climate change. It is definitely not a point of disagreement. Do not be tricked by the answer choice using similar language.

Choice D is a third strong answer choice. It restates the scientist's conclusion, and it is reasonable to infer that the politician would disagree with it. Although the politician does not mention whether America needs to take the lead on climate change, he basically says that climate change is natural, so nothing needs to be changed. The politician would disagree with it even being an issue. This is stronger than Choices A and B, but now look at Choice E.

Choice E is very strong. The scientist definitely believes that human beings cause and can impact climate change, or else he would not advocate for the dire need for policy changes. In contrast, the politician's conclusion is that climate change is natural, and nothing can be done about it. The politician would strongly disagree that humans have anything to do with climate change aside from living on the planet. This is stronger than Choice D since it best describes the main point of disagreement between the two.

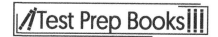

Argument Proceeds By

These arguments focus on the author's reasoning, whether logical or flawed, rather than picking out premises or conclusions. Removing the fluff and focusing on the essentials will make these questions much easier. Since the concept of **Argument Proceeds By** questions is so simple, the test makers utilize even more exaggerated language than usual. The arguments will use overly intellectual language. Look for an answer that describes the steps made by the author in justifying or presenting their argument. Once the distractions are stripped away, these questions will be some of the easiest in the Logical Reasoning section.

Here are some examples of *Argument Proceeds By* questions:

- Which of the following most accurately describes how the argument proceeds?
- Which of the following statements describes how the argument proceeds?
- The argument proceeds by:
- Which of the following is the author's method of reasoning?

An example of a question asking how an argument proceeds is:

> Darren is the world's most terrible human being. He comes from a loving and supportive family. People coming from this background are much more likely to be loving and supportive people themselves. However, this does not apply to Darren. He continues to sell drugs, catch charges, and serve time behind bars.

Which of the following most accurately describes how the argument proceeds?
  a. The argument presents a universal rule and then shows how Darren is an exception.
  b. The argument starts and finishes with different conclusions.
  c. The argument leads with a conclusion, offers evidence of Darren's terrible deeds, and draws on an analogy for additional support.
  d. The argument presents a common trend and then shows how Darren is an exception.
  e. The argument absolves Darren's family of responsibility for his actions.

Choice *A* is incorrect. The argument does not present a universal rule. Universal rule implies that something is always true. What the argument does say is that people from loving and supportive families are *much more likely* to be that way. It is showing a trend or correlation. Universal rule does not accurately describe how the argument proceeds. Eliminate this choice.

Choice *B* is clearly incorrect. The argument first states the conclusion and the entire remainder is devoted to justifying premises. Furthermore, the last sentence is the strongest premise and definitely not a conclusion. Eliminate this choice.

Choice *C* contains two correct statements with a third incorrect statement. The argument does lead with a conclusion and then offers evidence of Darren's terrible deeds—the drug dealing, criminal history, and prison time. However, the argument does not contain an analogy. Eliminate this choice.

Choice *D* looks good. It is similar to Choice *A*, but contains less strong language. In particular, "universal rule" is replaced with "common trend" in Choice *D*. The author definitely shows a common trend—that loving and supportive families are likely to produce loving and supportive people—and then depicts Darren as an exception. This is strong, but first review Choice *E*.

Choice *E* is trickier than the other incorrect answer. It could be argued that the *purpose* of the argument is to absolve Darren's family of responsibility. They provided a loving and supportive environment that, more often than not, succeeds. The author definitely wants to lay the blame on Darren. However, this does not describe how the argument proceeds. It does not pertain to the structure or reasoning. Therefore, Choice *E* is not as strong as Choice *D*.

THE UNCOMMON QUESTIONS		
Question Type	**Phrasing**	**Task**
Passage Completion	• Which of the following best completes the passage? • Which of the following statements best completes the last sentence according to the author's argument?	Complete the last sentence of the argument.
Must Be True & Deductions	• Which one of the following statements can be deduced from the passage? • Based on the passage, which one of the following must be true?	Choose the answer choice that is a proper and accurate extension of the argument.
Point at Issue	• Jack and Jill disagree on which of the following statements? • Jack and Jill would most likely agree on which of the following statements? • What is the main point of dispute in the two arguments?	Given two opposing arguments, identify the point of contention or how the two conflicting views could be reconciled.
Argument Proceeds By	• Which of the following most accurately describes how the argument proceeds? • Which of the following statements describes how the argument proceeds? The argument proceeds by: • Which of the following is the author's method of reasoning?	Select the answer best summarizing the author's reasoning.
Syllogism	• Assuming all of the statements above are correct, which of the following must be true? • According to the argument above, what must follow: • If the above argument is correct, then what cannot be true?	Similar to Inference, Must Be True, and Deduction questions. Test the answer choices against the syllogism to determine what must be true.

Syllogism

A **syllogism** contains two premises and a conclusion. Syllogisms are a classic method of argumentation in formal logic. An example of a basic syllogism is:

John always wears a green shirt on Tuesday.

It is Tuesday.

John is wearing a green shirt.

The test makers usually include one or two syllogism questions. The argument will consist of a short syllogism, and the question will ask, "If the syllogism is true, what answer choice must also be true?"

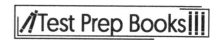

Due to their brevity and simplicity, test takers generally find these questions some of the easiest questions. However, if the syllogism is complex, then it can be helpful to draw a diagram representing the syllogism.

Here are some examples of how syllogism questions will appear on the test:

- Assuming all of the statements above are correct, which of the following must be true?
- According to the argument above, what must follow:
- If the above argument is correct, then what cannot be true?

Here's an example of a syllogism question:

Patricia is lactose intolerant.

Some foods contain lactose.

Patricia cannot safely eat every type of food.

Assuming all of the statements above are correct, which of the following must be true?
a. Patricia cannot eat any food.
b. Some types of food do not contain lactose.
c. Patricia can eat any food.
d. Patricia does not enjoy the taste of lactose.
e. Patricia chose to be lactose intolerant.

Choice *A* is incorrect. Based on the conclusion, it can be reasonably inferred that Patricia can eat some type of food. If there are some foods that she cannot eat safely, then it follows that she can safely eat some other food. Eliminate this choice.

Choice *B* looks very promising. If some food contains lactose, then it means that not all food contains lactose. Therefore, some types of food do not contain lactose. This is a really strong answer choice but examine the rest of the answer choices for a stronger candidate.

Choice *C* is clearly incorrect. The syllogism's conclusion is that Patricia cannot safely eat every type of food. There is no way that Patricia can eat any type of food. Eliminate this choice.

Choice *D* is irrelevant. The argument makes no mention of enjoyment. Eliminate this choice.

Choice *E* is also irrelevant. The argument does not discuss whether lactose intolerance is a result of Patricia's diet, health condition, or allergy, etc.

Catch-All

The Law School Admissions Council will occasionally experiment with a new question type. There is no reason to panic when encountering a question type not included in this discussion. The skills learned and internalized for the common questions will be applicable to solving the new ones. Many of the new questions will focus on the same skills as more common variants. Think of how the **Conclusions** questions are almost identical to the **Main Point** questions. The former is just phrased differently and less common. The rules and application of logic remain unchanged, and the skills learned in this guide will prepare the test taker for all question types.

Analytical Reasoning

The problems in the **Analytical Reasoning** section of the LSAT are like little brainteasers or logic puzzles. For that reason, the Analytical Section is often referred to as the "Logic Games" section.

Most test takers find the Analytical Reasoning questions to be the most time-consuming. There are usually four problems in the Analytical Reasoning section of the test. Because of this, there will be four problems for you to complete in the allotted 35 minutes. Each problem will include five to seven related questions, which amounts to 20 to 28 questions. These questions are usually quite involved, requiring test takers to keep track of a lot of information and identify relationships between items. This effectively makes time the most pressing challenge in the Analytical Reasoning section, which is designed to be virtually impossible to fully complete in the allotted time. This guide will be invaluable in teaching the methods and skills necessary to conserve precious time. Before delving into specifics, more background information on this section will be covered.

At the top of a problem, the test will provide a short setup. The setup will contain two major parts. First, it will contain elements, which are informational facts about people, places, or things. This is the universe of items that will be used to answer the questions. Second, the setup will contain conditions, which limit the elements in a way that facilitates their manipulation. People sometimes refer to these conditions as *rules* or *clues*.

For example, an Analytical Reasoning problem might be about taking people to a movie. The setup might list six possible moviegoers and then explain that there are only four tickets available to distribute. The rules would then be things such as: "Alice will only go to the movie if she can sit next to Bob" and "Bob and Carol won't both go." Then the questions under that problem might ask you things such as: "If Alice sits in Seat 2, which other guest can't come?" or "How many different combinations of guests are possible if Carol attends and sits in Seat 1?"

One thing that distinguishes Analytical Reasoning questions from the other types of LSAT questions is that there is always one, and only one, objectively correct answer. There is never a request to choose "the best answer," which might be requested in other sections. If test takers enjoy using cold, hard logic, this might be their favorite section. Even if not, the advice listed below will give them a systematic way to attack these problems and improve their score.

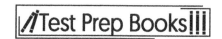

Some people enjoy Analytical Reasoning problems. However, most test takers find the Analytical Reasoning section to be the hardest of the test. Often, this is because the brainteaser concept is the least familiar to them. Other sections of the LSAT are more like something seen on a college entrance exam; however, Analytical Reasoning problems may be puzzles of a type never previously encountered before picking up this book.

For those who initially struggle with these problems, the good news is that the Analytical Reasoning section is the top place to improve scores. Students typically find that as they learn what to expect from an Analytical Reasoning section, completing answers for that section becomes easier with every practice problem. It's all about familiarity with the thought processes required. In fact, there are only a handful of different types of Analytical Reasoning problems. Once students have seen them all, they are prepared for them all. Likewise, the LSAT uses the same types of questions repeatedly. Each time a practice question is attempted, it provides insight into how that type of question works. When that type of question is encountered on test day, the test taker will recognize it and know just what to do with it.

For the reasons discussed above, most test takers would be prudent to dedicate a significant amount of practice time to the Analytical Reasoning section. Readers of this guide should do as many practice problems as possible. How many? The sky is the limit, but it's recommended to complete at least ten Analytical Reasoning sections—that's forty problems, or around two hundred questions—before test day. More is even better. Some people like to set aside an hour each night and just do one section (plus looking over the solutions once finished) each day. It seems like a lot, but once students get used to them, it can be a fun activity—like doing a daily crossword puzzle. Plus, they will become easier.

Analytical Reasoning questions are particularly suitable for group study. It's recommended that an entire Analytical Reasoning section be completed individually without helping each other, then the entire group can go back and compare answers. Additionally, a discussion of respective approaches is helpful, especially when one or more group members did not get the correct answer. Also, a review of the sketches made to address each question and which sketch worked best is helpful. Why that person decided to draw it that way is a question to be asked. Don't be intimidated by the idea of sketching out the problem. It doesn't need to be an artistic masterpiece—just helpful in solving the question. The best sketching techniques will be discussed later in this section.

It's worth emphasizing again that test takers are given thirty-five minutes to answer more than twenty very involved questions. That might not feel like enough time, and it's not. However, the people who design the LSAT intentionally make it very hard, if not impossible, to completely figure every answer to every problem. Along with the specific instructions provided below, here are a few general tips to help make the most of the limited time provided for the test section.

Time Tip #1: Advice on Skipping Problems

In the Analytical Reasoning section, a good chunk of time is going to be spent reading and getting a handle on the setup and rules for a given problem. Once those factors are in the mind and sketched on paper, answering the questions for that problem begins. A first read of the setup and the rules should be done before a sketch is drawn.

It's like building the foundation of a house. Build the foundation right since it will be used repeatedly for each question under that problem. It's best to avoid repeating that initial effort for the same problem, so avoid leaving any problem in the middle of it with plans to come back to it later. Instead, it's better to stick with a problem, get all you can out of the questions under that problem, and then leave the problem behind. It's okay if that means taking an extra minute or two on a problem. Don't worry if there's not going to be enough time to do a thorough job on the last problem and related set of questions; most test takers do not complete this section. Just stick with the problem until it's answered as much as reasonably possible before moving on. If a couple of minutes are left at the end of the section, it is certainly okay to go back and try to answer questions.

Keep in mind that while it is a bad idea to leave a *problem* in the middle, it can be a good idea to leave a *question* in the middle. Take our movie example. If that first question about Alice isn't easily answered, it's okay to move on to the next question. The movie setup will still be in the mind, and the previously completed sketch should help with the answer. When other questions under that problem are completed, any unanswered questions can be figured out. In the example, avoid leaving the movie problem before getting to all of the questions, at least until that problem is ready to be left behind for good.

Some people recommend reading all four problems and starting with the one that looks the easiest. However, there are two reasons to avoid this approach. First, as explained in the preceding paragraphs, you don't have time to read all four problems once, then choose one, then read them again when you return to them. There's just simply not enough time, even for the most efficient test taker. Second, it is just about impossible to quickly determine whether a problem is easy or hard before wading into it. A problem that looks short initially can turn out to be very difficult because its rules are more complex to offset their brevity. Conversely, a problem that looks long initially can be one that includes several rules that help eliminate incorrect choices and offers a faster path toward the correct answer. Rather than spending even two or three of the thirty-five minutes deciding where to start, it's best to start at the beginning. With enough practice, it's possible to move quickly enough to work through all four problems within the allotted time.

Time Tip #2: Tough Questions

There are no penalties for guessing on the LSAT, so it's always worth taking a shot at an answer. This is especially useful in the Analytical Reasoning section, where test takers must make the best use of their limited time.

Among the multiple choices for a given question, one or two choices are often obviously wrong because they directly contradict one of the rules. Choices like these can be ruled out without referring to a sketch or making advanced applications of the rules. For example, in the movie problem given previously, there was a rule that said, "Bob and Carol won't both go." If a question asked, "Which of these combinations of moviegoers would work?" and one of the choices was "Alice, Bob, Carol, and David," then that choice can be obviously ruled out immediately, since Bob and Carol cannot be in the correct answer choice.

We'll discuss these "easy eliminations" further, but for now, just consider how they affect the strategic approach to each question. Before looking at a question, randomly selecting a choice carries no penalty. However, eliminating even one obviously wrong choice tilts the odds in the test taker's favor. After that step, selecting from the remaining choices will add points to a score. So, when stumped, don't feel compelled to struggle to find the one and only right answer. Instead, try to rule out any choices that are obviously wrong, then make a best guess from the remaining choices and move on.

How to Read, Understand, and Correctly Answer Analytical Reasoning Questions

Reading the Setup
Each Analytical Reasoning problem will start with a paragraph that is just a few sentences in length. This paragraph will describe the scenario and identify the people or items meant to be ordered, sorted, chosen, or otherwise handled. It's tempting to just skim the setup and jump down to the rules, but don't be tricked. A key piece of information, which essentially functions as a rule, often can be included in the setup.

Reading the Rules
Underneath the setup, a handful of rules will be provided. There's usually between four and six individual rules, and the rules are usually indented or set aside from the text above and questions below. Rules are typically short and fairly straightforward, but the difficulty arises from applying the rules simultaneously and drawing conclusions. Although the rules tend to be short, they need to be read very carefully. Nearly everything needed to answer Analytical Reasoning questions is contained in these rules.

Some rules will provide a fixed relationship. In the movie example, a rule with a fixed relationship might be, "Carol must sit in Seat 2." Other rules will provide a variable relationship. For example, "Carol must sit in Seat 2 or 4."

Loose vs. Tight Rules
The rule and its implications are sometimes quite subtle. Make sure to always pay close attention to the exact wording of the rules. Rules can often be classified as **loose** or **tight**. Loose rules only provide vague details, while tight rules are much more specific. In general, tight rules are much more helpful because they provide more information, which enables necessary decisions to be made more easily.

Compare the following two rules: "Tyson sits in the seat to Alice's immediate left," and "Bob sits in a seat to the left of Alice." The first rule is tight because it clearly defines where Tyson is sitting. If it's known where Alice is sitting, then it's known where Tyson is sitting as well. The second is a loose rule because it only communicates that Tyson is to the left of Alice. Thus, it leaves open the possibility that there might be other people sitting between them.

Double Negatives
Another thing to watch for in the rules is **double** (or even triple) **negatives**. In other words, a rule will occasionally say something such as, "Alice is not one of the moviegoers who will not sit on the end of the row." When a sentence has multiple words or prefixes indicating "not," test takers should take time to read it carefully and figure out exactly what is being stated. In this example, if Alice is NOT among the group that will NOT sit on the end, then that means she is willing to sit on the end.

Face Value
However, it's important to not obsess over double negatives; the LSAC doesn't try to write trick questions. The questions are often quite difficult, but they are meant to be read in one clear way. There are not multiple interpretations to a rule. Lawyers are notorious for trying to find loopholes and technicalities, but that kind of effort will backfire on the LSAT. If it appears there might be more than one way to read a rule, question, or choice, stick with the most natural reading.

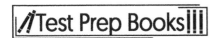

Read Carefully

Each question will have multiple choices, one and only one of which is correct. Pay close attention to any new information introduced in a question. For example, consider the question, "If Alice sits in Seat 2, which other guest can't come?" For that question, and that question ONLY, you must assume Alice is sitting in Seat 2. For all other questions, consider only the information from the setup, the rules, and each of those specific questions.

Key to Success on the Analytical Reasoning Section

After figuring out the setup and rules, test takers might be tempted to try to figure out how all of the rules fit together while they are being read, but they shouldn't. The problems have too many pieces of information and are too complicated to organize at one time. If this is attempted, it's easy to lose track of rules, get confused, use up time unnecessarily, and answer fewer questions correctly.

Instead, drawing a sketch before solving most problems is the best approach. The type of sketch will differ depending on the type of problem, but each sketch should be a simple representation of the relationships expressed in the setup and rules. The idea is to have somewhere to write out the relationships spotted in the rules. Additionally, sketches are valuable places to test out possible answer choices.

The Fine Art of Diagramming

Keep in mind that sketches should always be as simple as possible. A sketch is functional; there are no extra points allotted for the most artistic rendition. If a blank line will suffice to represent a seat in a movie theater, then draw a blank line. There's no need for legs, a chair back, upholstery, etc. It should just be big and clear enough for room to write in the information provided in the setup and rules.

Sketches will improve dramatically in terms of both time and accuracy as problems are practiced. For now, let's look at a couple of basic sketches.

For the movie problem described previously, it might be as simple as four blanks to represent the four seats at the movie theater:

     —— —— —— ——

     1   2   3   4

For a problem in which seven activities the seven days of a week need to be arranged, a drawing can be done with seven squares, with each square representing a day, similar to a week from a calendar page:

After sketching the "playing field," whether that means a row of movie seats or days on a calendar, make sure to accurately label the sketch. This will ensure the sketch accurately illustrates what the rules are expressing. For example, a rule in the movie problem might be, "David is sitting in Seat #3," and a

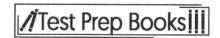

second rule in that problem might be, "Carol does not sit on the end of a row." A proper update to the sketch would be as follows:

___	C	D	___
1	2	3	4

This is an example of how drawing a simple sketch provides immense benefits. After merely reading the two rules, it isn't quite clear where Carol is sitting. However, after placing David in Seat #3, it is clear that Carol must be in Seat #2 since she cannot be on the end row.

Symbols

Note that a "D" was placed in Seat #3, and not "David." Never waste time writing a whole word or name on a sketch. The LSAT will often make it easy on test takers and only use initials in the problem, but if it uses full names, just abbreviate. Additionally, the LSAT test developers do not typically use names beginning with the same letter within the same problem. Abbreviation is encouraged, and necessary, in this section.

Also note that while including the positive information that David is in Seat 3 just meant writing "D" in the appropriate place, the negative information about Carol was a little more complicated to depict. An "X" can be used to indicate "not," and written smaller to leave room for additional information that might be learned or deduced later about those chairs. (It was not necessary to write "D" small in Seat 3, since it was already known who was sitting there.) For this reason, it's generally a good idea to draw large blanks in sketches, since it's better to have too much room than too little.

Not every rule will be easy to represent visually in a simple sketch. For example, if a rule says, "Bob sits in the seat to Alice's immediate left," it wouldn't be known into which seat to draw that relationship. Instead, a "BA" might be placed next to the sketch as a reminder that wherever A is, B must be on the immediate left. Or, if a rule says, "Bob sits in a seat to the left of Alice," we might put a "B ← A" next to our sketch.

As discussed above, there may be additional information introduced in a question, such as, "If Alice sits in Seat #2 . . ." When this kind of question-specific information is presented, it might be best to draw a fresh version of a sketch, such as a mini-sketch, for use in that question only.

Scratch Paper

All sketches should be in the test booklet, along with any other necessary notes. Test takers are allowed to use the booklet for any writing, so they should make the most of it. However, the focus should be on keeping things simple and well-organized. There's a finite amount of space in the test booklet. Furthermore, if you make a sketch too complex, it's easy to get lost in the details of it. The idea is to strip away the distractions to help focus on the information that will lead to a correct answer.

Answer Selection

On other tests, it's usually a matter of reading the question, figuring out the answer, and then looking for it in the answer choices. That approach makes a lot of sense on other tests or other sections of the LSAT, but it is almost always the wrong approach on an Analytical Reasoning question.

The reason is that the rules of Analytical Reasoning problems rarely give enough information to figure out the absolute correct answer. Instead, enough information is given to deduce or rule out a couple of certain things; however, it leaves many possibilities open that "could be true." It's unnecessary to try to make sense of an entire gamut of possibilities.

Instead, it's best to turn to the answer choices. Consider a possible question for the movie scenario mentioned previously:

Which of the following could be an arrangement of moviegoers in Seats 1, 2, 3, and 4, respectively?
   a. Alice, Carol, Elizabeth, David
   b. Carol, Fred, David, Elizabeth
   c. Fred, Bob, Alice, David
   d. Alice, Elizabeth, Bob, David
   e. Alice, Carol, David, Bob

This question is asking for just one arrangement that *could* be true. It's much easier to approach *could be true* questions as "process of elimination" questions. Once it's realized that a choice is not true for whatever reason, eliminate it without a second thought. Then seek the one choice that could conceivably be true, given the information provided.

It would be disastrous to stop after reading the question and try to figure out every possible combination of moviegoers for the four seats. That's partly because it would waste loads of time considering possibilities that aren't applicable to any question. It's also a waste of time because the LSAC usually doesn't provide enough information to figure out every possibility. Problems only provide enough information to address the specific questions.

Rule Busters

Instead, just look at each choice in progression. Some choices can be ruled out immediately because they contradict one of the given rules. For instance:

- If a rule said, "Alice has only one person sitting next to her," Choice *C* can be ruled out because it has Alice between Bob and David.

- Or, if a rule said, "David sits in Seat #4," Choices *B* and *E* can be ruled out because those choices have David in Seat #3.

When a choice can be ruled out, cross it off and move on to the remaining choices. This brings the correct answer one step closer. These easy eliminations are going to help immensely in the Analytical Reasoning section. In fact, as more practice problems are done, patterns can be noted that help spot easy eliminations more quickly. Certain types of rules become apparent and lend themselves to easy eliminations. Rules that simply say something is always true or always false are an example.

In the moviegoer problem, a rule that states, "David sits in Seat #4" enables the elimination of all choices without David in Seat #4. As soon as a rule like that is read, start eliminating the inappropriate choices. By contrast, a conditional rule such as, "If Alice goes to the movie, David will sit in one of the middle two seats" is not as helpful for eliminating answer choices immediately. Similarly, the more abstract rules such as, "Bob sits next to David or Alice, but not both," are not as helpful because they don't provide concrete information.

Some answers will initially appear to be correct answers. In other words, an answer might seem obviously right based on direct application of just one of the rules. It's tempting to mark that choice as the answer and move to the next question, but don't be too quick to do so. While it is common that a rule might directly rule out one of the choices, it is rare that rules will easily and directly require a certain choice to be right. If an easy answer seems apparent, take a good hard look at the question, rules, and answer choices. Read through the other answer choice just in case something is being missed. If it seems too obvious and direct, it is likely incorrect.

When reading through answer choices for the first time, it might be easy to eliminate one or two based on an obvious contradiction of the rules. This is when a good sketch can be helpful. All remaining choices should be reviewed and penciled into a sketch. See how they do or don't fit the relationships and rules sketched out. One or more additional choices can usually be ruled out because they contradict the rules as they're represented in the sketch.

Common Sense

Of course, it's wonderful to be able to get to one right answer. It's time to mark that answer and move to the next question. If not, keep looking at the setup, the rules, and the choices, filtering everything in a sketch where it feels helpful to do so. Keep trying to get down to one right answer. The good news is that impossible leaps of logic to reach a solution should never be necessary. Trust in common sense when reading the problem and rules to keep moving toward a solution.

Final Notes

It's important to be aware of the passing time. Sooner or later, a point will be reached when time is better spent on the next question rather than trying to eliminate that next-to-last choice. With practice, test takers can improve their ability to realize when additional effort isn't worth the time. Remember, for every answer choice that can be eliminated, the better the odds of guessing the correct answer. These questions are meant to be time-consuming brainteasers, so test takers should remain positive. It's best to pick what appears to be the correct answer, declare victory, and move on to the next question.

Basic Types of Analytical Reasoning Problems

Problems in the Analytical Reasoning section usually fall into one of the following five recognizable types. Sometimes a problem will combine a couple of these types.

- **Selection**: The setup will request a smaller group of people, items, or things be selected from a larger group, and the conditions will provide the criteria for selecting the group.

- **Assignment**: The setup will request various people, items, or things are assigned into smaller groups, while the conditions will provide the criteria for divvying them into groups.

- **Ordering**: The setup will ask that people, items, or things be placed in some clearly defined order, and the conditions will provide rules governing the relationships. Days of the week are a common structure for an ordering question.

- **Connecting**: The setup and conditions will provide specific criteria or instructions for connecting people, items, or things in some particular way.

- **Hybrid**: Some setups will combine two or more of the types of problems. Test developers also occasionally devise a novel setup; however, skills attained to solve other types of test problems will still be applicable and important.

An overview of what to expect from each of these problem types now will be presented, including how to efficiently draw a sketch and approach the related questions.

Selection Problems

In a **selection problem**, a list of items will be given. The questions will ask you to select certain items from that list. For example, a list of students might be provided with a request to follow rules given to select some of those students and place them in a study group. Alternatively, a list of food dishes might be provided with a request to follow the rules and select certain dishes for a menu. The rules in a selection problem will place conditions on which items can or cannot be grouped together.

As an example, here is the setup and four rules for a selection problem:

> The CDC needs to send a three-person team of professionals to the site of a disease outbreak. The available personnel are three containment specialists, Amber, Brandon, and Cameron; three quarantine specialists, Denise, Edgar, and Fitz; and two generalists, Greg and Heather. The following conditions apply to the formation of the team:
>
>> - The team must have one and only one generalist.
>>
>> - Either Brandon or Edgar, but not both, are on the team.
>>
>> - There are not three of any one specialty on the same team.
>>
>> - If Amber is on the team, then no quarantine specialist is on the team.

This should be immediately identified as a selection problem because a list of names is given with a request to select a smaller group from the big list. When a sorting problem is recognized, start by sketching out the structure of the groups identified in the setup. Here, it's necessary to pick a team of three people, so sketching three blank lines on which to place the initials of the people would be appropriate. Note: a sketch with five more blank lines also could be drawn on which the initials of the people you do NOT choose could be written.

___ ___ ___   c: A, B, C

q: D, E, F

g: G, H

Selection problems often work this way. Sometimes answers can be determined by looking at which members of the large group are selected. At other times, answers can be found by looking at which members are excluded. (For this reason, some people refer to these kinds of problems as "In/Out" problems.) Sketches should be drawn to look at both perspectives.

As rules are read, each sketch should be drawn. The first rule states that one of the slots on the team must be filled with one of the generalists. This fact can be visualized by noting a small "g" next to one of the three blanks representing the team members. The rule also states that there is "only one" generalist on the team. Since two generalists, Greg and Heather, are given, it's known that if one is on the team, then the other must be off the team. Alternatively, a small "g" can also be used next to one of the five blanks representing the people who are not going to make the team. The more information from the rules that can be visualized in a sketch, the easier it will be to answer the selection problem's questions.

After incorporating as much information from the rules into a sketch as possible, it's time to start looking at the questions. A common type of selection question might ask which of several teams is possibly a valid group. That question could be approached by filling in each of the possible choices into a

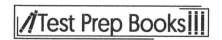

sketch to determine which choices violate the rules. Another common type of selection question might provide an additional rule (such as, "If two quarantine specialists are on the team . . .") and then ask for a selection among choices under that scenario. Again, that question could be approached by filling the choices into a sketch (including the note that two slots are needed for quarantine specialists for this question only) and seeing which ones break rules.

Assignment Problems

An assignment problem is a lot like a selection problem. The difference is that instead of having just one group to select from the larger group, sorting the larger group into several subgroups will instead be necessary. Here's an example setup of an assignment problem:

> A non-profit organization has 10 fundraising volunteers and needs to form teams of those volunteers to work on the organization's four fundraising events for the year. Each team must have at least two members, and no volunteer is willing to be on more than one team. The following rules govern the selection of the teams:

For this problem, the selection of people from the group of 10 volunteers is required, but instead of just one group, they will be formed into four groups. In this respect, grouping problems are a bit more complicated than selection problems, but the LSAC usually compensates by making the rules a little less complex than in a selection problem. The approach, however, should be the same. Visualize the situation. Here, four teams of at least two people are needed and—because three of the smallest possible teams would leave only four volunteers—no team will have more than four people. Sketch it out, with blanks for each person, incorporating information from the rules where possible. Then head to the questions, ruling out choices that violate rules until an answer is found.

Ordering Problems

In an **ordering problem**, a list of items is provided. Questions will request that the list of items be placed in order. For example, a list of television programs might be provided with a request to schedule and arrange them into a television network's night of programming. Or, a list of students might be given with a request to place them in the order they will stand up to give book reports.

Here's an example of the setup for an ordering problem:

> A film studies class at the local college will show eight movies, one each week over the first eight weeks of the semester. The eight movies are called April Showers, Bananas, Cruise Ship, Dog Park, Echoes, Fight Game, Giraffe Games, and Holiday Party. The schedule for the movies must obey the following conditions:

Remember, any time a setup involves a schedule, sequence, or order of items, it's likely to be an ordering problem. Terms such as class schedules, lines of people at grocery stores, books arranged in order on shelves, and similar wording will often be included in the setup. In all of these cases, it's best to start with a simple sketch that lays out the possible schedule, position, or order to work with before filling in additional information.

Ordering problems are often fairly straightforward because there is usually just one specified order to fill in. In other words, unlike a grouping problem with odd-sized subgroups, in an ordering problem, there's often a request such as having eight movies for eight weeks, six individuals for six spots in a line, or something similar. However, the complexity in an ordering problem arises from rules that specify fairly complex relationships between the various items that need to be placed in order. It's best to use sketching skills to visualize the possibilities, and then use trial and error to rule out combinations that violate one or more rules.

Connecting Problems

In a **connecting problem**, a short list of items will be provided, along with a list of criteria or characteristics that have to be connected to those items. For example, a list of people dining at a restaurant might be given with a request to list which people order which items off of a menu. Another example might be when a list of high school athletes is given with a request of which sports they play.

Here's an example of the setup and rules for a connecting problem:

> Andrew, Becca, Chris, and Drea are students who played intramural sports this school year. The sports they played are baseball, football, basketball, and soccer, consistent with the following rules:
>
> - Each student played at least one sport.
> - No student played all four sports.
> - Chris and Becca played at least one sport together.
> - Drea and Chris played no sports together.
> - Becca did not play soccer.
> - Drea played football.

In this problem, there is a group of items (the four students) and a group of characteristics (the four sports) that the students may or may not share. These are common characteristics of a connecting problem. The goal with this problem is to connect the students with the sports they played.

As always, approach this type of problem by sketching it out. Specifically, arrange the items in the first category in one vertical list, and the items in the second category in another vertical list. Leave lots of space between the columns since each item in these problems can connect to multiple characteristics. Thus, plenty of room to draw in multiple, clear connections will be needed. Then, sketch what the rules describe about the relationships between the members of the two categories by drawing lines between items. Make sure to use a symbol that will distinguish between a line that indicates a valid connection and one illustrating that there is no connection. Finally, turn to the questions and use the process of elimination to arrive at the answers.

Hybrid Problems

The LSAT test writers will occasionally add a problem that doesn't neatly fit into any one category, or they may combine elements of multiple problem types. Because these problems are outside the usual categories, they are often written with less complexity than a more standard problem. This can make them ideal problems to grab some "low-hanging fruit," scoring easy points while making up some time. As always, the trick is to visualize what is being asked. Make a simple sketch, fill in what is known by the setup and rules given, and start trying the choices to see what works.

Final Thoughts

A first Analytical Reasoning set can be very daunting. It may even seem impossible. Just remember that 90 percent of the battle with this section is familiarity. Analytical Reasoning problems include the same sorts of problem types, patterns, clues, and logical reasoning over and over again. Once ten or more Analytical Reasoning sets are completed, students often find that they are recognizing problem types faster, deciding how to sketch a diagram quicker, getting more answers correct, and finishing more questions. Remember, the majority of practice time should be spent on this one section, especially if a test taker is initially weakest in Analytical Reasoning. It is the easiest section to improve a score through practice and repetition alone.

Reading Comprehension

The Reading Comprehension section of the LSAT provides a passage to read and asks you to answer questions relating to the passage after you've read it. There are four subsections of readings, each containing five to eight questions. One of the four sections contains two shorter passages, which are meant to be comparative. The purpose of the Reading Comprehension section is to test whether students are able to understand, analyze, and/or synthesize complex text information given a certain set of questions. Lawyers are constantly confronted with difficult texts that require tedious analysis, so this section is important for test takers to learn.

The passages you will encounter on the LSAT will be drawn from the social sciences, law-related subjects, humanities, and biological and physical sciences. The sections below provide a comprehensive list of characteristics you will encounter in the passages. Some of the sections, such as Main Idea or Words used in Context, should be familiar to you. However, other sections, such as Principles that Function in the Selection or The Impact of New Information, are subjects that may be unfamiliar to new LSAT test takers.

It's important to remember that it is not necessary to have outside knowledge of the passage information before you enter the test. Every question relies on the universe of the passage; therefore, it's important to read the whole passage first and at least designate what the primary purpose or main idea of the passage is. If you delve straight into the questions, you may not have a sense of the passage's entirety and thus will waste time reading answers that have no meaning to you.

Main Idea or Primary Purpose

On the LSAT, some questions may ask you to identify the **main idea** or **primary purpose** of the passage. The main idea is what the writer wants to say about that topic. A writer may make the point that global warming is a growing problem that must be addressed in order to save the planet. Therefore, the topic is global warming, and the main idea is that it's *a serious problem needing to be addressed*. The **topic** can be expressed in a word or two, but the main idea should be a complete thought.

In order to illustrate the main idea, a writer will use **supporting details**—the details that provide evidence or examples to help make a point. Supporting details are typically found in nonfiction texts that seek to inform or persuade the reader.

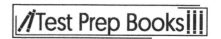

For example, in the example of global warming, where the author's main idea is to show the seriousness of this growing problem and the need for change, the use of supporting details would be critical in effectively making that point. Supporting details used here might include statistics on an increase in global temperatures and studies showing the impact of global warming on the planet. The author could also include projections regarding future climate change in order to illustrate potential lasting effects of global warming.

Some questions may also ask you what the best title is for the passage. Going back to the topic, for these questions, it's important to give a narrower answer that still encompasses the main idea of the passage. Asking for the appropriate title for passages is rare, but it's best to be prepared for anything.

Finally, the LSAT may ask to you summarize the passage you've read. Giving a summary is different than pointing out the main idea; in a **summary**, expect to choose a more comprehensive answer, one that includes the most important points in the passage that you've read. In our example of global warming, the summary might be the main idea merged with the most important supporting details. Reading the passage in its entirety before approaching the questions is key to obtaining a comprehensive idea of the text's most important aspects.

Information that is Explicitly Stated

As a reader, you will want to draw a conclusion about what the author has presented. **Drawing a conclusion** will help you to understand what the writer intended as well as whether you agree with what he or she has said. There are a few ways to determine the logical conclusion, but careful reading is the most important. Read the passage a few times and highlight or take notes on the details that you deem important to the meaning of the piece. You may draw a conclusion that is different than what the writer intended, or you may draw more than one conclusion. Look carefully at the details to see if your conclusion matches up with what the writer has presented and intended for readers to understand. Of course, in the test itself, you may not have time to take notes or compare. However, it may be helpful to practice this on your own to make sure your comprehension skills are strong.

Textual evidence can help readers to draw a conclusion about a passage. Textual evidence refers to information such as facts and examples that support the main point; it will likely come from outside sources and can be in the form of quoted or paraphrased material. Look at this evidence and its credibility and validity in relation to the main idea to draw a conclusion about the writing.

Consider that the author may state the conclusion directly in the passage. Inferring the author's conclusion is useful, especially when it is not overtly stated, but inferences should not outweigh the information that is directly stated. Alternatively, when readers are trying to draw a conclusion about a text, it may not always be directly stated.

As mentioned, a summary is another effective way to draw a conclusion from a passage. A **summary** is a shortened version of the original text, written in one's own words. It should focus on the main points of the original text, including only the relevant details. It's important to be brief but thorough in a summary. While the summary should always be shorter than the original passage, it should still retain the meaning of the original source.

Like summarizing, paraphrasing can also help a reader to fully understand a part of a reading. **Paraphrasing** requires the reader to take a small part of the passage and to say it in their own words. Paraphrasing is more than rewording the original passage, though. It should be written in one's own way, while still retaining the meaning of the original source. When a reader's goal is to write something in their own words, deeper understanding of the original source is required. Again, working to summarize or paraphrase each passage on the test may not be the most efficient use of your time. However, think about these tools when practicing comprehending passages. Once you are familiar with carefully selecting important aspects of the passage, it will come easier to you on test day.

The Purpose of Words or Phrases as Used in Context

Knowledge of synonyms and antonyms is crucial for writing and identifying a good paraphrase and also helps readers expand their mental vocabulary network. Another useful vocabulary skill is being able to understand meaning in context. A word's **context** refers to all the other words and information surrounding it, and the context of a word can have an impact on how readers interpret that word's meaning. Of course, many words have more than one definition. For example, consider the meaning of the word *engaged*. The first definition that comes to mind might be "promised to be married," but consider the following sentences:

A: The two armies engaged in a conflict that lasted all night.

B: The three-hour lecture flew by because students were so engaged in the material.

C: The busy executive engaged a new assistant to help with his workload.

As you can see, *engaged* has a variety of other meanings. In these sentences, respectively, it can mean: "battled," "interested or involved," and "appointed or employed." With so many possible definitions, readers may wonder how to decide which one to apply in a given sentence. The appropriate meaning is prioritized based on context. For example, sentence *C* mentions "executive," "assistant," and "workload," so readers can assume that *engaged* has something to do with work—in which case, "appointed or employed" would be the best definition for this context. Context clues can also be found in sentence *A*. Words like "armies" and "conflicts" show that this sentence is about a military situation (and not about marriage or the office), so in this context, *engaged* is closest in meaning to "battled." By using context clues—the surrounding words in the sentence—readers can easily select the most appropriate definition for the word in question.

In addition to helping readers select the best meaning for a word with many definitions, context clues can also help readers when they don't know any meanings for a certain word. Test writers will deliberately ask about vocabulary that test takers are probably unfamiliar with in order to measure their ability to use context to make an educated guess about a word's meaning.

Which of the following is the closest in meaning to the word *loquacious* in the following sentence?

The loquacious professor was notorious for always taking too long to finish his lectures.
   a. Knowledgeable
   b. Enthusiastic
   c. Approachable
   d. Talkative
   e. Inexperienced

Even if the word *loquacious* seems completely new, it is still possible to utilize context to make a good guess about the word's meaning. Grammatically, it is apparent that *loquacious* is an adjective that modifies the noun "professor"—so *loquacious* must be some kind of quality or characteristic. A clue in this sentence is "taking too long to finish his lectures." Readers should then brainstorm qualities that might cause a professor to be late. Perhaps he is "disorganized," "slow," or "talkative"—all words that might still make sense in this sentence. After brainstorming some ideas for the word's definition, take a look at the choices for the question. Choice *D* matches one word from the brainstorming session, and it is a logical choice for this sentence—the professor talks too much, so his lectures run late. In fact, *loquacious* means "talkative" or "wordy."

One way to use context clues is to think of potential replacement words before considering the answer choices given in the question. However, if it is truly a struggle to come up with any possibilities, turn to the answer choices first and try to replace each of them in the sentence to see if the sentence is still logical and retains the same meaning.

Which of the following is the closest in meaning to the word *dogma* in the following sentence?

Martin Luther was a revolutionary religious figure because he argued against Catholic dogma and encouraged a new interpretation of Christianity.
   a. Punishments
   b. Doctrines
   c. Leadership
   d. Procedures
   e. History

Based on context, this sentence has something to do with religious conflict and interpretations of Christian faith. The only word related to religious belief is Choice *B*, *doctrines*, which is in fact the best synonym for *dogma*.

Yet another way to use context clues is to consider clues in the word itself. Most students are probably familiar with prefixes, suffixes, and root words—the building blocks of many English words. A little knowledge goes a long way when it comes to these components of English vocabulary, and they can point readers in the right direction when they need help finding an appropriate definition.

Which of the following is the closest in meaning to the word *antipathy* in the following sentence?

A strong antipathy existed between Margaret and her new neighbor, Susan.
   a. Enmity
   b. Resemblance
   c. Relationship
   d. Alliance
   e. Persuasion

In this case, the sentence does not provide much context for the word *antipathy*. However, the word itself gives some useful clues. The prefix *anti-* means "opposite or against," so *antipathy* probably has a negative meaning. Also, if readers already know words like "sympathy" or "empathy," they might guess that the root word "path" is related to emotions. So, antipathy must be a feeling *against* something. *Alliance* is a positive connection, *relationship* is too neutral, and *resemblance* means two things are similar to each other. *Persuasion* usually relates to a set of beliefs or the act of coercing someone of something, so this is choice is nonsensical for the provided sentences. The only word that shows a negative or opposite feeling is Choice *A*, enmity (the feeling of being enemies). In this way, even an unfamiliar word may contain clues that can indicate its meaning.

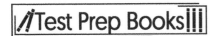

The Author's Attitude in the Tone of a Passage

Style, tone, and mood are often thought to be the same thing. Though they're closely related, there are important differences to keep in mind. The easiest way to do this is to remember that style creates and affects tone and mood. More specifically, style is *how the writer uses words* to create the desired tone and mood for their writing.

Style

Style can include any number of technical writing choices, and some may have to be analyzed on the test. A few examples of style choices include:

- **Sentence Construction**: When presenting facts, does the writer use shorter sentences to create a quicker sense of the supporting evidence, or does he or she use longer sentences to elaborate and explain the information?

- **Technical Language**: Does the writer use jargon to demonstrate their expertise in the subject, or does he or she use ordinary language to help the reader understand things in simple terms?

- **Formal Language**: Does the writer refrain from using contractions such as *won't* or *can't* to create a more formal tone, or does he or she use a colloquial, conversational style to connect to the reader?

- **Formatting**: Does the writer use a series of shorter paragraphs to help the reader follow a line of argument, or does he or she use longer paragraphs to examine an issue in great detail and demonstrate their knowledge of the topic?

On the test, examine the writer's style and how their writing choices affect the way the text comes across.

Tone

Tone refers to the writer's attitude toward the subject matter. For example, the tone conveys how the writer feels about the topic he or she is writing about. A lot of nonfiction writing has a neutral tone, which is an important tone for the writer to take. A neutral tone demonstrates that the writer is presenting a topic impartially and letting the information speak for itself. On the other hand, nonfiction writing can be just as effective and appropriate if the tone isn't neutral. For instance, consider this example:

> Seat belts save more lives than any other automobile safety feature. Many studies show that airbags save lives as well; however, not all cars have airbags. For instance, some older cars don't. Furthermore, airbags aren't entirely reliable. For example, studies show that in 15% of accidents, airbags don't deploy as designed; but, on the other hand, seat belt malfunctions are extremely rare. The number of highway fatalities has plummeted since laws requiring seat belt usage were enacted.

In this passage, the writer mostly chooses to retain a neutral tone when presenting information. If the writer would instead include their own personal experience of losing a friend or family member in a car accident, the tone would change dramatically. The tone would no longer be neutral and would show that the writer has a personal stake in the content, allowing them to interpret the information in a different way. When analyzing tone, consider what the writer is trying to achieve in the text and how they *create* the tone using style.

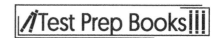

Mood

Mood refers to the feelings and atmosphere that the writer's words create for the reader. Like tone, many nonfiction texts can have a neutral mood. To return to the previous example, if the writer chose to include information about a person they knew dying in a car accident, the text would carry an emotional component that is absent in the previous example. Depending on how they present the information, the writer can create a sad, angry, or even hopeful mood. When analyzing the mood, consider what the writer wants to accomplish and whether the best choice was made to achieve that end.

Types of Appeals

In nonfiction writing, authors employ argumentative techniques to present their opinion to readers in the most convincing way. Persuasive writing usually includes at least one type of appeal: an appeal to logic (**logos**), emotion (**pathos**), or credibility and trustworthiness (**ethos**). When a writer appeals to logic, they are asking readers to agree with them based on research, evidence, and an established line of reasoning. An author's argument might also appeal to readers' emotions, perhaps by including personal stories and anecdotes (a short narrative of a specific event). A final type of appeal—appeal to authority—asks the reader to agree with the author's argument on the basis of their expertise or credentials. Consider three different approaches to arguing the same opinion:

Logic (Logos)

Below is an example of an appeal to logic. The author uses evidence to disprove the logic of the school's rule (the rule was supposed to reduce discipline problems, but the number of problems has not been reduced; therefore, the rule is not working) and he or she calls for its repeal.

> Our school should abolish its current ban on campus cell phone use. The ban was adopted last year as an attempt to reduce class disruptions and help students focus more on their lessons. However, since the rule was enacted, there has been no change in the number of disciplinary problems in class. Therefore, the rule is ineffective and should be done away with.

Emotion (Pathos)

An author's argument might also appeal to readers' emotions, perhaps by including personal stories and anecdotes. The next example presents an appeal to emotion. By sharing the personal anecdote of one student and speaking about emotional topics like family relationships, the author invokes the reader's empathy in asking them to reconsider the school rule.

> Our school should abolish its current ban on campus cell phone use. If students aren't able to use their phones during the school day, many of them feel isolated from their loved ones. For example, last semester, one student's grandmother had a heart attack in the morning. However, because he couldn't use his cell phone, the student didn't know about his grandmother's condition until the end of the day—when she had already passed away, and it was too late to say goodbye. By preventing students from contacting their friends and family, our school is placing undue stress and anxiety on students.

Credibility (Ethos)

Finally, an appeal to authority includes a statement from a relevant expert. In this case, the author uses a doctor in the field of education to support the argument. All three examples begin from the same

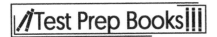

opinion—the school's phone ban needs to change—but rely on different argumentative styles to persuade the reader.

> Our school should abolish its current ban on campus cell phone use. According to Dr. Bartholomew Everett, a leading educational expert, "Research studies show that cell phone usage has no real impact on student attentiveness. Rather, phones provide a valuable technological resource for learning. Schools need to learn how to integrate this new technology into their curriculum." Rather than banning phones altogether, our school should follow the advice of experts and allow students to use phones as part of their learning.

Rhetorical Questions
Another commonly used argumentative technique is asking **rhetorical questions**, questions that do not actually require an answer but that push the reader to consider the topic further.

> I wholly disagree with the proposal to ban restaurants from serving foods with high sugar and sodium contents. Do we really want to live in a world where the government can control what we eat? I prefer to make my own food choices.

Here, the author's rhetorical question prompts readers to put themselves in a hypothetical situation and imagine how they would feel about it.

The Organization or Structure

Good writing is not merely a random collection of sentences. No matter how well written, sentences must relate and coordinate appropriately to one another. If not, the writing seems random, haphazard, and disorganized. Therefore, good writing must be organized, where each sentence fits a larger context and relates to the sentences around it.

Text Structures
Depending on what the author is attempting to accomplish, certain formats or text structures work better than others. For example, a sequence structure might work for narration but not for identifying similarities and differences between concepts. Similarly, a comparison-contrast structure is not useful for narration. It's the author's job to put the right information in the correct format.

Readers should be familiar with the five main literary structures:

Sequence Structure
Sequence structure (sometimes referred to as the order structure) is when the order of events proceeds in a predictable order. In many cases, this means the text goes through the plot elements: exposition, rising action, climax, falling action, and resolution. Readers are introduced to characters, setting, and conflict in the **exposition**. In the **rising action**, there's an increase in tension and suspense. The **climax** is the height of tension and the point of no return. **Tension** decreases during the falling action. In the **resolution**, any conflicts presented in the exposition are resolved, and the story concludes. An informative text that is structured sequentially will often go in order from one step to the next.

Problem-Solution
In the **problem-solution structure**, authors identify a potential problem and suggest a solution. This form of writing is usually divided into two paragraphs and can be found in informational texts. For

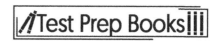

example, cell phone, cable, and satellite providers use this structure in manuals to help customers troubleshoot or identify problems with services or products.

Comparison-Contrast

When authors want to discuss similarities and differences between separate concepts, they arrange thoughts in a **comparison-contrast paragraph structure**. **Venn diagrams** are an effective graphic organizer for comparison-contrast structures because they feature two overlapping circles that can be used to organize similarities and differences. A comparison-contrast essay organizes one paragraph based on similarities and another based on differences. A comparison-contrast essay can also be arranged with the similarities and differences of individual traits addressed within individual paragraphs. Words such as *however*, *but*, and *nevertheless* help signal a contrast in ideas.

Descriptive

Descriptive writing is designed to appeal to your senses. Much like an artist who constructs a painting, good descriptive writing builds an image in the reader's mind by appealing to the five senses: *sight, hearing, taste, touch,* and *smell.* However, overly descriptive writing can become tedious; likewise, sparse descriptions can make settings and characters seem flat. Good authors strike a balance by applying descriptions only to facts that are integral to the passage.

Cause and Effect

Passages that use the **cause and effect structure** are simply asking *why* by demonstrating some type of connection between ideas. Words such as *if*, *since*, *because*, *then*, or *consequently* indicate a relationship. By switching the order of a complex sentence, the writer can rearrange the emphasis on different clauses. Saying, *If Sheryl is late, we'll miss the dance*, is different from saying *We'll miss the dance if Sheryl is late*. One emphasizes Sheryl's tardiness while the other emphasizes missing the dance. Paragraphs can also be arranged in a cause and effect format. Since the format—before and after—is sequential, it is useful when authors wish to discuss the impact of choices. Researchers often apply this paragraph structure to the scientific method.

Transition Words

The writer should act as a guide, showing the reader how all the sentences fit together. Consider this example:

> Seat belts save more lives than any other automobile safety feature. Many studies show that airbags save lives as well. Not all cars have airbags. Many older cars don't. Airbags aren't entirely reliable. Studies show that in 15% of accidents, airbags don't deploy as designed. Seat belt malfunctions are extremely rare.

There's nothing wrong with any of these sentences individually, but together they're disjointed and difficult to follow. The best way for the writer to communicate information is through the use of transition words. Here are examples of transition words and phrases that tie sentences together, enabling a more natural flow:

- To show causality: *as a result*, *therefore*, and *consequently*
- To compare and contrast: *however*, *but*, and *on the other hand*
- To introduce examples: *for instance*, *namely*, and *including*
- To show order of importance: *foremost*, *primarily*, *secondly*, and *lastly*

NOTE: This is not a complete list of transitions. There are many more that can be used; however, most fit into these or similar categories. The point is that the words should clearly show the relationship between sentences, supporting information, and the main idea.

Here is an update to the previous example using transition words. These changes make it easier to read and bring clarity to the writer's points:

> Seat belts save more lives than any other automobile safety feature. Many studies show that airbags save lives as well; however, not all cars have airbags. For instance, some older cars don't. Furthermore, airbags aren't entirely reliable. For example, studies show that in 15% of accidents, airbags don't deploy as designed; but, on the other hand, seat belt malfunctions are extremely rare.

Also, be prepared to analyze whether the writer is using the best transition word or phrase for the situation. Take this sentence for example: "As a result, seat belt malfunctions are extremely rare." This sentence doesn't make sense in the context above because the writer is trying to show the contrast between seat belts and airbags, not the causality.

Logical Sequence

Even if the writer includes plenty of information to support their point, the writing is only coherent when the information is in a logical order. **Logical sequencing** is really just common sense, but it's also an important writing technique. First, the writer should introduce the main idea, whether for a paragraph, a section, or the entire piece. Second, they should present evidence to support the main idea by using transitional language. This shows the reader how the information relates to the main idea and the sentences around it. The writer should then take time to interpret the information, making sure necessary connections are obvious to the reader. Finally, the writer can summarize the information in a closing section.

NOTE: Though most writing follows this pattern, it isn't a set rule. Sometimes writers change the order for effect. For example, the writer can begin with a surprising piece of supporting information to grab the reader's attention, and then transition to the main idea. Thus, if a passage doesn't follow the logical order, don't immediately assume it's wrong. However, most writing usually settles into a logical sequence after a nontraditional beginning.

Introductions and Conclusions

Examining the writer's strategies for introductions and conclusions puts the reader in the right mindset to interpret the rest of the text. Look for methods the writer might use for **introductions** such as:

- Stating the main point immediately, followed by outlining how the rest of the piece supports this claim.

- Establishing important, smaller pieces of the main idea first, and then grouping these points into a case for the main idea.

- Opening with a quotation, anecdote, question, seeming paradox, or other piece of interesting information, and then using it to lead to the main point.

- Whatever method the writer chooses, the introduction should make their intention clear, establish their voice as a credible one, and encourage a person to continue reading.

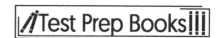

Conclusions tend to follow a similar pattern. In them, the writer restates their main idea a final time, often after summarizing the smaller pieces of that idea. If the introduction uses a quote or anecdote to grab the reader's attention, the conclusion often makes reference to it again. Whatever way the writer chooses to arrange the conclusion, the final restatement of the main idea should be clear and simple for the reader to interpret. Finally, conclusions shouldn't introduce any new information.

Information or Ideas that can be Inferred

Inference questions require drawing a conclusion using reasoning and evidence. Inference requires careful reading of the passage to determine the author's intended meaning. The author's main idea or overall meaning may be directly stated in the passage, but in some cases, it is not. The implied meaning is what is not explicitly stated in the passage, so it is necessary to use details from the passage to decipher the author's implications. Using the facts and evidence presented in the passage, it is possible to draw a logical conclusion about the author's intended meaning.

The Premise
Inference questions are based on the premises provided in the passage. **Premises** are the facts or evidence presented by the author. These premises should be taken as fact, even if they are based on the author's opinion. In some cases, the reader may disagree with the premises presented, or even know them to be untrue, but it is important to view the premises as fact. This is what the author believes and wants the reader to believe, so the premises will help lead the reader to the most logical conclusion.

There are certain clue words that can indicate the premises in a passage. These clue words include:

- because
- for
- since
- as
- given that
- in that
- as indicated by
- owing to

While these words can help the reader discover the author's premises, inference requires reading between the lines to find the implied meaning of the passage. The implications of the facts are what lead the reader to a logical conclusion.

Question Types
An inference question may focus on a word's meaning or ask the reader to draw a conclusion based on the evidence presented. It is helpful to know that a question calls for inference, so it is not confused with assumption.

Some clues to look for are questions that use statements like the following:

- If the previous statements are true, it logically follows that
- Must be true
- Author's conclusion
- Best supported by

It's important to remember that the facts presented should be taken as true, even if they aren't. When answering this type of question, answers that could be true, but not based on the facts presented in the passage, should be avoided. Instead, readers should look for the only answer that must be true based on the premises provided. Also avoid making assumptions, as this is a different type of question. Inference is about drawing a logical conclusion based on facts, not making assumptions.

Answer Types

Avoid answers that go too far in their value judgment. These answers are often distractors and can be identified by the use of words like *always*, *never*, *only*, and *must*. These absolutes are tough to prove, and likely not to be inferred. The words to look for in the answers to inference questions are *some*, *most*, *can*, and *possibly*, because these are far more likely to indicate an inferred conclusion. Another distractor is an answer that is based on a different subject altogether. This is likely not the answer to an inference question and can typically be thrown out.

Sample Question

Congress passed the Older Americans Act (OAA) in 1965 in response to concern by policymakers about a lack of community social services for older persons. The original legislation established authority for grants to States for community planning and social services, research and development projects, and personnel training in the field of aging. The law also established the Administration on Aging (AoA) to administer the newly created grant programs and to serve as the Federal focal point on matters concerning older persons.

Although older individuals may receive services under many other Federal programs, today, the OAA is considered to be the major vehicle for the organization and delivery of social and nutrition services to this group and their caregivers. It authorizes a wide array of service programs through a national network of 56 State agencies on aging, 629 area agencies on aging, nearly 20,000 service providers, 244 Tribal organizations, and 2 Native Hawaiian organizations representing 400 Tribes. The OAA also includes community service employment for low-income older Americans; training, research, and demonstration activities in the field of aging; and vulnerable elder rights protection activities.

Adapted from AOA.gov

1. Based on the above passage, which of the following must be true?
   a. The OAA is in need of additional funding from the private sector.
   b. Native Hawaiians are always underrepresented in the OAA.
   c. The elderly are in need of protection of their rights.
   d. Nutrition needs of the elderly are severely neglected in this country.
   e. Today, the OAA is has a fairly insignificant impact on the social services for the elderly.

The best answer here is Choice *C*. The author's main idea in this passage is that the OAA was created and exists to provide social services and protect the rights of the elderly. Based on this information, it can be logically inferred that the author believes the elderly are in need of protection of their rights.

Choice *A* is incorrect because the passage mentions that the OAA is funded through grants, and there is no indication of a need for additional funding. It would be an assumption, not an inference, to conclude that more funding is needed from the private sector.

Choice *B* uses an absolute with the use of "never." Use of an absolute could be an indicator of an incorrect answer. While there are only two Native Hawaiian organizations identified as being represented by the OAA in the passage, it states that they represent 400 Tribes. This does not suggest an underrepresentation of this group in the OAA.

Choice *D* requires an assumption, not inference, based on the author's premises. The passage states that the OAA was created in response to a lack of services for the elderly. The OAA has become the biggest organization meeting the nutritional needs of the elderly, so it cannot be inferred that their nutritional needs are being neglected. This answer requires assumption, not inference, based on the author's premises.

Choice *E* is incorrect because it contradicts the information provided in the second paragraph, which notes that while there are many Federal programs with a similar aim, the OAA is a major vehicle of services for the elderly in today's environment.

The Application of Information in the Selection to a New Context

A natural extension of being able to make an inference from a given set of information is also being able to apply that information to a new context. This is especially useful in nonfiction or informative writing. Considering the facts and details presented in the text, readers should consider how the same information might be relevant in a different situation. The following is an example of applying an inferential conclusion to a different context:

> Often, individuals behave differently in large groups than they do as individuals. One example of this is the psychological phenomenon known as the bystander effect. According to the bystander effect, the more people who witness an accident or crime occur, the less likely each individual bystander is to respond or offer assistance to the victim. A classic example of this is the murder of Kitty Genovese in New York City in the 1960s. Although there were over thirty witnesses to her killing by a stabber, none of them intervened to help Kitty or to contact the police.

Considering the phenomenon of the bystander effect, what would probably happen if somebody tripped on the stairs in a crowded subway station?
  a. Everybody would stop to help the person who tripped.
  b. Bystanders would point and laugh at the person who tripped.
  c. Someone would call the police after walking away from the station.
  d. Few, if any, bystanders would offer assistance to the person who tripped.
  e. Bystanders would quickly call the authorities

This question asks readers to apply the information they learned from the passage, which is an informative paragraph about the bystander effect. According to the passage, this is a concept in psychology that describes the way people in groups respond to an accident—the more people are present, the less likely any one person is to intervene. While the passage illustrates this effect with the example of a woman's murder, the question asks readers to apply it to a different context—in this case, someone falling down the stairs in front of many subway passengers. Although this specific situation is not discussed in the passage, readers should be able to apply the general concepts described in the paragraph. The definition of the bystander effect includes any instance of an accident or crime in front of a large group of people. The question asks about a situation that falls within the same definition, so the general concept should still hold true: in the midst of a large crowd, few individuals are likely to actually respond to an accident. In this case, answer Choice *D* is the best response.

Principles that Function in the Selection

A **principle** can be defined as a fundamental truth that functions as the foundation of a system of belief, behavior, or reasoning. Expressed another way, a principle is a core truth that cannot be violated. The LSAT test examiners write reading comprehension passages that rely on or express some principle, and the most common principle questions ask you to correctly identify the principle expressed in the passage. In addition, some question stems will provide a principle, state that it is true, and ask the test taker to select the answer choice that best describes how the stated principle impacts the passage. A reading comprehension section also might be composed of two passages, where one passage commonly states the principle, while the other applies it. Principle question stems are typically easy to identify since they will explicitly include the word *principle* or a synonym. Here is an example of a principle question stem:

The reasoning in the passage most conforms to which of the following principles?

The overwhelming majority of principle questions will list the principles as answer choices, and the test taker should select the principle that best matches the passage.

The LSAT test examiners require test takers to analyze and apply myriad concepts; however, determining a principle's validity will never be a question. If the author asserts the principle that all capitalist economic systems are doomed to fail and you are asked to identify the principle, then select the answer stating that all capitalist systems are doomed to fail. No matter how sensational, the real-world validity of the principle is never in question. Although this might seem silly or imprudent, assuming the fictitious as true is an essential part of legal jurisprudence, commonly referred to as **legal fiction**. By its very definition, a principle is outcome determinative for any situation falling within its universe. Thus, the question that a test taker must always ask is: assuming this principle is true, how does it impact or match the given situation? If the principle is valid, which is assumed in the LSAT, and the specific circumstances fall within the principle's criteria, then the conclusion must adhere to the principle. As a result, answering principle questions is just a matter of matching the passage's specifics with the most appropriate principle.

The first step to interpreting principles is determining whether each principle is broad or narrow. Since everything covered by the principle is true, determining the confines will change how many situations the principle controls. Test takers should pay close attention to limiting language, or lack thereof, in the stated principle. Keywords to consider include: *all, every, any, some, never, none, no, anyone, everyone*, and any other similar words that describe an amount of something. Difference in language will decide whether some action or statement will, could, or could not happen, or be true. In addition, look for limitations on the group required for the principle to be activated. If the principle's stated limitation excludes some category or requires some characteristic, then it will not apply in situations not covered by the limitation. Consider the difference between the following principles:

Every American will vote in the upcoming presidential election.

All Americans interested in politics will vote in the upcoming presidential election.

Some Americans will vote in the upcoming presidential election.

No Americans will vote in the upcoming presidential election.

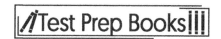

What do these principles say about an individual American? The first principle dictates that the simple fact that the individual is American necessitates that he or she will vote in the upcoming presidential election. As discussed at length above, the test taker must not consider external facts, such as the voting rate being substantially lower than one hundred percent in every American presidential election. This type of principle is outcome determinative for anyone who is an American. If you are an American, then you will vote in the upcoming presidential election.

Although the second principle begins with *all*, it includes a limiting requirement, "interested in politics," that must be accounted for in the analysis. It is unclear whether the individual American is interested in politics, and there is no way to find out that fact with the information provided; thus, this principle does not force any conclusion in this situation. The third principle only tells us that some Americans will vote; thus, it is both possible that the individual American will and will not vote, but no outcome is forced. The fourth principle is similar to the first principle since it is outcome determinative. The individual is American; no Americans will vote in the upcoming presidential election; thus, the individual will not be voting. This type of analysis should be used to determine what principle best matches the passage.

Principles can sometimes be converted into *if-then* statements, also known as conditional statements, which allow for inferences to be drawn. These inferences provide additional information that is useful for identifying the passage's principle. Before drawing an inference is possible, the principle must be converted into a conditional statement. For example:

Original: Every American will vote in the upcoming presidential election.

Conversion: If an individual is American, then that individual will vote in the upcoming presidential election.

Representation: A→ V (American →Vote)

In this scenario, the knowledge that an individual is an American, functions as a sufficient condition. Knowing that fact alone is sufficient to knowing something else occurred—that individual will vote. Voting is referred to as the necessary condition since it necessarily must occur if the sufficient condition is triggered. Conditional statements can also be negated and flipped to reveal a second inference. This is known as the contrapositive. The example can be restated as the following:

Contrapositive: If an individual will not vote in the upcoming presidential election, then that individual is not an American.

Representation: ~V→~A (Vote→ American)

When writing the contrapositive, crossing out the symbol is shorthand for *not*. Depending on the complexity of the principle, as well as the test taker's familiarity with conditional statements, converting the principle might not be feasible in terms of time management. However, if possible, test takers should be cognizant of the effectiveness of conditional statements in evaluating principle questions.

Analogies to Claims or Arguments in the Selection

Analogous questions challenge test takers' understanding of the passage by asking questions involving the recognition of structurally similar arguments. Test takers often struggle with analogies to claims within a reading comprehension passage for two reasons. First, analogies inherently test abstract reasoning. The questions ask test takers to draw comparisons between situations that appear entirely unrelated on the surface. Emphasis is placed on logical structure rather than substantive content. For this reason, analogies to claims in the reading comprehension section are most similar to the parallel reasoning questions that appear in the logical reasoning section. Second, these questions take up a disproportionate amount of finite time relative to other question types.

Due to the abstract nature of these analogy questions, all of the answer choices must be given special scrutiny. It will likely be more difficult to immediately eliminate a choice since every choice will form its own claim or element. Therefore, test takers must break down each answer choice into its corresponding elements and then compare those elements with the argument or claim from the passage. In addition, the smallest detail will often separate the correct answer from the second best option.

With that said, analogies to claims are not to be feared. Although admittedly cumbersome, they only require completing and repeating one of the most tested concepts on the LSAT—identifying conclusions and determining how premises operate to support those conclusions. The question stem will provide a quote or direct you to a set of lines from the passage. Sometimes the quote or line reference will isolate a single claim or argument from the passage, while other times, the required interpretation will rely on the passage's broader context. This skill is one of the most important for lawyers to grasp since analogies play an essential role in the American case law. When representing a client, lawyers must apply case law and argue from precedent to their client's particular claim or defense. This requires using abstract reasoning to draw analogies between situations, and the strongest analogy will typically prevail.

Analogies to claims questions will be easy to identify since *analogous* will almost always appear directly in the question stem. In less common instances, the question stem might include some derivation of application or ask what scenario is *most similar* to the logic deployed in the passage. Here is an example of an analogous question stem:

> Given Friedman's economic theory, as expressed between lines 32 and 45 in the passage, which one of the following is most analogous to the role monetary policy plays in his theory?

When initially reading through the passage, pay especially close attention to differing theories, arguments, or claims, especially from competing sources. For example, a passage about economics might include arguments from two or more economists. In this scenario, the analogous question will always identify which of the competing arguments to analogize. Never stray from the constraints provided in the question stem. If the economics passage includes arguments from John Maynard Keynes, Milton Friedman, and Karl Marx, but the question only asks how Friedman's theory applies to different scenarios, only focus on the portion of the passage devoted to Friedman. For the purposes of this question, the theories of Keynes and Marx are irrelevant.

The abstract reasoning behind analogous questions forces test takers to compare the logical structure of claims and arguments. The LSAT test examiners will often include answer choices that closely mirror the substance of the passage, rather than its structure. Do not fall for this trick—whether the passage and answer choice discuss the same substantive topic is irrelevant. As a result, test takers should be extremely cautious of answer choices that use similar language or cover identical topics as the claim in the passage. In fact, these types of similar substance answers are usually incorrect, functioning as red herrings to catch the less astute test takers who fail to analyze the structure.

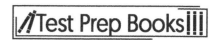

The table below contains some general frameworks that LSAT examiners use to analogize between the passage and answer choices. These are not an exhaustive list of analogous situations included in the reading comprehension section; however, reviewing these examples provides a framework for thinking about patterns in analogous questions.

General Structure	Example of an Analogy
Cause and effect	A scientist meticulously attempts a variety of methods and ultimately cures a deadly disease. A student reads her textbook, watches class lectures, and listens to an audio recording from a panel of experts, and she achieves the highest grade in her class.
Part and whole (subset)	All whales are mammals but not all mammals are whales. All prosecutors are lawyers but not all lawyers are prosecutors.
Unintended consequence	A town passes legislation outlawing the hunting of deer to increase their population, but the exploding deer population eats all of the vegetation, and their population decreases. An airline invests in a new silent plane to attract more customers, but their business decreases as customers become irritated with the noise from the bathroom and side conversations that had previously been blocked out by the engine noise.
Confusing causation (especially with correlation)	Ice cream sales rise at the same time that the murder rate similarly increases, but the actual cause of both is more people outside during the summer. A textbook company doubles its sales at the same time the company moves its headquarters to a more prestigious location, but the actual cause of both is an increase in capital investment.
Performance relative to a defined standard	A teenager loses his driver's license after amassing too many points as a result of accidents and speeding tickets. A doctor loses his medical license after a series of patients win medical malpractice actions against him.

To answer analogous questions, the test taker should first reread the passage's discussion of the quote or lines referenced by the question stem. Next, the test taker should generally summarize the structure of the presented claim or argument. For example, many analogous questions ask what logical error the author committed, so the summary would be a short description of that error. This summary should be a slightly more detailed version of what appears in the chart's left column. Lastly, the test taker should make similar summaries for each answer choice, and then the closest match will be the correct answer.

The Impact of New Information on Claims or Arguments in the Selection

Reading comprehension question stems will occasionally supplement the passage with **new information** in the answer choices. The new information will typically impact the conclusion of the entire passage or a supporting claim. The correct answer in a new information question will always do more than merely relate to the same substantive topic as the claim or argument in the passage; the new information will have a direct impact on the claim's plausibility or likelihood. Fortunately, new information questions are essentially strengthening or weakening questions, identical to those that appear in the Logical Reasoning section, and the question stem will explicitly specify which of the two is being asked.

Here is an example of a weakening question stem:

> Which of the following, if true, would most undermine the author's claim that *Infinite Jest* is the most rewarding book to read?

Here is an example of a strengthening question:

> Which of the following, if true, best supports the author's contention that capitalism is the most effective economic system?

Notice that the question stem includes the caveat "if true." All new information questions will include such a caveat, so the plausibility or validity of the new information should never be questioned based on real world knowledge. The new information will likely involve an unaccounted-for fact, expert opinion, recent discovery, or some other substantive statement related to the passage. The table below includes the most common synonyms for *strengthen* or *weaken* to help identify new information questions.

Strengthen	Weaken
Support	Undermine
Fortify	Challenge
Buttress	Diminish
Reinforce	Impair
Fortify	Erode
Bolster	Call into question
Underpin	Lessen
Augment	Undercut
Supplement	Damage

The easiest type of new information question will simply ask which of the following statements weakens or strengthens the claim or argument. If the question stem does not include a modifier, such as *best* or *most*, then only one of the answer choices will weaken or strengthen the claim; it would be impossible for more than one answer choice to strengthen or weaken the claim in such a situation. This makes the question much more approachable, since only one answer choice will impact the argument in the right direction.

When the question does include the *best* or *most* modifier, then multiple answer choices will provide new information that impacts the claim in the right direction. In this scenario, the test taker should immediately eliminate any answer choice that does the opposite. For example, if the question asks what best supports a claim, then eliminate any answer choice that weakens it. In addition, any answer choice that is neutral or irrelevant can be eliminated. Of the remaining answer choices, select the answer choice that is most relevant to the claim, which usually presents itself by directly addressing the conclusion or an important premise. Similarly, new information questions will occasionally come in the *except* variety. These questions are actually quite similar to the simple weaken or strengthen question, since there will only be one answer choice moving in the right direction. However, always make sure to read the question stem carefully, or else the question will be impossible to answer correctly.

Test takers often fret over new information questions, believing that the new information will completely fortify or totally deconstruct the argument. Although such extreme scenarios would actually be easier to answer, the correct answer will just make the argument more likely or less likely to be plausible. As with most of the other questions in the reading comprehension section, identifying conclusions and evaluating premises is by far the most important skill. The correct answers will almost always impact the conclusion by altering the premises.

For strengthen questions, test takers should review the claim or argument in the context of the passage and evaluate its logical strength. Where could the argument be improved? If the weakness is glaring, then the correct answer should be readily apparent amongst the options. The test taker should look out for any new information that validates a prediction or proves a generalization mentioned in the passage. Another possible way to strengthen an argument occurs when the new information provides support for a previously unjustified assumption. In addition, answers to strengthen questions will sometimes come in the form of principles, as discussed above. In these instances, the principle will provide some generalization that impacts a specific statement from the passage. For example, the passage might rely on a supporting claim without any justification, and the principle will strengthen the argument by stating that the claim is always true under those circumstances.

One of the most common answers to strengthen questions is an answer choice that offers new information that will impact the claim by providing a missing link between premises. The original claim or argument might not have connected these two premises, or the new information might strengthen the bridge between premises and the conclusion. Strengthening connections between premises is common when the relevant argument or claim does not immediately appear to be weak or lacking in some way. In the case of already strong arguments, another common correct answer will rule out possible alternatives. For example, the premises might all be airtight, but they collectively lead to two equally plausible conclusions. In this case, the correct answer will rule out the alternative conclusion, and therefore strengthen the conclusion actually included in the claim or argument.

Similarly, in weaken questions, the correct answer will make the argument less plausible by showing that the premises do not necessarily lead to the stated conclusion. This occurs when an important premise is invalidated or eliminated in some way. Special attention should be paid to any premises, suppositions, or statements that rely on some fact being true. Test takers should also pay special attention to how the premises relate to each other in support of the conclusion. Does one premise connect multiple other premises to the argument? If so, then this is the type of premise that is often invalidated by the new information, and the argument will completely fall apart. The more premises that fall off from supporting the conclusion, the weaker the argument. In addition, any new information that invalidates an important prediction or disproves a relied upon generalization will often be the correct answer. Arguments or claims can also be weakened if the new information creates a scenario where an equally plausible alternative conclusion can be drawn. Furthermore, it is possible to weaken arguments by attacking a relied upon assumption.

LSAT Practice Test #1

Section I: Logical Reasoning

Time – 35 minutes

25 Questions

1. John looks like a professional bodybuilder. He weighs 210 pounds and stands six feet tall, which is the size of an NFL linebacker. John looks huge when he enters the room. Years of gym time have clearly paid off in spades.

Which of the following, if true, weakens the argument?
   a. John prefers to work out in the morning.
   b. The average professional bodybuilder is considerably heavier and taller than the average NFL linebacker.
   c. John weighed considerably less before he started working out.
   d. John's father, brothers, and male cousins all look like professional bodybuilders, and none of them have ever worked out.
   e. John works out five times every week.

2. Hank is a professional writer. He submits regular columns at two blogs and self-publishes romance novels. Hank recently signed with an agent based in New York. To date, Hank has never made any money off his writing.

The strength of the argument depends on which of the following?
   a. Hank's agent works at the biggest firm in New York.
   b. Being a professional writer requires representation by an agent.
   c. Hank's self-published novels and blogs have received generally positive reviews.
   d. Being a professional writer does not require earning money.
   e. Hank writes ten thousand words per day.

3. Quillium is the most popular blood pressure-regulating prescription drug on the market. Giant Pharma, Inc., the largest prescription drug manufacturer in the country, owns the patent on Quillium. Giant Pharma stock is hitting unprecedented high valuations. As a result, Quillium is by far the most effective drug available in treating irregular blood pressure.

Which of the following, if true, most weakens the argument?
   a. The most lucrative and popular pharmaceuticals are not always the most effective.
   b. Quillium passed the FDA drug testing and screening faster than any other drug.
   c. Giant Pharma gouges its customers on Quillium's price.
   d. Giant Pharma's high stock prices are attributable to recent patent acquisitions other than Quillium.
   e. Quillium has numerous alternate applications.

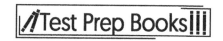
4. David Foster Wallace's *Infinite Jest* is the holy grail of modern literature. It will stand the test of time in its relevance. Every single person who starts reading *Infinite Jest* cannot physically put down the book until completing it.

Which of the following is the main point of the passage?
   a. David Foster Wallace's *Infinite Jest* is the holy grail of modern literature.
   b. *Infinite Jest* is a page-turner.
   c. David Foster Wallace wrote *Infinite Jest*.
   d. *Infinite Jest* will stand the test of time.
   e. *Infinite Jest* is a modern classic for good reason, and everybody should read it.

5. Julia joined Michael Scott Paperless Company, a small New York based tech start-up company, last month. Michael Scott Paperless recently received a valuation of ten million dollars. Julia is clearly the reason for the valuation.

Which of the following statements, if true, most weakens the argument?
   a. Michael Scott Paperless Company released an extremely popular mobile application shortly before hiring Julia.
   b. Michael Scott Paperless Company is wildly overvalued.
   c. Julia is an expert in her field.
   d. Julia only started working two weeks before the valuation.
   e. Julia completed two important projects during her first month with the company.

6. A famous children's author recently published a historical fiction novel under a pseudonym; however, it did not sell as many copies as her children's books. In her earlier years, she had majored in history and earned a graduate degree in Antebellum American History, which is the time frame of her new novel. Critics praised this newest work far more than the children's series that made her famous. In fact, her new novel was nominated for the prestigious Albert J. Beveridge Award but still isn't selling like her children's books, which fly off the shelves because of her name alone.

Which one of the following statements might be accurately inferred based on the above passage?
   a. The famous children's author produced an inferior book under her pseudonym.
   b. The famous children's author is the foremost expert on Antebellum America.
   c. The famous children's author did not receive the bump in publicity for her historical novel that it would have received if it were written under her given name.
   d. People generally prefer to read children's series than historical fiction.
   e. The children's author has started to decline in popularity and has probably reached her height in fame.

7. Ronan rarely attended class during his first semester at law school. Some of his professors didn't know he was in the class until the final exam. Ronan finished the year in the top 10 percent of his class and earned a spot on the school's prestigious law review.

Which of the following, if true, would explain the apparent paradox?
   a. Ronan is lazy.
   b. Ronan learns better through reading than listening, and he read the most relevant treatise on every class.
   c. Class attendance is optional in law school.
   d. Ronan is smart.
   e. Ronan's professors were unqualified to teach the law.

8. Advertisement: Cigarettes are deadly. Hundreds of thousands of people die every year from smoking-related causes, such as lung cancer or heart disease. The science is clear—smoking a pack per day for years will shorten one's life. Sitting in a room where someone is smoking might as well be a gas chamber in terms of damage to long-term health.

Which one of the following best describes the flaw in the author's reasoning?
   a. The advertisement confuses cause and effect.
   b. The advertisement uses overly broad generalization.
   c. The advertisement draws an unjustified analogy.
   d. The advertisement relies on shoddy science.
   e. The advertisement makes an unreasonable logical leap.

9. Jake works for Bank Conglomerate of America (BCA), the largest investment bank in the United States. Jake has worked at Bank Conglomerate of America for a decade. Every American investment bank employs dozens of lawyers to defend against insider-trading allegations. Some Bank Conglomerate of America employees must pass a certification course. However, all employees must complete a mandatory class on insider trading.

If the statements above are correct, which of the following must not be true?
   a. Jake took a class on insider trading.
   b. Jake passed a certification course.
   c. Jake has worked at Bank Conglomerate of America for a decade.
   d. Jake never took a class on insider trading.
   e. No investment bank has ever been formally charged with insider trading.

10. Leslie lost her job as a cashier at Locally Sourced Food Market because the store went out of business. Two days later, Randy's Ammunition Warehouse closed down for good in the same shopping center. Therefore, the Locally Sourced Food Market's closing clearly caused Randy's to close.

The flawed reasoning in which of the following arguments most mirrors the flawed reasoning presented in the argument above:
   a. The United States fought two wars while cutting taxes. The budget deficit continued to increase during that time, which increased national debt. Therefore, fighting two wars and cutting taxes clearly caused an increase in national debt.
   b. Tito's Taco Shop recently closed down due to lack of foot traffic. Nearby Bubba's Burrito Bowls also closed down later that month for the same reason. Therefore, a lack of foot traffic caused both businesses to close.
   c. Angela recently ran into some rotten luck. Last week she fell off her skateboard, and two days later, she crashed her car. Therefore, Angela needs to recover from her injuries.
   d. Theresa lost her job on Monday, but she received an unsolicited offer to consult for a hedge fund that same day. Therefore, losing one job led to another one.
   e. Tammy overslept and missed her early class. That same day, she experienced car trouble and missed her night class. Therefore, Tammy did not go to school today.

11. The assassination of Archduke Franz Ferdinand of Austria is often ascribed as the cause of World War I. However, the assassination merely lit the fuse in a combustible situation since many of the world powers were in complicated and convoluted military alliances. For example, England, France, and Russia entered into a mutual defense treaty seven years prior to World War I. Even without Franz Ferdinand's assassination _____.

Which of the following most logically completes the passage?
   a. A war between the world powers was extremely likely.
   b. World War I never would have happened.
   c. England, France, and Russia would have started the war.
   d. Austria would have started the war.
   e. The world powers would still be in complicated and convoluted military alliances.

12. Football is unsafe regardless of the precautions undertaken or rule changes implemented. Repeated head trauma always leads to long-term head injury. Parents are already refusing to allow their children to play youth football. Eventually, nobody will want to play football due to safety concerns. Therefore, the NFL will dramatically decline in popularity.

Which of the following, if true, most weakens the argument?
   a. Whether children play the sport has no impact on the NFL's popularity.
   b. Scientific studies of brain trauma are inconclusive as to long-term effects.
   c. The NFL's popularity will naturally decline as tastes change, like the decline in popularity of boxing and horse racing.
   d. Removing helmets would reduce head collisions by fifty percent.
   e. No matter the danger, there will always be players willing to sign waivers and play.

13. The following exchange occurred after the Baseball Coach's team suffered a heartbreaking loss in the final inning.

Reporter: The team clearly did not rise to the challenge. The reason the team lost the game is entirely attributable to the fact that they got zero hits in twenty at-bats with runners in scoring position. What are your thoughts on this devastating loss?

Baseball Coach: Hitting with runners in scoring position was not the reason we lost this game. We made numerous errors in the field, and our pitchers gave out too many free passes. Also, we did not even need a hit with runners in scoring position. Many of those at-bats could have driven in the run by simply making contact. Our team did not deserve to win the game.

Which of the following best describes the main point of dispute between the reporter and baseball coach?
   a. Whether the loss was heartbreaking.
   b. Whether getting zero hits in twenty at-bats with runners in scoring position caused the loss.
   c. Numerous errors in the field and pitchers giving too many free passes caused the loss.
   d. Whether the team deserved to win the game.
   e. Whether the team rose to the challenge.

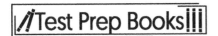

14. Kimmy is a world-famous actress. Millions of people downloaded her leaked movie co-starring her previous boyfriend. Kimmy earns millions through her television show and marketing appearances. There's little wonder that paparazzi track her every move.

What is the argument's primary purpose?
   a. Kimmy does not deserve her fame.
   b. Kimmy starred in an extremely popular movie.
   c. Kimmy earns millions of dollars through her television show and marketing appearances.
   d. Kimmy is a highly compensated and extremely popular television and movie actress.
   e. The paparazzi track Kimmy's every move for good reason.

15. Although China considers him a threat against the state, the Dalai Lama is one of the most popular world leaders according to recent polls. People across the globe respect the Dalai Lama's commitment to religious harmony, self-determination, and humanistic values. The Dalai Lama believes that gun violence in America can only be solved by stricter background check legislation. With any luck, Congress will pass the bill during its next session.

Which one of the following best describes the flaw in the author's reasoning?
   a. The argument relies on *ad hominem* attacks to discredit the Dalai Lama.
   b. The argument's extreme language detracts from its logical coherence.
   c. The argument cites an inappropriate expert.
   d. The argument makes a hasty generalization.
   e. The argument confuses correlation with causation.

16. Dwight works at a mid-sized regional tech company. He approaches all tasks with unmatched enthusiasm and leads the company in annual sales. The top salesman is always the best employee. Therefore, Dwight is the best employee.

Which of the following most accurately describes how the argument proceeds?
   a. The argument proceeds by first stating a conclusion and then offering several premises to justify that conclusion.
   b. The argument proceeds by stating a universal rule and then proceeds to show how this situation is the exception.
   c. The argument proceeds by stating several facts that serve as the basis for the conclusion at the end of the argument.
   d. The argument proceeds by stating a general fact, offering specific anecdotes, and then drawing a conclusion.
   e. The argument proceeds by stating several facts, offering a universal rule, and then drawing a conclusion by applying the facts to the rule.

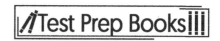

17. Julian plays the lottery every day. Julian always manages to buy his daily ticket, but he often struggles to pay his rent. Despite the billion-to-one odds, Julian is always close to hitting the power ball. The Local Lottery Commission's commercials state that the more lottery tickets an individual purchases, the better their chances are at winning. Thus, Julian wisely spends his money and will likely win the lottery in the near future.

What is the flaw in the argument's reasoning?
    a. The argument justifies its conclusion based on a hasty generalization.
    b. The argument's extreme language detracts from its logical coherence.
    c. The argument makes several logical leaps and assumptions.
    d. The argument confuses correlation with causation.
    e. The argument relies on an inappropriate expert.

18. Bobo the clown books more shows and makes more money than Gob the magician. Despite rampant coulrophobia—an irrational fear of clowns—Bobo still books more parties and receives higher rates of compensation per show. Gob's magic shows are no worse than Bobo's clown performances.

Which of the following statements, if true, best explains the apparent paradox?
    a. Bobo is an experienced clown.
    b. Despite rampant coulrophobia, statistical data shows that people generally prefer clowns to magicians for children's birthday parties.
    c. Bobo goes out of his way to appear non-threatening.
    d. Gob is a below average magician.
    e. Bobo works in a densely populated city, while Gob works in a rural town.

19. Cindy always braids her hair on Christmas.

Today is Easter.

Cindy's hair is braided.

If the statements above are correct, then what cannot be true?
    a. Cindy braids her hair every day.
    b. Cindy dislikes braiding her hair since it takes too long.
    c. Cindy never braids her hair during July or August.
    d. Cindy only braids her hair on Christmas.
    e. Cindy only braids her hair on holidays.

LSAT Practice Test #1 | Section I: Logical Reasoning

20. Musician: Some fans enjoy dancing in front of the stage, while others like to listen from a distance. The best music venues offer a mix of standing room and seats. If a suitable mix is impossible, then it's always best for the venue to be standing room only. Our band will never play at a concert hall without at least some standing room.

Which of the following arguments most closely parallels the musician's argument?
    a. Chef: Some diners enjoy eating Chinese food with traditional chopsticks, while others like to use a fork. The best restaurants offer both utensils as options.
    b. Coach: Some players respond to yelling, while others thrive in a more nurturing environment. The best coaches alternate between yelling and nurturing, depending on the player and situation. If the coach doesn't know how a player will respond, then it's always best to only be nurturing. I will never yell at my players without first offering a nurturing approach.
    c. Businessman: Some suits have two buttons, while others have three. The best suits always have two buttons. I will never wear a three-button suit.
    d. Lawyer: Some clients enjoy written updates, while others prefer to be updated on the phone. The best lawyers adapt to their clients' needs. If a client's preference can't be discerned, then it's always best to first call and then follow up with written notice. I highly prefer talking on the phone.
    e. Writer: Some writers prefer to type their stories, while others prefer handwriting them. The best writers always type since they can easily identify errors and edit more effectively. If a writer only writes by hand, then their work is always worse than those who type. I will never write my stories by hand.

21. All executive council members must have a law degree. Additionally, no felon can serve as an executive council member. Although she's a successful attorney, Jackie cannot serve as the President of the Executive Council since she has committed a felony.

The argument's conclusion follows logically if which one of the following is assumed?
    a. Anyone with a law degree and without a felony conviction is eligible to serve as an executive council member.
    b. Only candidates eligible to serve as an executive council member can serve as the President of the Executive Council.
    c. A law degree is not necessary to serve as an executive council member.
    d. If Jackie did not have a felony conviction, she would be serving as the President of the Executive Council.
    e. The felony charge on which Jackie was convicted is relevant to the President of the Executive Council's duties.

22. Mouth guards are increasingly becoming required equipment for contact sports. Besides the obvious benefit of protecting an athlete's teeth, mouth guards also prevent concussions. Youth league referees should penalize teams with players participating without a sanctioned mouth guard.

Which of the following most accurately expresses the argument's main conclusion?
    a. Mouth guards protect teeth and prevent concussions.
    b. Youth leagues should make mouth guards mandatory.
    c. Mouth guards save lives.
    d. It is generally preferable to wear mouth guards while playing contact sports.
    e. Mouth guards should always be worn during contact sports.

84

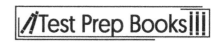

23. Law student: Law students cannot have a social life if they have any hope of succeeding academically. The daily reading and never-ending exam preparation frustrate all aspects of friendships. My friends sometimes invite me to watch a movie or go to a baseball game, but I can't go. Our professors warned us of the workload and its effect on free time at the start of the semester. It's completely impossible to budget fun into my busy schedule. I don't know any law students who have any fun whatsoever.

The reasoning in the law student's argument is most vulnerable to criticism on the grounds that the argument:
a. Improperly relies on a personal anecdote.
b. Improperly relies on an inappropriate authority.
c. Improperly draws a hasty generalization.
d. Improperly uses extreme language.
e. Dismisses all evidence that contradicts the law student's argument.

24. It is now common for people to identify as gluten intolerant. In ancient societies, it was common for people to identify as poultry intolerant. This eventually ended when people realized they were misdiagnosing poultry intolerance with food poisoning caused by mistakes in the birds' preparation. Eventually, people will realize that they are not actually gluten-sensitive.

The reference to the ancient civilization's poultry intolerance plays which of the following roles in the argument?
a. It serves as a historical example of food intolerance.
b. It functions as the argument's conclusion.
c. It provides an example of how societies can misdiagnose food intolerances.
d. It ties the argument's reasoning together.
e. It distracts the reader from the argument's primary purpose.

25. Doctor: Recent pharmaceutical advances will lead the way in weight loss. Prior to these advancements, obesity-related deaths outnumbered all other causes of death by a wide margin. The new drugs will curb appetite and increase metabolism. Thanks to these advancements, obesity will dramatically decline in the near future.

Each of the following, if true, strengthens the doctor's argument EXCEPT:
a. Increasing metabolism would significantly reduce obesity across the country.
b. Participants in several studies reported significant appetite reductions.
c. Double blind studies prove that participants lost significantly more weight using the drug compared to those participants given a placebo.
d. Most people will not be able to afford these prescriptions since the majority of healthcare plans will not cover the new drugs.
e. Nutritious food is not readily available to many people suffering from obesity.

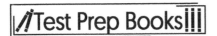

Section II: Analytical Reasoning

Time – 35 minutes

24 Questions

Problem 1

The administrator of a small music school has to assign six numbered parking spaces in front of the school to six music teachers employed there: Nan, Olivia, Pablo, Quincy, Robert, and Sasha. The six spaces are laid out adjacent to each other and in numerical order. Space #1 is closest to the front door of the school.

Sasha's space is next to Nan's space.

Nan's space is closer to the door than Quincy's space.

Olivia's space is next to only one other space.

There are exactly three other teachers' spaces between Pablo's and Sasha's spaces.

1. Which of the following must be true?
    a. Quincy is in one of the middle two spaces.
    b. Pablo's space is on one of the two ends.
    c. Pablo's space is farther from the door than Quincy's space.
    d. Robert's space is farther from the door than Quincy's space.
    e. Olivia's space is next to Sasha's space.

2. Which of the following teachers could be in space #4?
    a. Nan
    b. Olivia
    c. Pablo
    d. Quincy
    e. Sasha

3. If Olivia's space is closest to the door, which teacher's space must be farthest from the door?
    a. Nan
    b. Pablo
    c. Quincy
    d. Robert
    e. Sasha

4. If Robert's space is adjacent to Pablo's space, which of the following cannot be true?
    a. Sasha is in space #1.
    b. Quincy is in space #5.
    c. Olivia's space is next to Sasha's.
    d. Olivia's space is next to Pablo's.
    e. Nan is in one of the two middle spaces.

5. Which one of the following is a possible layout of the order of the school's parking spaces, starting with the space closest to the door?
 a. Sasha, Nan, Robert, Quincy, Pablo, Olivia
 b. Robert, Sasha, Nan, Quincy, Pablo, Olivia
 c. Olivia, Nan, Robert, Sasha, Quincy, Pablo
 d. Olivia, Sasha, Nan, Quincy, Pablo, Robert
 e. Pablo, Sasha, Quincy, Robert, Olivia, Nan

6. Which teacher's space must be next to Quincy's?
 a. Nan
 b. Olivia
 c. Pablo
 d. Robert
 e. Sasha

Problem 2

The kitchen at a Mexican restaurant has prepared taco orders for three customers, Kim, Lester, and Marlo. The tacos ordered—four tofu, three steak, two avocado, and one fish—are ready, but the customers' waiter has misplaced the ticket containing the taco orders.

 Each customer ordered at least one tofu taco and at least one non-tofu taco.

 The customer who ordered the fish taco also ordered at least two steak tacos.

 Lester did not order any steak or fish tacos.

 No two customers ordered the same number of tacos.

 Marlo ordered at least one of each type of taco.

7. Which of these is a possible distribution of taco orders?
 a. Kim: One tofu, one avocado, one steak
  Lester: Two tofu
  Marlo: One tofu, two steak, one avocado, one fish
 b. Kim: One tofu, two steak
  Lester: Two tofu, one avocado
  Marlo: One tofu, one steak, one avocado, one fish
 c. Kim: One tofu, one steak
  Lester: One tofu, one avocado
  Marlo: Two tofu, two steak, one avocado, one fish
 d. Kim: One tofu, one steak
  Lester: One tofu, one avocado, one fish
  Marlo: Two tofu, two steak, one avocado
 e. Kim: Two tofu, one steak
  Lester: One tofu, one avocado
  Marlo: One tofu, two steak, one avocado, one fish

8. If Kim has not ordered more than one of any single type of taco, which of the following must be true?
  a. Marlo ordered four tacos.
  b. Lester ordered three tacos.
  c. Kim ordered a steak and a fish taco.
  d. Marlo ordered two tofu tacos.
  e. Marlo ordered two avocado tacos.

9. Which of these is a complete list of diners who could have ordered more than one of the same type of taco?
  a. Marlo
  b. Kim and Lester
  c. Kim and Marlo
  d. Lester and Marlo
  e. Kim, Lester, and Marlo

10. Which of the following could be true?
  a. Marlo ordered two avocado tacos.
  b. Marlo ordered two steak tacos.
  c. Marlo ordered three steak tacos.
  d. Marlo ordered two tofu tacos.
  e. Marlo ordered three tofu tacos.

11. Which of the following cannot be true?
  a. Kim ordered one tofu taco.
  b. Kim ordered two tofu tacos.
  c. Exactly one customer ordered more than one of the same type of taco.
  d. Exactly two customers ordered more than one of the same type of taco.
  e. Marlo ordered more steak tacos than he ordered tofu tacos.

12. If Kim orders more tacos than Lester, which of the following must be Lester's order?
  a. One tofu, two avocado
  b. Two tofu, one avocado
  c. One tofu, one avocado
  d. Two tofu
  e. One tofu, one fish

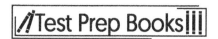

Problem 3

A political organizer has to assemble a team of volunteers to go to the town square and register new voters. She has six volunteers available to her: Malcolm, Zoe, Jayne, Kaylee, Simon, and Bridget. She wants to send at least two volunteers to the town square, while always keeping at least two volunteers back at the campaign office.

> If Malcolm goes to register voters, Zoe stays at the campaign office.

> If Zoe goes to register voters, then Jayne does too.

> If Zoe stays at the campaign office, Simon does too.

> Jayne and Kaylee are not assigned to both go or both stay.

13. Which one of the following could be a list of all volunteers assigned to go register voters?
    a. Simon, Bridget, and Zoe
    b. Zoe, Kaylee, Bridget
    c. Jayne, Kaylee, Simon, Bridget
    d. Zoe, Jayne, Bridget
    e. Malcolm, Simon

14. Which of the following pairs of volunteers could both go register voters together, with or without the accompaniment of other volunteers?
    a. Malcolm and Zoe
    b. Zoe and Kaylee
    c. Malcolm and Simon
    d. Kaylee and Jayne
    e. Zoe and Bridget

15. If Zoe goes to register voters, which of the following could be a complete list of volunteers who stay in the office?
    a. Jayne, Malcolm, and Simon
    b. Kaylee and Malcolm
    c. Bridget, Kaylee, Malcolm, and Zoe
    d. Bridget, Jayne, and Zoe
    e. Bridget, Jayne, Malcolm, and Simon

16. Which of the following cannot be a complete list of volunteers who stay in the office?
    a. Kaylee, Simon, and Zoe
    b. Kaylee and Malcolm
    c. Bridget, Kaylee, Simon, and Zoe
    d. Bridget, Kaylee, and Zoe
    e. Bridget, Kaylee, Malcolm, and Simon

17. If exactly two volunteers stay in the office, which of the following could be true?
    a. Kaylee goes to register voters.
    b. Malcolm stays in the office.
    c. Zoe stays in the office.
    d. Malcolm goes to register voters.
    e. Bridget stays in the office.

18. If Simon and Malcolm get the same assignment, then which of the following is a valid selection of the largest possible team to go register voters?
    a. Bridget, Malcolm, and Simon
    b. Jayne, Malcolm, and Simon
    c. Bridget, Jayne, and Zoe
    d. Bridget, Jayne, Kaylee, and Zoe
    e. Malcolm, Simon, Zoe, and Kaylee

Problem 4

Four companies, T, U, V, and W, are planning to make presentations at an industry conference. The four time slots available for their presentations are 9 a.m., 11 a.m., 2 p.m., and 4 p.m. Lunch is served at 1 p.m. The companies are asked to give their preferences for time slots, and they respond in order of preference as follows:

T: 2 p.m., 11 a.m., 4 p.m., 9 a.m.

U: 11 a.m., 4 p.m., 9 a.m., 2 p.m.

V: 2 p.m., 4 p.m., 11 a.m., 9 a.m.

W: 11 a.m., 2 p.m., 4 p.m., 9 a.m.

The conference then assigns time slots by giving one company its first choice, another company its first choice from the remaining three time slots, and so on until all four companies are assigned a time slot.

19. Which of the following could be true?
    a. Exactly three companies get their second choice.
    b. Exactly two companies get their third choice.
    c. Exactly three companies get their third choice.
    d. Exactly two companies get their fourth choice.
    e. Exactly three companies get their fourth choice.

20. Which of these is a possible order in which the companies' presentations could be assigned?
    a. W, V, T, U
    b. U, V, T, W
    c. U, T, W, V
    d. V, W, U, T
    e. T, U, W, V

21. If Company V makes their presentation before lunch, which of the following cannot be true?
    a. W picked second.
    b. T picked first.
    c. T picked before U.
    d. V picked second.
    e. W picked before U.

22. If Company V's presentation goes first, which of the following could be true?
    a. Company T presents at 11 a.m.
    b. Company U presents at 4 p.m.
    c. Exactly three companies got their first choice.
    d. Exactly two companies got their second choice.
    e. Exactly two companies got their third choice.

23. Which of these must be true?
    a. At least one company got their second choice.
    b. At most one company got their first choice.
    c. At least one company got their fourth choice.
    d. At least one company got their third choice.
    e. At least one company got their first choice.

24. Which of the following cannot be true?
    a. Company V goes at 11 a.m.
    b. Company T goes at 11 a.m.
    c. Company W goes at 2 p.m.
    d. Company U goes at 4 p.m.
    e. Company W goes at 11 a.m.

Section III: Logical Reasoning

Time – 35 minutes

25 Questions

1. Historian: Roman nobles, known as patricians, often owned dozens of slaves. It was extremely common in ancient Rome. Roman society did not consider the practice to be immoral or illegal in any way. Rome would simply enslave the many people conquered by the Empire. A fresh supply of slaves was integral to sustaining the Roman Empire.

Which one of the following is most strongly supported by the historian's argument?
    a. Slavery is not immoral.
    b. Romans treated their slaves with more humanity, compassion, and respect than any other contemporary civilization.
    c. Slavery was a necessary evil for the Romans.
    d. The Roman Empire would have collapsed earlier without enslaving new peoples.
    e. Conquered people welcomed their new lives as slaves.

2. College Administrator: The recent evaluation of our students' academic performance revealed that in general, the students who are on full scholarships have higher grade point averages than those students who must finance school via loans and/or jobs. When school expenses are covered by scholarships, students evade the stress induced by the financial burden of paying tuition bills. It also frees up their time, which enables them to study more instead of work.

The administrator's conclusion follows logically if which one of the following is assumed?
    a. Students who have to maintain a job to finance their education cannot achieve high grade point averages.
    b. The scholarships were not primarily awarded on the basis of the student's high grade point average.
    c. Intensive studying is more influential on a student's academic performance than is controlling one's stress level.
    d. Financial stress and restricted study time affect students' academic performance similarly.
    e. Students who take out loans maintain higher grade point averages than those who work to finance school.

3. A decade can be characterized just like an individual. Decades have specific character and unique quirks. They all start with a departure from the past decade and develop their personality throughout their timespans. Just as people in their twilight years start to look back on the events of their lives, people at decade's end_____.

Which one of the following most logically completes the argument?
    a. Reminisce about their lives.
    b. Fear they're about to die.
    c. Focus on what the next decade will bring.
    d. Become very interested in evaluating the events of the last decade.
    e. Throw a big party.

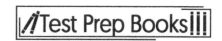

4. Religious Scholar: Truly moral people are naturally inclined to benefit their fellow man. People who act morally solely as a means to garner some divine benefit or avoid cosmic retribution are not, in fact, moral. They are blind sheep. To be moral requires true selflessness, rather than following any specific religious text.

Which one of the following individual's actions best adheres to the religious scholar's moral code?
   a. Jorge caught his wife in the midst of an extra-marital affair with a coworker. Naturally, he was extremely angry. Jorge wanted to physically harm his unfaithful wife and her treacherous coworker. But he remembered the words of the Sixth Commandment—*thou shall not kill*—and walked out of the room before he lost control.
   b. Elizabeth babysat her sister's four kids over the weekend. She had recently been studying Eastern religious practices and learned of the karmic principle, which states that an individual will be rewarded for their good deeds. Elizabeth hoped babysitting would help her chances at getting an overdue promotion at work.
   c. Tyler always tips 40 percent regardless of the quality of service provided. He follows an obscure ancient religion that values common laborers as the purest form of good. Tyler believes that waiters, doormen, and the like will determine his fate in the afterlife.
   d. Carlos visits his grandmother every weekend. She's an old bitter woman, and the rest of her family refuses to visit her except on special occasions. However, Carlos started practicing a new religion, which demands its followers respect the elderly.
   e. Every weekend, Arianna volunteers at a soup kitchen run by her church. She also donates a substantial part of her paycheck to children's cancer charities.

5. Angela's Hair Salon no longer takes reservations. Foot traffic already draws enough customers into the business. The Hair Salon's success is solely due to their terrific location.

Which one of the following, if true, most significantly weakens the argument?
   a. All of the nearby businesses are not profitable.
   b. Foot traffic is greater across the street.
   c. Angela's Hair Salon used to be located at a different location, and the business was significantly less successful.
   d. Angela's Hair Salon employs the town's best hairdresser, whose skills are well known in the community.
   e. Angela's Hair Salon has an enormous sign that is visible for miles down the road.

6. Situation: Sometimes people follow unhealthy diets to lose weight more quickly.

Analysis: People sometimes prioritize perceived beauty over health.

The analysis provided for this situation is most similar to which of the following situations?
   a. A musician buys a new leather jacket in preparation for an upcoming show.
   b. A model undergoes an elective cosmetic procedure to appear thinner.
   c. An actress applies massive amounts of make-up to hide her acne.
   d. An actor starts brushing his teeth with new special whitening toothpaste that contains several known carcinogens.
   e. A couple joins a gym to start running more.

7. After years of good health, Jacob finally visited the doctor for the first time in a decade. Immediately after his doctor's appointment, Jacob fell ill with the flu.

Each of the following, if true, explains the apparent paradox, EXCEPT:
   a. Jacob's doctor administered him several vaccines that temporarily weakened his immune system.
   b. Jacob's flu was dormant and didn't show symptoms until after the doctor's visit.
   c. Jacob's immune system did not worsen after the doctor's visit.
   d. It was below freezing during the week before his doctor's appointment, and Jacob did not wear his winter coat.
   e. Jacob's wife was sick with the flu during the week before his appointment.

8. Many new tech companies follow the Orange Company's model. Orange Company often utilizes lavish release parties to market their products. New tech companies are now doing the same. However, almost all new tech companies cannot afford to throw parties as lavish as Orange's parties. Therefore, these companies are foolish to throw parties if they can't afford to market their products.

The reasoning in the argument is most vulnerable to criticism on the grounds that the argument:
   a. Fails to consider that new tech companies would throw lavish release parties without Orange Company's example.
   b. Takes for granted that, with respect to their products, tech companies are not all the same.
   c. Fails to consider that new tech companies could benefit from applying Orange Company's marketing strategy on a smaller and more affordable scale.
   d. Does not adequately address the possibility that lavish release parties are still cheaper than national marketing campaigns.
   e. Fails to consider that even if new tech companies threw lavish release parties, they would still not match Orange Company's profitability.

9. Businessman: Sales are the most important part of any business. Marketing and communications are never as effective as a strong sales team. Persuasive salesmen can sell as many units of an inferior product as average salesmen with better quality products. Our company should eliminate every department except the sales team.

Which one of the following is an assumption on which the businessman's argument depends?
   a. The sales team's effectiveness is unaffected by contributions from the other departments.
   b. Companies often separate their departments into distinct teams.
   c. The company would be better off with only a sales team.
   d. Businesses often have other departments besides marketing, communications, and sales.
   e. The company in question has a strong sales team.

10. Conservative Politician: Social welfare programs are destroying our country. These programs are not only adding to the annual deficit, which increases the national debt, but they also discourage hard work. Our country must continue producing leaders who bootstrap their way to the top. None of our country's citizens truly *need* assistance from the government; rather, the assistance just makes things easier.

Liberal Politician: Our great country is founded on the principle of hope. The country is built on the backs of immigrants who came here with nothing, except for the hope of a better life. Our country is too wealthy not to provide basic necessities for the less fortunate. Recent immigrants, single mothers, historically disenfranchised, disabled persons, and the elderly all require an ample safety net.

What is the main point of dispute between the politicians?
    a. Spending on social welfare programs increases the national debt.
    b. Certain classes of people rely on social welfare programs to meet their basic needs.
    c. Certain classes of people would be irreparably harmed if the country failed to provide a social welfare program.
    d. All of the country's leaders have bootstrapped their way to the top.
    e. Immigrants founded the country.

11. Geoffrey never attends a movie without watching the trailer and generally tries to read the reviews prior to the show. At the theater, Geoffrey sometimes buys popcorn and always buys a bottle of water. Geoffrey recently saw the eighth installment of the *Boy Wizard Chronicles*.

Based on these true statements, which of the following must be true?
    a. Geoffrey ate popcorn during the *Boy Wizard Chronicles*.
    b. Geoffrey has read the critics' reviews of the *Boy Wizard Chronicles*.
    c. Geoffrey watched the *Boy Wizard Chronicles*' trailer and purchased popcorn at the theater.
    d. Geoffrey read the *Boy Wizard Chronicles*' reviews and drank a bottle of water during the show.
    e. Geoffrey watched the *Boy Wizard Chronicles*' trailer and drank a bottle of water during the show.

12. All advertising attempts to tie positive attitudes with their product. Companies experiencing a backlash would be wise to invest in a large marketing campaign. Advertising is especially important if potential customers have neutral or negative attitudes toward the product.

What is the argument's conclusion?
    a. All advertising attempts to tie positive attitudes with their product.
    b. Companies experiencing a backlash would be wise to invest in a large marketing campaign.
    c. Advertising is especially important if potential customers have neutral or negative attitudes toward the product.
    d. Advertising is extremely important.
    e. Advertising is extremely manipulative.

13. Professor: The United States faces several threats, and of those threats, terrorism is by far the most dangerous. Instability across the Middle East breeds extremism. The United States must be proactive in protecting itself and its allies.

The professor would most likely agree that:
   a. Extremism is even more dangerous than terrorism.
   b. The United States is responsible for stabilizing the Middle East.
   c. The United States should spread democracy in the Middle East.
   d. The United States should pre-emptively invade the Middle East.
   e. The United States should make a strategic plan to employ, should an imminent threat to its security develop.

14. Teacher: Students don't need parental involvement to succeed. In my class of twenty kids, the two highest achieving students come from foster homes. There are too many children in the foster homes for their parents to monitor homework and enforce study habits. It's always the case that students can overcome their parents' indifference.

What mistake does the teacher commit in his reasoning?
   a. The teacher incorrectly applies a common rule.
   b. The teacher's conclusion is totally unjustified.
   c. The teacher relies on an unreasonably small sample size in drawing his conclusion.
   d. The teacher fails to consider competing theories.
   e. The teacher is biased.

15. Trent is a member of the SWAT Team, the most elite tactical unit at the city's police department. SWAT apprehends more suspected criminals than all other police units combined. Taken as a whole, the police department solves a higher percentage of crime than ever before in its history. Within the SWAT team, Trent's four-man unit is the most successful. However, the number of unsolved crime increases every year.

Which of the following statements, if true, most logically resolves the apparent paradox?
   a. Trent's SWAT team is the city's best police unit.
   b. Violent crime has decreased dramatically, while petty drug offenses have increased substantially.
   c. The total number of crimes increases every year.
   d. Aside from the SWAT units, the police department is largely incompetent.
   e. The police department focuses more on crimes involving serious injury or significant property damage.

16. Scientist: The FDA has yet to weigh in on the effects of electronic cigarettes on long-term health. Electronic cigarettes heat up a liquid and produce the vapor inhaled by the user. The liquid consists of vegetable glycerin and propylene glycerol in varying ratios. Artificial flavoring is also added to the liquid. Although the FDA has approved vegetable glycerin, propylene glycerol, and artificial flavors for consumption, little is known about the effects of consuming their vapors. However, electronic cigarettes do not produce tar, which is one of the most dangerous chemicals in tobacco cigarettes.

Which one of the following most accurately expresses the scientist's main point?
   a. The FDA is inefficient and ineffective at protecting public health.
   b. Electronic cigarettes' liquid is probably safer than tobacco.
   c. Smokers should quit tobacco and start using electronic cigarettes.
   d. Tar is the reason why cigarettes are unhealthy.
   e. Although all of the information is not yet available, electronic cigarettes are promising alternatives to tobacco since the former does not produce tar.

17. All Labrador retrievers love playing fetch. Only German shepherds love protecting their home. Some dogs are easy to train. Brittany's dog loves playing fetch and loves protecting her home.

Which one of the following statements must be true?
   a. Brittany's dog is a Labrador retriever.
   b. Brittany's dog is a German shepherd.
   c. Brittany's dog is easy to train.
   d. Brittany's dog is half Labrador retriever and half German shepherd.
   e. Brittany's dog is half Labrador retriever and half German shepherd, and her dog is also easy to train.

18. Sociologist: Poverty is the number one cause of crime. When basic needs, like food and shelter, are not met, people become more willing to engage in criminal activity. The easiest way to reduce crime is to lessen poverty.

Which one of the following statements, if true, best supports the sociologist's argument?
   a. The typical criminal is less wealthy than the average person.
   b. The easiest way to lessen poverty is to redistribute wealth.
   c. Drug addiction and substance abuse is the second largest cause of crime, and drug users who struggle with addiction are more impoverished than the average person.
   d. Moral societies should guarantee that all their members' basic needs are met.
   e. Studies show that most crimes involve food theft and trespassing.

19. Regular weightlifting is necessary for good health. Weightlifting with heavy resistance, especially with compound movements, helps break down and rebuild stronger muscle fibers, resulting in strength and size gains.

Which one of the following is an assumption required by the argument?
   a. Strength and size gains are indicators of good health.
   b. Compound movements are the only way to increase strength and size.
   c. Performing compound movements is necessary for good health.
   d. Performing compound movements is the only way to break down and rebuild stronger muscle fibers.
   e. Regular weightlifting is necessary for good health.

20. West Korea's economy is experiencing high rates of growth for the sixth consecutive quarter. An autocratic despot dominates all aspects of West Korean society, and as a result, West Koreans enjoy less civil liberties and freedom than neighboring countries. Clearly, civil liberties do not impact economic gains.

The following, if true, strengthens the argument, EXCEPT:
    a. Neighboring countries' democratic processes are often deadlocked and unable to respond to immediate economic problems.
    b. The autocratic despot started governing the country six quarters ago.
    c. West Korea found a massive oil reserve under the country shortly before the autocratic despot seized power.
    d. Political protests in neighboring countries often shorten workdays and limit productivity.
    e. The West Korean autocratic despot devotes all of his time to solving economic problems.

21. Sociologist: Marriage is one of the most important societal institutions. The marital relationship provides numerous structural benefits for married couples and their offspring. Studies consistently show that children born out of wedlock are less likely to attend college and more likely to work low-paying jobs. Additionally, married people are more likely to be homeowners and save for retirement. Therefore, if marriage rates decline, _____.

Which one of the following most logically completes the sociologist's argument?
    a. Society will collapse.
    b. Everyone would have less money.
    c. Nobody would own homes.
    d. People would be happier.
    e. College attendance would probably decline.

22. Economist: Countries with lower tax rates tend to have stronger economies. Although higher taxes raise more revenue, highly taxed consumers have less disposable income. An economy can never grow if consumers aren't able to purchase goods and services. Therefore, the government should lower tax rates across the board.

The economist's argument depends on assuming that:
    a. The top five world economies have the lowest tax rates in the world.
    b. Consumers' disposable income is directly related to their ability to purchase goods and services.
    c. Lower tax rates will be much more popular with consumers.
    d. Increasing disposable income is the only way to ensure economic growth.
    e. Economic growth is more important than supporting social welfare programs.

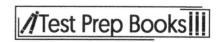

23. The United States' economy continues to grow. Over the last decade, the country's Gross Domestic Product—the monetary value of all finished goods and services produced within a country's borders—has increased by between 2 and 4 percent. The United States' economy is guaranteed to grow between 2 and 4 percent next year.

The flawed reasoning in which of the following arguments most mirrors the flawed reasoning presented in the argument above?

a. Ted is obsessed with apple pie. He's consumed one whole pie every day for the last decade. Ted will probably eat a whole apple pie tomorrow.

b. Last year Alexandra finished as the top salesperson at her company. She will undoubtedly be the top salesperson next year.

c. George always brushes his teeth right before getting into bed. His bedtime routine has remained the same for two decades. It's more probable than not that George brushes his teeth right before getting into bed tomorrow night.

d. Germany's economy is the strongest it's been since the end of World War II. Over the last decade, the country's Gross Domestic Product—the monetary value of all finished goods and services produced within a country's borders—has increased by between 2 and 4 percent. Germany's economic growth is a result of inclusive democratic processes.

e. Tito is the top ranked surfer in the world. Las Vegas bookmakers listed him as a clear favorite to win the upcoming invitational tournament. Tito is more likely to win the invitational than any other surfer.

24. Zookeeper: Big cats are undoubtedly among the smartest land mammals. Lions, tigers, and jaguars immediately adjust to their new surroundings. Other animals refuse to eat or drink in captivity, but the big cats relish their timely prepared meals. Big cats never attempt to escape their enclosures.

Which one of the following, if true, most weakens the zookeeper's argument?

a. Big cats don't attempt to escape because they can't figure out their enclosures' weak spots.

b. No qualified expert believes that adjusting to captivity is a measure of intelligence.

c. Bears also do not have any trouble adjusting to captivity.

d. A recent study comparing the brain scans of large mammals revealed that big cats exhibit the most brain activity when stimulated.

e. Zoos devote exponentially more resources to big cats relative to other animals.

25. Tanya is a lawyer. Nearly all lawyers dutifully represent their clients' best interests, but a few unethical ones charge exorbitant and fraudulent fees for services. Some lawyers become millionaires, while others work in the best interest of the public. However, all lawyers are bound by extensive ethical codes, which vary slightly by jurisdiction.

If the statements above are true, which one of the following must also be true?

a. Tanya dutifully represents her clients' best interests.

b. Tanya charges exorbitant fees for her services.

c. Tanya is bound by extensive ethical codes.

d. Tanya is a millionaire.

e. Tanya works for the public sector.

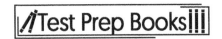

Section IV: Reading Comprehension

Time – 35 minutes

27 Questions

Questions 1–6 are based on the following passage.

Dana Gioia argues in his article that poetry is dying, now little more than a limited art form confined to academic and college settings. Of course poetry remains healthy in the academic setting, but the idea of poetry being limited to this academic subculture is a stretch. New technology and social networking alone have contributed to poets and other writers' work being shared across the world. YouTube has emerged to be a major asset to poets, allowing live performances to be streamed to billions of users. Even now, poetry continues to grow and voice topics that are relevant to the culture of our time. Poetry is not in the spotlight as it may have been in earlier times, but it's still a relevant art form that continues to expand in scope and appeal.

Furthermore, Gioia's argument does not account for live performances of poetry. Not everyone has taken a poetry class or enrolled in university—but most everyone is online. The Internet is a perfect launching point to get all creative work out there. An example of this was the performance of Buddy Wakefield's *Hurling Crowbirds at Mockingbars*. Wakefield is a well-known poet who has published several collections of contemporary poetry. One of my favorite works by Wakefield is *Crowbirds*, specifically his performance at New York University in 2009. Although his reading was a campus event, views of his performance online number in the thousands. His poetry attracted people outside of the university setting.

Naturally, the poem's popularity can be attributed both to Wakefield's performance and the quality of his writing. *Crowbirds* touches on themes of core human concepts such as faith, personal loss, and growth. These are not ideas that only poets or students of literature understand, but all human beings: "You acted like I was hurling crowbirds at mockingbars / and abandoned me for not making sense. / Evidently, I don't experience things as rationally as you do" (Wakefield 15-17). Wakefield weaves together a complex description of the perplexed and hurt emotions of the speaker undergoing a separation from a romantic interest. The line "You acted like I was hurling crowbirds at mockingbars" conjures up an image of someone confused, seemingly out of their mind . . . or in the case of the speaker, passionately trying to grasp at a relationship that is fading. The speaker is looking back and finding the words that described how he wasn't making sense. This poem is particularly human and gripping in its message, but the entire effect of the poem is enhanced through the physical performance.

At its core, poetry is about addressing issues/ideas in the world. Part of this is also addressing the perspectives that are exiguously considered. Although the platform may look different, poetry continues to have a steady audience due to the emotional connection the poet shares with the audience.

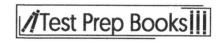

1. Which one of the following best explains how the passage is organized?
    a. The author begins with a long definition of the main topic, and then proceeds to prove how that definition has changed over the course of modernity.
    b. The author presents a puzzling phenomenon and uses the rest of the passage to showcase personal experiences in order to explain it.
    c. The author contrasts two different viewpoints, then builds a case showing preference for one over the other.
    d. The passage is an analysis of another theory that the author has no stake in.
    e. The passage is a summary of a main topic from its historical beginnings to its contemplated end.

2. The author of the passage would likely agree most with which of the following?
    a. Buddy Wakefield is a genius and is considered at the forefront of modern poetry.
    b. Poetry is not irrelevant; it is an art form that adapts to the changing time while containing its core elements.
    c. Spoken word is the zenith of poetic forms and the premier style of poetry in this decade.
    d. Poetry is on the verge of vanishing from our cultural consciousness.
    e. Poetry is a writing art. While poetry performances are useful for introducing poems, the act of reading a poem does not contribute to the piece overall.

3. Which one of the following words, if substituted for the word *exiguously* in the last paragraph, would LEAST change the meaning of the sentence?
    a. Indolently
    b. Inaudibly
    c. Interminably
    d. Infrequently
    e. Impecunious

4. Which of the following is most closely analogous to the author's opinion of Buddy Wakefield's performance in relation to modern poetry?
    a. Someone's refusal to accept that the Higgs Boson will validate the Standard Model.
    b. An individual's belief that soccer will lose popularity within the next fifty years.
    c. A professor's opinion that poetry contains the language of the heart, while fiction contains the language of the mind.
    d. An individual's assertion that video game violence was the cause of the Columbine shootings.
    e. A student's insistence that psychoanalysis is a subset of modern psychology.

5. What is the primary purpose of the passage?
    a. To educate readers on the development of poetry and describe the historical implications of poetry in media.
    b. To disprove Dana Gioia's stance that poetry is becoming irrelevant and is only appreciated in academia.
    c. To inform readers of the brilliance of Buddy Wakefield and to introduce them to other poets that have influenced contemporary poetry.
    d. To prove that Gioia's article does have some truth to it and to shed light on its relevance to modern poetry.
    e. To recount the experience of watching a live poetry performance and to look forward to future performances.

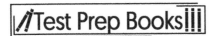

6. What is the author's main reason for including the quote in the passage?
   a. To give an example of speaking meter, the writing style of spoken word poets.
   b. To demonstrate that people are still writing poetry even if the medium has changed in current times.
   c. To prove that poets still have an audience to write for even if the audience looks different than from centuries ago.
   d. To illustrate the complex themes poets continue to address, which still draw listeners and appreciation.
   e. To open up opportunity to disprove Gioia's views.

Questions 7–14 are based on the following passage.

In the quest to understand existence, modern philosophers must question if humans can fully comprehend the world. Classical western approaches to philosophy tend to hold that one can understand something, be it an event or object, by standing outside of the phenomena and observing it. It is then by unbiased observation that one can grasp the details of the world. This seems to hold true for many things. Scientists conduct experiments and record their findings, and thus many natural phenomena become comprehendible. However, several of these observations were possible because humans used tools in order to make these discoveries.

This may seem like an extraneous matter. After all, people invented things like microscopes and telescopes in order to enhance their capacity to view cells or the movement of stars. While humans are still capable of seeing things, the question remains if human beings have the capacity to fully observe and see the world in order to understand it. It would not be an impossible stretch to argue that what humans see through a microscope is not the exact thing itself, but a human interpretation of it.

This would seem to be the case in the "Business of the Holes" experiment conducted by Richard Feynman. To study the way electrons behave, Feynman set up a barrier with two holes and a plate. The plate was there to indicate how many times the electrons would pass through the hole(s). Rather than casually observe the electrons acting under normal circumstances, Feynman discovered that electrons behave in two totally different ways depending on whether or not they are observed. The electrons that were observed had passed through either one of the holes or were caught on the plate as particles. However, electrons that weren't observed acted as waves instead of particles and passed through both holes. This indicated that electrons have a dual nature. Electrons seen by the human eye act like particles, while unseen electrons act like waves of energy.

This dual nature of the electrons presents a conundrum. While humans now have a better understanding of electrons, the fact remains that people cannot entirely perceive how electrons behave without the use of instruments. We can only observe one of the mentioned behaviors, which only provides a partial understanding of the entire function of electrons. Therefore, we're forced to ask ourselves whether the world we observe is objective or if it is subjectively perceived by humans. Or, an alternative question: can man understand the world only through machines that will allow them to observe natural phenomena?

LSAT Practice Test #1 | Section IV: Reading Comprehension

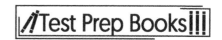

Both questions humble man's capacity to grasp the world. However, those ideas don't take into account that many phenomena have been proven by human beings without the use of machines, such as the discovery of gravity. Like all philosophical questions, whether man's reason and observation alone can understand the universe can be approached from many angles.

7. The word *extraneous* in paragraph two can be best interpreted as referring to which of the following?
   a. Indispensable
   b. Bewildering
   c. Fallacious
   d. Exuberant
   e. Superfluous

8. What is the author's motivation for writing the passage?
   a. To bring to light an alternative view on human perception by examining the role of technology in human understanding.
   b. To educate the reader on the latest astroparticle physics discovery and offer terms that may be unfamiliar to the reader.
   c. To argue that humans are totally blind to the realities of the world by presenting an experiment that proves that electrons are not what they seem on the surface.
   d. To reflect on opposing views of human understanding.
   e. To disprove classical philosophy by comparing more accurate technology to the speculations of the ancient philosophers.

9. Which of the following most closely resembles the way in which paragraph four is structured?
   a. It offers one solution, questions the solution, and then ends with an alternative solution.
   b. It presents an inquiry, explains the detail of that inquiry, and then offers a solution.
   c. It presents a problem, explains the details of that problem, and then ends with more inquiry.
   d. It gives a definition, offers an explanation, and then ends with an inquiry.
   e. It presents a problem, offers an example, and then ends with a solution.

10. For the classical approach to understanding to hold true, which of the following must be required?
   a. A telescope.
   b. A recording device.
   c. Multiple witnesses present.
   d. The person observing must be unbiased.
   e. The person observing must prove their theory beyond a doubt.

11. Which best describes how the electrons in the experiment behaved like waves?
   a. The electrons moved up and down like actual waves.
   b. The electrons passed through both holes and then onto the plate.
   c. The electrons converted to photons upon touching the plate.
   d. The electrons were seen passing through one hole or the other.
   e. The electrons were glowing during the experiment, indicating light waves were moving them.

103

12. The author mentions "gravity" in the last paragraph in order to do what?

    a. In order to show that different natural phenomena test man's ability to grasp the world.

    b. To prove that since man has not measured it with the use of tools or machines, humans cannot know the true nature of gravity.

    c. To demonstrate an example of natural phenomena humans discovered and understood without the use of tools or machines.

    d. To show an alternative solution to the nature of electrons that humans have not thought of yet.

    e. To look toward the future of technology so that we may understand the dual nature of all phenomena, including gravity.

13. Which situation best parallels the revelation of the dual nature of electrons discovered in Feynman's experiment?

    a. Ancient Greeks believed that Zeus hurled lightning down to Earth. In reality, lightning is caused by supercharged electrons, and happens either inside the clouds or between the cloud and the ground.

    b. The coelacanth was thought to be extinct, but a live specimen was just recently discovered. There are now two living species of coelacanth known to man, and both are believed to be endangered.

    c. In the Middle Ages, blacksmiths added carbon to iron, thus inventing steel. The consequences of this important discovery would have its biggest effects during the industrial revolution.

    d. In order to better examine and treat broken bones, the x-ray machine was invented and put to use in hospitals and medical centers.

    e. A man is born color-blind and grows up observing everything in lighter or darker shades. With the invention of special goggles he puts on, he discovers that there are other colors in addition to different shades.

14. Which statement about technology would the author likely disagree with?

    a. Technology can help expand the field of human vision.

    b. Technology renders human observation irrelevant.

    c. Developing tools used in observation and research indicates growing understanding of our world in itself.

    d. Studying certain phenomena necessitates the use of tools and machines.

    e. Classical observation still serves a function in our world.

Questions 15–19 are based on the following passage.

The Middle Ages were a time of great superstition and theological debate. Many beliefs were developed and practiced, while some died out or were listed as heresy. Boethianism is a Medieval theological philosophy that attributes sin to gratification and righteousness with virtue and God's providence. Boethianism holds that sin, greed, and corruption are means to attain temporary pleasure, but that they inherently harm the person's soul as well as other human beings.

In *The Canterbury Tales,* we observe more instances of bad actions punished than goodness being rewarded. This would appear to be some reflection of Boethianism. In the "Pardoner's Tale," all three thieves wind up dead, which is a result of their desire for wealth. Each wrong doer pays with their life, and they are unable to enjoy the wealth they worked to steal. Within his tales, Chaucer gives reprieve to people undergoing struggle, but also interweaves stories of contemptible individuals being cosmically punished for their wickedness. The thieves idolize physical wealth, which leads to their downfall. This same theme and ideological principle of Boethianism is repeated in the "Friar's Tale," whose summoner character attempts to gain

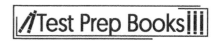

further wealth by partnering with a demon. The summoner's refusal to repent for his avarice and corruption leads to the demon dragging his soul to Hell. Again, we see the theme of the individual who puts faith and morality aside in favor for a physical prize. The result, of course, is that the summoner loses everything.

The examples of the righteous being rewarded tend to appear in a spiritual context within the *Canterbury Tales*. However, there are a few instances where we see goodness resulting in physical reward. In the Prioress' Tale, we see corporal punishment for barbarism *and* a reward for goodness. The Jews are punished for their murder of the child, giving a sense of law and order (though racist) to the plot. While the boy does die, he is granted a lasting reward by being able to sing even after his death, a miracle that marks that the murdered youth led a pure life. Here, the miracle represents eternal favor with God.

Again, we see the theological philosophy of Boethianism in Chaucer's *The Canterbury Tales* through acts of sin and righteousness and the consequences that follow. When pleasures of the world are sought instead of God's favor, we see characters being punished in tragic ways. However, the absence of worldly lust has its own set of consequences for the characters seeking to obtain God's favor.

15. What would be a potential reward for living a good life, as described in Boethianism?
    a. A long life sustained by the good deeds one has done over a lifetime.
    b. Wealth and fertility for oneself and the extension of one's family line.
    c. Vengeance for those who have been persecuted by others who have a capacity for committing wrongdoing.
    d. The act of reaching Sainthood.
    e. God's divine favor for one's righteousness.

16. What might be the main reason why the author chose to discuss Boethianism through examining *The Canterbury Tales*?
    a. *The Canterbury Tales* is a well-known text.
    b. *The Canterbury Tales* is the only known fictional text that contains use of Boethianism.
    c. *The Canterbury Tales* presents a manuscript written in the medieval period that can help illustrate Boethianism through stories and show how people of the time might have responded to the idea.
    d. Within each individual tale in *The Canterbury Tales*, the reader has the opportunity to read about different levels of Boethianism and how each level leads to greater enlightenment.
    e. Chaucer, who wrote *The Canterbury Tales,* was a devoted Boethianist.

17. What "ideological principle" is the author referring to in the middle of the second paragraph when talking about the "Friar's Tale"?
    a. The principle that the act of ravaging another's possessions is the same as ravaging one's soul.
    b. The principle that thieves who idolize physical wealth will be punished in an earthly sense as well as eternally.
    c. The principle that fraternization with a demon will result in one losing everything, including their life.
    d. The principle that a desire for material goods leads to moral malfeasance punishable by a higher being.
    e. The principle that wealth is impossible to enjoy when one has been corrupted in the pursuit of it.

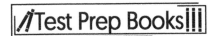

18. Which of the following words, if substituted for the word *avarice* in paragraph two, would LEAST change the meaning of the sentence?
  a. Perniciousness
  b. Pithiness
  c. Covetousness
  d. Pompousness
  e. Capriciousness

19. Based on the passage, what view does Boethianism take on desire?
  a. Desire does not exist in the context of Boethianism.
  b. Desire is a virtue and should be welcomed.
  c. Having desire is evidence of demonic possession.
  d. Desire for pleasure can lead toward sin.
  e. Desire is the result of original sin.

Questions 20–27 are based on the following passages.

Passage I

Lethal force, or deadly force, is defined as the physical means to cause death or serious harm to another individual. The law holds that lethal force is only accepted when you or another person are in immediate and unavoidable danger of death or severe bodily harm. For example, a person could be beating a weaker person in such a way that they are suffering severe enough trauma that could result in death or serious harm. This would be an instance where lethal force would be acceptable and possibly the only way to save that person from irrevocable damage.

Another example of when to use lethal force would be when someone enters your home with a deadly weapon. The intruder's presence and possession of the weapon indicate mal-intent and the ability to inflict death or severe injury to you and your loved ones. Again, lethal force can be used in this situation. Lethal force can also be applied to prevent the harm of another individual. If a woman is being brutally assaulted and is unable to fend off an attacker, lethal force can be used to defend her as a last-ditch effort. If she is in immediate jeopardy of rape, harm, and/or death, lethal force could be the only response that could effectively deter the assailant.

The key to understanding the concept of lethal force is the term *last resort*. Deadly force cannot be taken back; it should be used only to prevent severe harm or death. The law does distinguish whether the means of one's self-defense is fully warranted, or if the individual goes out of control in the process. If you continually attack the assailant after they are rendered incapacitated, this would be causing unnecessary harm, and the law can bring charges against you. Likewise, if you kill an attacker unnecessarily after defending yourself, you can be charged with murder. This would move lethal force beyond necessary defense, making it no longer a last resort but rather a use of excessive force.

Passage II

Assault is the unlawful attempt of one person to apply apprehension on another individual by an imminent threat or by initiating offensive contact. Assaults can vary, encompassing physical strikes, threatening body language, and even provocative language. In the case of the latter, even if a hand has not been laid, it is still considered an assault because of its threatening nature.

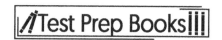

Let's look at an example: A homeowner is angered because his neighbor blows fallen leaves into his freshly mowed lawn. Irate, the homeowner gestures a fist to his fellow neighbor and threatens to bash his head in for littering on his lawn. The homeowner's physical motions and verbal threat heralds a physical threat against the other neighbor. These factors classify the homeowner's reaction as an assault. If the angry neighbor hits the threatening homeowner in retaliation, that would constitute an assault as well because he physically hit the homeowner.

Assault also centers on the involvement of weapons in a conflict. If someone fires a gun at another person, it could be interpreted as an assault unless the shooter acted in self-defense. If an individual drew a gun or a knife on someone with the intent to harm them, it would be considered assault. However, it's also considered an assault if someone simply aimed a weapon, loaded or not, at another person in a threatening manner.

20. What is the purpose of the second passage?
   a. To inform the reader about what assault is and how it is committed
   b. To inform the reader about how assault is a minor example of lethal force
   c. To disprove the previous passage concerning lethal force
   d. To argue that the use of assault is more common than the use of lethal force
   e. To recount an incident in which the author was assaulted

21. Which of the following situations, according to the passages, would not constitute an illegal use of lethal force?
   a. A disgruntled cashier yells obscenities at a customer.
   b. A thief is seen running away with stolen cash.
   c. A man is attacked in an alley by another man with a knife.
   d. A woman punches another woman in a bar.
   e. A driver accidently slams into another person's car and injures them.

22. Given the information in the passages, which of the following must be true about assault?
   a. All assault is considered an expression of lethal force.
   b. There are various forms of assault.
   c. Smaller, weaker people cannot commit assault.
   d. Assault is justified only as a last resort.
   e. Assault charges are more severe than unnecessary use of force charges.

23. Which of the following, if true, would most seriously undermine the explanation proposed by the author in the third paragraph of Passage I?
   a. An instance of lethal force in self-defense is not absolutely absolved from blame. The law takes into account the necessary use of force at the time it is committed.
   b. An individual who uses necessary defense under lethal force is in direct compliance of the law under most circumstances.
   c. Lethal force in self-defense should be forgiven in all cases for the peace of mind of the primary victim.
   d. The use of lethal force is not evaluated on the intent of the user but rather the severity of the primary attack that warranted self-defense.
   e. It's important to note that once lethal force goes beyond the necessary attempt to protect oneself, there's a chance it could turn into a deadly assault of excessive force.

24. Based on the passages, what can we infer about the relationship between assault and lethal force?
    a. An act of lethal force always leads to a type of assault.
    b. An assault will result in someone using lethal force.
    c. An assault with deadly intent can lead to an individual using lethal force to preserve their well-being.
    d. If someone uses self-defense in a conflict, it is called deadly force; if actions or threats are intended, it is called assault.
    e. Assault and lethal force have no conceivable connection.

25. Which of the following best describes the way the passages are structured?
    a. Both passages open by defining a legal concept and then continue to describe situations in order to further explain the concept.
    b. Both passages begin with situations, introduce accepted definitions, and then cite legal ramifications.
    c. The first passage presents a long definition while the second passage begins by showing an example of assault.
    d. Both cite specific legal doctrines, then proceed to explain the rulings.
    e. The first passage explains both concepts and then focuses on lethal force. The second passage picks up with assault and explains the concept in depth.

26. What can we infer about the role of intent in lethal force and assault?
    a. Intent is irrelevant. The law does not take intent into account.
    b. Intent is vital for determining the lawfulness of using lethal force.
    c. Intent is only taken into account for assault charges.
    d. The intent of the assailant is the main focus for determining legal ramifications; it is used to determine if the defender was justified in using force to respond.
    e. Intent is very important for determining both lethal force and assault; intent is examined in both parties and helps determine the severity of the issue.

27. The author uses the example in the second paragraph of Passage II in order to do what?
    a. To demonstrate two different types of assault by showing how each specifically relates to the other.
    b. To demonstrate a single example of two different types of assault, then adds in the third type of assault in the example's conclusion.
    c. To prove that the definition of lethal force is altered when the victim in question is a homeowner and his property is threatened.
    d. To suggest that verbal assault can be an exaggerated crime by the law and does not necessarily lead to physical violence.
    e. To demonstrate that threatening body language is only considered a type of assault if it leads to physical violence.

Answer Explanations #1

Section I: Logical Reasoning

1. D: Choice *A* is irrelevant. The argument makes no mention as to when John works out. Would it weaken the conclusion—which is that years of gym time have clearly paid off—if he works out in the morning instead of the afternoon? No, of course not. Eliminate this choice.

Choice *B* preys on those who incorrectly identify the conclusion. Test takers who identify the first sentence as the conclusion will find this answer very appealing. If John is the size of an NFL linebacker, but linebackers are much smaller than professional bodybuilders, then John doesn't look like a professional linebacker. However, Choice *B* is irrelevant as to whether years of working out have paid off. Eliminate this choice.

Choice *C* actually strengthens the argument. If John weighed considerably less before working out and now he looks like a professional bodybuilder, then years of working out have definitely paid off. Eliminate this choice.

Choice *D* looks very appealing. If John's family members are all similar in size without weightlifting, then it's possible that it doesn't matter that John regularly spends time in the gym. Even without lifting, John would likely be the same size as his male family members. Therefore, years of working out would not be the reason why he looks like a professional bodybuilder. Don't be concerned that Choice *D* is unlikely in reality. If a question says something's true, then treat it as true. Keep this choice for now.

Choice *E* reinforces the argument's conclusion. The argument already states that John has gone to the gym for years. Whether he goes three, five, or seven times per week does not weaken the argument. Eliminate this choice.

Therefore, Choice *D* is the correct answer.

2. D: Choice *A* is irrelevant. The argument's conclusion is that Hank is a professional writer. The argument does not depend on whether Hank's agent is the best or worst in the business. Eliminate this choice.

Choice *B* seems fairly strong at first glance. It feels reasonable to say that being a professional writer requires representation. However, the argument would still be strong if being a professional writer did not require an agent. Hank would still be a professional writer. Eliminate this choice.

Choice *C* is irrelevant. Whether Hank is a professional writer does not depend on his reviews. Eliminate this choice.

Choice *D* is strong. Negate it to determine if the argument falls apart. If being a professional writer requires earning money, then Hank would not be a professional writer. The argument falls apart. This is almost definitely the correct answer.

Choice *E* is irrelevant. The argument does not attempt to tie Hank's professionalism with a word count. For the purposes of this argument, it does not matter if Hank writes ten or ten thousand words per day. Eliminate this choice.

Therefore, Choice *D* is the correct answer.

3. A: Choice *A* looks very strong. The argument devotes most of its time discussing Quillium's popularity and monetary value. It uses these facts to conclude that Quillium is the most effective drug in treating blood pressure. If the most lucrative and popular drugs are not necessarily the most effective, then it seriously weakens the argument. Leave this choice for now, and look at the other answer choices.

Choice *B* strengthens the argument. Moving through the screening process at record time supports the conclusion. It definitely does not weaken it. Eliminate this choice.

Choice *C* is irrelevant. Whether Giant Pharma gouges its customers does not affect the conclusion concerning the drug's effectiveness. Eliminate this choice.

Choice *D* is misleading. This choice would greatly weaken the argument if the argument's conclusion was that Quillium is the reason for Giant Pharma's high valuation. However, this is only a premise. Choice *D* weakens this premise, but it does not weaken the argument as much as Choice *A*, which attacks the heart of the argument. Eliminate this choice.

Choice *E* is irrelevant. The argument's conclusion is that Quillium is the most effective drug for treating irregular blood pressure. Does it matter if Quillium has alternate applications? Of course not, so eliminate this choice.

Therefore, Choice *A* is the correct answer.

4. E: Choice *A* restates the author's conclusion. The correct answer to main point questions will often be closely related to the conclusion. Choice *A* should jump off the page as a possibility. Keep it for now.

Choice *B* restates a premise. Is the author's main point that *Infinite Jest* is a page-turner? No, he uses readers' obsession with the book as a premise. Eliminate this choice.

Choice *C* is definitely not the main point of the passage. It's a simple fact underlying the argument. It certainly cannot be considered the main point. Eliminate this choice.

Choice *D* restates a premise, just like Choice *B*. Whether the book stands the test of time is not the main point of the passage.

Choice *E* looks like a strong answer. This answer choice references the argument's main points—*Infinite Jest* is a modern classic, the book deserves its praise, and everybody should read it. In contrast, Choice *A* merely restates the conclusion. Choice *E* better expresses the argument's main point.

Therefore, Choice *E* is the correct answer.

5. A: Choice *A* is very strong since it provides an alternate explanation for the high valuation other than Julia. If the Michael Scott Paperless Company released an extremely popular application, then the application is the real reason for the 10-million-dollar valuation. Furthermore, this answer choice explicitly states that the application was released before Julia's hiring. Keep this choice for now.

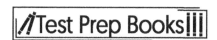

Choice *B* is irrelevant. Whether investors are properly evaluating the Michael Scott Paperless Company's price does not affect Julia's role in that valuation. Eliminate this choice.

Choice *C* strengthens the argument. If Julia is an expert in her field, then her skills could have been the reason for the valuation. Investors could have factored in Julia's expertise in their valuation. It definitely does not weaken the argument. Eliminate this choice.

Choice *D* is another strong answer choice. If Julia only worked at Michael Scott Paperless Company for two weeks, then it is less likely that she's the reason for the 10-million-dollar valuation. However, if she's a renowned expert or extreme talent, then her hiring alone could have affected the valuation. This answer choice is less strong than Choice *A*, which provides a clear alternative explanation for the sudden increase in valuation. Since Choice *A* is stronger, eliminate Choice *D*.

Choice *E* strengthens the argument. If Julia completed two important projects during her first month, then she could very well be the reason for the valuation. It definitely does not weaken the argument; eliminate Choice *E* as well.

Therefore, Choice *A* is the correct answer.

6. C: We are looking for an inference—a conclusion that is reached on the basis of evidence and reasoning—from the passage that will likely explain why the famous children's author did not achieve her usual success with the new genre (despite the book's acclaim). Choice *A* is incorrect because the statement is false according to the passage.

Choice *B* is incorrect because, although the passage says the author has a graduate degree on the subject, it would be an unrealistic leap to infer that she is the foremost expert on Antebellum America.

In contrast, Choice *C* can be logically inferred since the passage speaks of the great success of the children's series and the declaration that the fame of the author's name causes the children's books to "fly off the shelves." Thus, she did not receive any bump from her name since she published the historical novel under a pseudonym, which makes Choice *C* correct.

Choice *D* is incorrect because there is nothing in the passage to lead us to infer that people generally prefer a children's series to historical fiction.

Choice *E* is incorrect. The passage tells us that the author wrote under a pseudonym. If the author's name is different on the novel than on the children's books, then the popularity of the author cannot be said to be declining. Since the author is unknown or less known under the pseudonym, this is an unfair comparison. Additionally, the phrase "has probably reached her height in fame," is a prediction rather than an inference.

7. B: Choice *A* fails to explain the apparent paradox. Eliminate this choice.

Choice *B* is a strong answer choice. It helps explain how Ronan succeeded in law school without attending class. Choice *B* states that Ronan learns better through reading, and he read relevant treatises. It expresses how Ronan finished in the top 10 percent of his class without attending school. This is almost certainly the correct answer, but work through the remaining choices first.

Choice *C* is irrelevant. This answer choice explains that Ronan was not penalized by his repeated absence, but it does not explain how he still succeeded despite his attendance record. Eliminate this choice.

Choice *D* is almost definitely true, but it does not explain the paradox. Simply being smart does not seem like enough of an explanation. This does not explain the paradox as well as Choice *B*. Eliminate this choice.

Choice *E* looks somewhat promising. It's possible that Ronan did not go to class since his professors could not teach him anything. However, like Choice *D*, it is not as strong as Choice *B*, which explains *how* Ronan succeeded.

Therefore, Choice *B* is the correct answer.

8. C: Choice *A* does not identify a flaw in the advertisement's reasoning. The advertisement connects smoking with fatal disease. At no point does the advertisement confuse the cause and effect. Eliminate this choice.

Choice *B* is incorrect. The advertisement does not make any overly broad generalizations. Eliminate this choice.

Choice *C* correctly identifies the argument's flaw. The argument analogizes secondhand smoke with a gas chamber without offering any evidence concerning secondhand smoke's health risk. The advertisement is clearly relying on hyperbole. The advertisement's argument properly justifies smoking with adverse health effects, but it does not do the same for secondhand smoke. This is most likely the correct answer.

Choice *D* is incorrect. Nothing in the argument states that there's real dispute over smoking's effect on health. Eliminate this choice.

Choice *E* is not present in the argument. Eliminate this choice.

Therefore, Choice *C* is the correct answer.

9. D: Choice *A* is true. According to the argument, all of the employees must complete a mandatory class on insider trading. Jake is an employee. Therefore, he must have taken a class on insider trading. Eliminate this choice.

Choice *B* is not necessarily true; however, it could be true. According to the argument, some employees must pass a certification course, but it does not mention whether Jake is one of those employees. This choice may or may not be true, so it cannot be the correct answer. Eliminate this choice.

Choice *C* restates a premise, so it is true. Therefore, it is incorrect for the purposes of this question. Eliminate this choice.

Choice *D* must be incorrect according to the argument. As previously discussed, all of the employees must take a class on insider trading. Jake is an employee, so he must have taken the class. Therefore, Choice *D* must not be true.

Choice *E* could be true. The argument states that investment banks hire dozens of lawyers. It does not mention whether any investment bank has ever been charged. Since this choice could be true, it's not the correct answer. Eliminate this choice.

Therefore, Choice *D* is the correct answer.

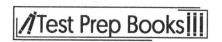
10. D: Choice *A* is incorrect, because it follows logically. This answer choice tells us that the United States increased spending while cutting taxes, which increased debt. This cannot be the correct answer since there's no flawed reasoning.

Choice *B* is similar to the argument since both the argument and answer choice involve a nearby business closing down. However, Choice *B* states that both businesses closed for the same reason. It does not claim that one closing caused the other like the flawed reasoning present in the argument. Rather, it claims that both businesses closed as a result of a single factor. Eliminate this choice.

Choice *C* does not rely on flawed reasoning. It states that Angela fell off her skateboard and crashed her car so she needs to recover from her injuries. This answer choice does not confuse causation with correlation like the argument. Eliminate this choice.

Choice *D* looks promising. The answer choice claims that losing her job caused her to receive another job offer on the same day. This mixes causation with correlation. The argument claims that Locally Sourced Food Market's caused Randy's Ammunition Warehouse to close without offering any evidence aside from time and location. Both share the same flaw—confusing correlation and causation—so it is the correct answer.

Choice *E* is incorrect since it's logically sound. There is no flaw in the choice's reasoning, so it cannot be the correct answer. Eliminate this choice.

Therefore, Choice *D* is the correct answer.

11. A: Choice *A* is consistent with the argument's logic. The argument asserts that the world powers' military alliances amounted to a lit fuse, and the assassination merely lit it. The main point of the argument is that any event involving the military alliances would have led to a world war. This is a very strong answer.

Choice *B* runs counter to the argument's tone and reasoning. It can immediately be eliminated.

Choice *C* is also clearly incorrect. At no point does the argument blame any single or group of countries for starting World War I. This can also be immediately eliminated.

Choice *D* is wrong for the same reason as Choice *C*. Eliminate this choice.

Choice *E* is a better option than the previous three, but it fails to complete the passage in any meaningful way. The argument is contending that the assassination was a sufficient cause for the war, rather than a necessary cause. Choice *A* more logically completes the passage. Eliminate this choice.

Therefore, Choice *A* is correct.

12. E: Choice *A* weakens the argument, but it does not address the argument's main point that football is inherently dangerous. This answer choice negates the premise concerning parents allowing their children to play youth football, but it fails to decimate the argument. Eliminate this choice.

Choice *B* severely weakens the argument, which hinges on football being so dangerous that, eventually, nobody will want to play it for fear of long-term brain injury. If the scientific studies are inconclusive, then all of the concerns could be irrelevant. This is a very strong answer choice.

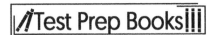

Choice *C* is irrelevant. The argument contends that the NFL will decline in popularity due to safety concerns. It is not contending that football will decline naturally. Eliminate this choice.

Choice *D* weakens the argument but not dramatically so. Even if removing helmets improved the sport's safety, it still would face concerns from the remaining head collisions. This choice does not weaken the argument as much as Choice *A*.

Choice *E* states that a pool of players will always be willing to play regardless of health concerns. Therefore, the safety concerns are irrelevant. It doesn't matter whether repeated head trauma causes brain injury or if parents allow their children to play youth football, if it's true that some people will always be willing to sign waivers and play. This really weakens the argument against football's danger. It is stronger than Choice *B*, which merely states that the studies are inconclusive. Choice *E* unravels the whole argument.

Therefore, Choice *E* is the correct answer.

13. B: Choice *A* uses similar language, but it is not the main point of disagreement. The reporter calls the loss devastating, and there's no reason to believe that the coach would disagree with this assessment. Eliminate this choice.

Choice *B* is strong since both passages mention the at-bats with runners in scoring position. The reporter asserts that the team lost *because* the team failed to get such a hit. In contrast, the coach identifies several other reasons for the loss, including fielding and pitching errors. Additionally, the coach disagrees that the team even needed a hit in those situations.

Choice *C* is mentioned by the coach, but not by the reporter. It is unclear whether the reporter would agree with this assessment. Eliminate this choice.

Choice *D* is mentioned by the coach but not by the reporter. It is not stated whether the reporter believes that the team deserved to win. Eliminate this choice.

Choice *E* is clearly incorrect. Although the coach would probably disagree that his team rose to the challenge, he does not explicitly express this opinion. Do not make that assumption. Eliminate this choice.

Therefore, Choice *B* is the correct answer.

14. D: Choice *A* is irrelevant. The argument does not address whether Kimmy deserves her fame. Eliminate this choice.

Choice *B* restates a premise. Kimmy starring in an extremely popular movie is only one piece of the argument. It is not the main purpose. Eliminate this choice.

Choice *C* also restates a premise, and it is incorrect for the same reasons as Choice *B*. Eliminate this choice.

Choice *D* accurately expresses the argument's conclusion, and it best describes the argument's primary purpose. The argument concludes that Kimmy is a world-famous actress. Choice *D* is the best expression of the argument's purpose.

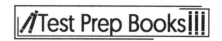

Choice *E* is yet another restatement of a premise. Don't be fooled by the three answer choices that restate premises. They are all equally incorrect since a single premise will almost never be the primary purpose.

Therefore, Choice *D* is the correct answer.

15. C: Choice *A* is incorrect. The argument does not attack the Dalai Lama's credibility. Eliminate this choice.

Choice *B* is incorrect since the argument does not use extreme language. Eliminate this choice.

Choice *C* correctly identifies the flaw in the author's reasoning. The argument builds the Dalai Lama's credibility as a world leader who's committed to religious harmony, national self-determination, and humanistic values. However, the argument then commits a logical flaw by relying on the Dalai Lama as a domestic policy expert. The Dalai Lama's expertise, as stated by the argument, does not support him being authority on curtailing gun violence. This is almost certainly the correct answer.

Choice *D* is incorrect since the argument does not make use of a hasty generalization. Eliminate this choice.

Choice *E* is incorrect. There's no discussion of causation in the argument, so it can't be confused with correlation. Eliminate this choice.

Therefore, Choice *C* is the correct answer.

16. E: Choice *A* is clearly incorrect. The argument does not start with a conclusion. Eliminate this choice.

Choice *B* is incorrect. Although the argument states a universal rule—the top salesman is always a company's best employee—it does not argue that Dwight is the exception. Eliminate this choice.

Choice *C* is fairly strong. The argument does state several facts and offers a conclusion based on those facts. Leave this choice for now.

Choice *D* is clearly incorrect. The argument does not contain any specific anecdotes. Eliminate this choice.

Choice *E* looks extremely promising. The argument first states several facts—Dwight works at a mid-sized regional tech company and leads the company in sales—then states a rule. Lastly, the argument applies the facts to the rule and concludes that Dwight is the best employee. This is a better fit than Choice *C* since it includes the rule and its application.

Therefore, Choice *E* is the correct answer.

17. A: Choice *A* looks like a strong answer choice. A hasty generalization relies on insufficient data or makes an unreasonable generalization. In this case, the conclusion is based on the advertisement's claims that the more one plays, the better their chances are at winning. However, this is clearly erroneous. The argument states that the odds are a billion-to-one. Technically, Julian is more likely to win the lottery if he buys seven tickets per week instead of zero, but it is unreasonable to claim that Julian will likely win the lottery in the near future. This is very likely the answer, but examine the other options first.

Choice *B* is incorrect. The argument does not rely on any extreme language. Eliminate this choice.

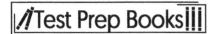

Choice *C* is also incorrect. The argument does not make multiple logical leaps and assumptions. The claim that Julian is more likely to win the lottery in the near future could be considered a logical leap, but the answer choice mentions multiple leaps and assumptions. Choice *A* remains the stronger choice.

Choice *D* is clearly incorrect since there's no mention of a causal relationship anywhere in the argument. Eliminate this choice.

Choice *E* is also clearly incorrect. The argument does not rely on any expert. Even if the Local Lottery Commission is considered an expert, Choice *A* is still the better choice.

Therefore, Choice *A* is the correct answer.

18. E: Choice *A* is irrelevant since the argument states that Gob and Bobo are equally talented. Therefore, it does not matter if Bobo is an experienced clown since both Bobo and Gob are equally talented. Eliminate this choice.

Choice *B* looks promising. This choice offers a reason why Bobo is more successful than Gob, even though they're equally talented. It explains the paradox by showing that people still generally prefer clowns despite rampant coulrophobia.

Choice *C* is a strong answer choice. This answer choice attempts to explain how Bobo is more successful despite rampant coulrophobia by claiming that Bobo is non-threatening. However, Choice *B* is the better explanation since it's more specific.

Choice *D* is irrelevant for the same reason as Choice *A*, which is that the argument claims that Bobo and Gob are equally talented. If Gob is a below average magician, Bobo is a below average clown. This does not explain the paradox.

Choice *E* is a third strong answer choice. It resolves the paradox by explaining that the two equally talented performers work in areas with different population densities. This is the best answer. Choice *B* only mentions preferences to children's birthday parties, and Choice *C* is too general.

Therefore, Choice *E* is the correct answer.

19. D: Choice *A* is incorrect since it could be true. According to the argument, we know that Cindy braids her hair on Christmas and Easter. It's not stated if there is any time that she doesn't braid her hair. Therefore, it could be true that she braids her hair every day. Eliminate this choice.

Choice *B* is irrelevant. The argument makes no mention of Cindy's preferences toward braiding. Therefore, there's no way to say that this answer choice cannot be true. Eliminate this choice.

Choice *C* is incorrect since it could be true. The argument leaves open this possibility. Eliminate this choice.

Choice *D* is correct since it absolutely cannot be true based on the facts. It is stated that Cindy braided her hair on Easter. Therefore, it cannot be true that Cindy only braids her hair on Christmas.

Choice *E* is incorrect since it could be true. The argument leaves open this possibility, so it could possibly be true. Eliminate this choice.

Therefore, Choice *D* is the correct answer.

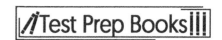

20. B: Choice *A* is clearly incorrect. The argument describes how fans have two preferences and then describes how venues handle those preferences before concluding with the band's preference. Choice *A* similarly describes diners' preferences and how the best restaurants offer those preferences. This choice doesn't parallel the reasoning of how restaurants handle the preferences. Eliminate this choice.

Choice *B* looks very promising. This choice starts by describing two ways to coach players, and then describes how those preferences play out. The concluding sentence is nearly identical to the argument's final sentence. This is a very strong answer choice.

Choice *C* is clearly incorrect. This answer choice fails to include the If/Then sentence included in the argument. Eliminate this choice.

Choice *D* is similar to the argument, but the final sentence does not parallel the argument. Eliminate this choice.

Choice *E* is clearly incorrect. It does not parallel the argument's reasoning. Eliminate this choice.

Therefore, Choice *B* is the correct answer.

21. B: Choice *A* looks appealing since it summarizes the argument's information. However, it does not describe an assumption necessary to the argument. Eliminate this choice.

Choice *B* is a strong answer choice. It is a necessary assumption since the argument does not follow logically without it. The argument does not directly address the qualifications to be President of the Executive Council. The argument merely describes the qualifications to be an executive council member. It must be assumed that the qualifications are the same if Jackie can't be the President of the Executive Council.

Choice *C* is incorrect since it is directly contradicted by the argument. The first sentence tells us that all Executive Council members must have a law degree. Eliminate this choice.

Choice *D* is incorrect. Although it might be true that Jackie would serve as the president if not for her felony, the argument's logic does not depend on this being true. Eliminate this choice.

Choice *E* is irrelevant. Any felony conviction is sufficient to bar an individual from serving as president. The felony's relevance to serving as president is inconsequential. Eliminate this choice.

Therefore, Choice *B* is the correct answer.

22. E: Choice *A* looks promising, but fails to express the argument's main conclusion. This choice merely states reasons why mouth guards provide important protection during contact sports. Eliminate this choice.

Choice *B* is a strong answer choice. The author clearly believes this to be true since the argument's last sentence advocates the enforcement of penalties for players who don't wear a mouth guard. However, this is not the main conclusion. Eliminate this choice.

Choice *C* is too extreme. The argument clearly supports the use of mouth guards, but the argument does not support the notion that mouth guards save lives. Eliminate this choice.

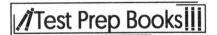

Choice *D* is incorrect since it uses weak language. The argument does not think that mouth guards are merely preferable. Rather, it advocates the enforcement of penalties for failing to wear mouth guards. The main conclusion must match the argument's tone and force. Eliminate this choice.

Choice *E* looks extremely promising. It encompasses the argument's relevant information—mouth guards protect teeth and prevent concussions—and matches the argument's tone, which advocates penalties for non-compliance.

Therefore, Choice *E* is the correct answer.

23. D: Choice *A* is incorrect. Even though the law student does in fact rely on personal anecdotes, the anecdotes are relevant. The law student is a member of the class that she describes. This is not the part of the argument most vulnerable to criticism. Eliminate this choice.

Choice *B* is incorrect. The law student's reference to an authority, the law school professor, is relevant to the argument. The professor is charged with assisting law students in balancing schoolwork and their lives. It is not the biggest source of criticism. Eliminate this choice.

Choice *C* looks promising. The argument does draw hasty generalizations by applying the law student and classmates' experience as a blanket characterization. Keep this choice.

Choice *D* also looks extremely promising. The law student definitely uses extreme language. Look at how these phrases are used in the argument: *any hope*, *all aspects*, and *completely impossible.* Additionally, the final sentence is the epitome of extreme language. Although the law student makes a hasty generalization, the extreme language is much more vulnerable to criticism.

Choice *E* is clearly incorrect. At no point does the law student address and then dismiss contradicting arguments. Eliminate this choice.

Therefore, Choice *D* is the correct answer.

24. C: Choice *A* is a strong answer choice. The reference to the ancient civilization's poultry intolerance definitely serves as a historical example. Examine the other choices first.

Choice *B* is clearly incorrect. The argument's conclusion is that people will eventually realize that they are not actually gluten insensitive. Eliminate this choice.

Choice *C* is also a strong answer choice. The reference to the ancient civilization illustrates how a society can wrongly attribute food intolerance. The argument contends that ancient societies believed they were poultry intolerant, but in reality, they were misdiagnosing the issue. In fact, they were never poultry intolerant. The perceived intolerance was due to poor preparation and food poisoning. The argument asserts that contemporary people will eventually come to a similar realization. Although Choice *A* is technically accurate, Choice *C* better explains the reference's role.

Choice *D* does not make any sense. The reference to ancient societies ties the argument together in the sense that it serves as a historical example that supports the conclusion, but this choice is too vague. Eliminate this choice.

Choice *E* is clearly incorrect. The reference does not distract the reader from the argument's primary purpose. It supports the argument's conclusion. Eliminate this choice.

Therefore, Choice *C* is the correct answer.

25. D: Choice *A* strengthens the argument by connecting increased metabolism with weight loss. Eliminate this choice.

Choice *B* strengthens the argument by providing evidence of the drug's efficacy across several studies. It supports the argument's contention that the new drugs decrease appetite. Eliminate this choice.

Choice *C* is similar to Choice *B*. This answer choice is incorrect since it strengthens the doctor's argument by proving the new drug's efficacy. Eliminate this choice.

Choice *D* definitely weakens the doctor's argument, unlike the other answer choices. If healthcare plans won't cover the new drugs and people cannot afford them, it is unlikely that the drugs will lead to a decline in obesity.

Choice *E* also strengthens the doctor's argument. If nutritious food is unavailable to many people battling obesity, the drug advancement is particularly important. Eliminate this choice.

Therefore, Choice *D* is the correct answer.

Section II: Analytical Reasoning

Problem 1

Because there's a request to place six teachers' parking spaces in order, this should be recognized as an ordering problem. As always, start with a diagram. Here, starting with just six blank spaces, one for each of the six parking spots, is a good first step.

_____ _____ _____ _____ _____ _____

(DOOR)

Writing "DOOR" underneath the first blank serves as a reminder that the first space is the one closest to the door. In a problem with a complex numbering system, a label for each blank with the appropriate parking space number could be used. However, this problem simply states that the numbers go from 1 to 6 in order, so it's unnecessary to label the already ordered numbers and would only add clutter.

No other useful information is in the problem setup, so it's best to turn to the problem's rules. Finding the most restrictive rule is a good next step. In other words, start with the rule that narrows down the possible scenarios.

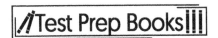

Here, the third rule, "Olivia's space is next to only one other space" is the most restrictive. The only two spaces that are next to only one other space are the two on the ends: space #1 and space #6. We now have two possibilities, so making a second copy of the diagram (without wasting time writing "DOOR" over again) is helpful. Then, fill in what was learned to represent those two possibilities:

O _____ _____ _____ _____ _____

(DOOR)

_____ _____ _____ _____ _____ O

At this point, it's wise to look for a rule that ties in with what has already been placed in the diagrams. However, none of the other three rules mention Olivia, the only teacher in the diagrams so far. So instead, a search for the next most restrictive rule should be done.

At first glance, none of the rules seems exceptionally helpful. Yet, as we look at the state of the diagrams, the fourth rule, "There are exactly three other teachers' spaces between Pablo's and Sasha's spaces," tells us something important. Since it's known that Olivia is on the end, there is only one place in each diagram where there is room for Pablo or Sasha, three empty spaces, and then Sasha or Pablo. Accordingly, a second copy of each of the two diagrams is needed—one with Sasha/empty/empty/empty/Pablo, and one with the reverse:

O S _____ _____ _____ P

(DOOR)

O P _____ _____ _____ S

S _____ _____ _____ P O

P _____ _____ _____ S O

Of the two rules remaining, only one mentions someone in a diagram—the first rule, "Sasha's space is next to Nan's space." In each of the four diagrams, there is only one possible space for Nan that is next to Sasha, so Nan should be penciled in the diagram:

O S N _____ _____ P

(DOOR)

O P _____ _____ N S

S N _____ _____ P O

P _____ _____ N S O

The final rule, "Nan's space is closer to the door than Quincy's space," should give us something solid regarding Quincy. However, two of the diagrams (the second and fourth) don't have any spaces available that are farther from the door than Nan's. That means these diagrams aren't possible anymore, so they must be crossed out. This leaves the following possibilities:

O S N _____ _____ P

(DOOR)

S N _____ _____ P O

There are just two spaces left, and there are only two teachers to go in each space. At this point, filling in the possibilities for each of the two viable scenarios is prudent:

#1	O S N Q R P
#2	O S N R Q P
#3	S N Q R P O
#4	S N R Q P O

It's great to reach a point of no more blanks. This signifies success at diagramming all valid possible answers, if done correctly, and makes answering the questions much easier.

1. C: This question asks which of the five choices *must* be true. Accordingly, this means that one of the five answer choices is true in ALL of the diagrams. If there is even one diagram in which an answer is not true, then it cannot be the correct answer.

Working through the choices, Choice *A* states, "Quincy is in one of the middle two spaces," but in Diagram 2, Quincy is in the 5th space. Eliminate Choice *A*. Choice *B* states, "Pablo's space is on one of the two ends," but in Diagrams 3 and 4, Pablo is not on the end. Choice *B* is out.

Choice *C* states, "Pablo's space is farther from the door than Quincy's space," and that is how it is in all four diagrams—Pablo's space is farther to the right than Quincy's. Thus, this is probably the correct answer.

When pressed for time and feeling somewhat comfortable with an answer, a test taker could stop here, mark Choice *C* as the answer, and head to the next question. But, it's usually worth a couple of extra seconds to rule out the remaining possibilities. So, Choice *D* states, "Robert's space is farther from the door than Quincy's space," but it's obvious that Quincy's space is actually farther from the door than Robert's space in Diagrams 2 and 4, so Choice *D* is out. And finally, Choice *E* states, "Olivia's space is next to Sasha's space." It's apparent in Diagrams 3 and 4 that Sasha and Olivia are on opposite ends, so Choice *E* is out.

2. D: Question 2 asks which teacher *could* be in space #4. Accordingly, when looking at space #4 in the four diagrams, Diagrams 1 and 4 show Quincy in space #4, while Diagrams #2 and #3 show Robert there. Robert is not one of the five choices; thus, Quincy must be the correct answer.

3. B: Question 3 asserts an additional condition: "If Olivia's space is closest to the door . . ." That means to ignore any diagrammed possibilities in which that condition is not true (Diagrams 3 and 4 show Sasha is closest to the door). Thus, Diagrams 1 and 2 are the only choices to analyze further. In the context of the remaining diagrams, the question becomes, "Which teacher's space *must* be farthest from the door?" In both Diagrams 1 and 2, Pablo is farthest from the door, so it has to be Choice *B*, Pablo.

4. B: Again, another condition is provided: "If Robert's space is adjacent to Pablo's space . . ." This time, the new condition rules out the diagrammed possibilities where Robert and Pablo's spaces are not next to each other—Diagrams 2 and 4. Then, the question is which of the five choices *cannot* be true. Accordingly, if the choice is true in either Diagram 1 or 3 (or true in both), it can be ruled out.

Choice *A* states, "Sasha is in space #1." That is true in Diagram 3, so it's not Choice *A*. Choice *B* states, "Quincy is in space #5," but we can see that Quincy is not in space #5 in either Diagram 1 or 3. He is in space #5 in Diagram 2, but the extra condition rules out Diagram 2, so it appears the answer is Choice *B*.

Just to be sure, though, further analysis can be done. Choice *C* states, "Olivia's space is next to Sasha's." That's true in Diagram 1, so Choice *C* is out. Choice *D* states, "Olivia's space is next to Pablo's," which is true in Diagram 3, so Choice *D* is out. And last, Choice *E* states, "Nan is in one of the two middle spaces." She is indeed in space #3 in Diagram 1, so Choice *E* is wrong as well. Choice *B* is correct.

5. A: This question asks which layout is *possible*, so each choice needs to be reviewed until one possibility is found among the four diagrammed choices. Note, this question specifies the order by stating, "starting with the space closest to the door." That's the order the diagrams are in, but always be careful. If it had stated, "starting with the space farthest from the door," then reading the diagrams backward would have been necessary.

After reviewing the five choices, it's apparent that Choice *A* matches Diagram 4. A couple others are close, such as Choice *D*, but Choice *A* is the only perfect match.

6. D: The last question for this problem asks which teacher's space *must* be next to Quincy's. Accordingly, the diagrams need to be analyzed to see which teacher appears next to Quincy in all four of them. Diagram 1 has Nan and Robert on either side of Quincy, Diagram 2 has Robert and Pablo, Diagram 3 has Nan and Robert, and Diagram 4 has Robert and Pablo. Robert is the only teacher next to Quincy in all of the diagrams. Thus, Choice *D* (Robert) is the correct answer.

Problem 2

This looks like a grouping problem. We have three customers who ordered a total of ten tacos. A good approach is to draw blanks for each taco next to the name of each customer, and then apply the most concrete rule, which is, "Each customer ordered at least one tofu taco and at least one non-tofu taco." That means that all three customers have at least two tacos, one of which is a tofu taco.

T _____

T _____

T _____

Looking for another rule with some solid information, "No two customers ordered the same number of tacos" fits that need. It's known that there are ten tacos, and six are already accounted for in the diagram. The last four tacos need to be distributed so that no customer gets the same number. Further analysis of splitting up the tacos shows the following: 4/0/0 doesn't work; 3/1/0 does; 2/2/0 doesn't;

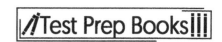
and neither does 2/1/1. There is no other way to split up four tacos among three people, so three customers are going to get the two tacos already in the diagram, plus an extra 3, 1, and 0, respectively.

T _____ _____ _____ _____

T _____ _____

T _____

Now the rule that "Marlo ordered at least one of each type of taco" comes to the forefront when trying to solve this problem. Clearly, his order must be the five-taco order. It's also known what four of those five tacos are. Since the remaining tacos are beginning to be narrowed down, listing them to the side is helpful:

M: T S A F _____

     T _____ _____   TSFA

     T _____

The customer who ordered the fish taco is also identified (Marlo), and it's known that he "also ordered at least two steak tacos."

M: T S A F S

     T _____ _____   TS~~F~~A

     T _____

The last rule states that Lester did not order steak or fish. Additionally, using the first rule, it's known that Lester did order at least one non-tofu taco. Therefore, he must have ordered an avocado taco, since that's the only one left. Unfortunately, it's still not known if he represents the two-taco or three-taco order. This means a tweak of the diagram would be helpful by labeling the two unknown orders and putting the third taco in parentheses, since it's not known whether Kim or Lester gets it:

M: T S A F S

K: T _____ (_____)   TS~~FA~~

L: T A (_____)

The same situation encountered with Lester a moment ago is now encountered with Kim. More specifically, Kim has a non-tofu taco, and there is only one non-tofu taco available to her. Therefore, the last steak taco goes to Kim, and the extra taco is left to go to either Kim or Lester:

M: T S A F S

K: T S (T)   ~~TSFA~~

L: T A (T)

Answer Explanations #1 | Section II: Analytical Reasoning

7. E: The question asks which choice is *possible,* so which four choices are impossible is something that needs to be figured out; i.e., cannot match the diagram. Choice A shows Kim with an avocado taco and Lester without one, so it cannot be right. Choice B shows Kim with two steak tacos and Marlo with only one, so it cannot be right. Choice C shows Marlo with two tofu tacos (and six total), so it must not be correct. Choice D shows Kim and Lester both with two tofu tacos, but they can only have three total tofu tacos, so it is incorrect. That leaves Choice E, which matches the diagram with the extra tofu taco going to Kim.

8. B: The question adds a rule by providing that Kim has not ordered more than one of any single type of taco. Since the diagram shows a definite tofu taco for Kim, it's known that the new rule means she cannot get the extra tofu taco, which must then go to Lester.

M: T   S   A   F   S

K: T   S

L: T   A   T

Turning to the choices, Choice A is not correct because the diagram shows Marlo with five tacos, not four. Choice B is correct, since it's known that Lester has a tofu taco and an avocado taco, and the new rule means he has a second tofu taco as well. Choice C is incorrect because Kim cannot have a fish taco. Choices D and E are incorrect because Marlo only ordered one tofu taco and one avocado taco.

9. E: Looking at the diagram, it's known that Marlo definitely ordered two steak tacos, so he is on the list. It is possible that Kim or Lester ordered two tofu tacos; however, both of those scenarios cannot be simultaneously true. The problem is asking for a list of diners who _could_ have ordered more than one of the same type of taco. It is possible that Kim did order two tacos of the same type, and the same is true for Lester. Therefore, both should be included on the list along with Marlo. Thus, Choice E is correct since it lists all three diners.

10. B: The diagram makes this one easy because it's known exactly what tacos Marlo ordered: one tofu, two steak, one avocado, and one fish. Thus, Choice B is correct because Marlo ordered two steak tacos.

11. C: The choice that is never true needs to be found. The diagram shows that Kim definitely ordered one tofu taco, and may have ordered a second, so neither Choice A nor B is correct because both could be true. Marlo is the only customer known to have ordered more than one of the same type of taco (two steak tacos). It's also known that Kim and Lester both ordered one tofu taco, and that one or the other of them must have ordered a second tofu taco, so Choice D is incorrect. Choice E is incorrect because Marlo did indeed order more steak tacos (two) than tofu tacos (one).

Thus, Choice C is the correct answer because it cannot be true that only one customer ordered more than one of the same type of taco. Marlo definitely ordered more than one of a single type of taco, and either Lester or Kim, but not both, must have done the same. It's important to note that all of the choices, except for Choices C and D, could have been crossed out, since they directly contradict each other. Therefore, it's known that only one choice can be true (making the other definitively false). This is the type of recognition that becomes second nature with practice.

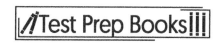

12. C: The question adds a new rule: "Kim orders more tacos than Lester." Therefore, here's the diagram for this question:

M: T S A F S

K: T S T

L: T A

Again, the diagram makes the question easy. Kim gets the extra tofu taco, which means Lester's order is just one tofu taco and one avocado taco. Thus, Choice *C* is correct.

Problem 3

After being given a big group of volunteers and asked to choose some number from that group, it's easy to recognize this as a selection problem. It's important to note there's a key limitation in the problem setup: at least two volunteers will be sent to register voters and at least two will remain in the office. This can be represented by drawing two blanks next to "go" and two next to "stay."

Accordingly, drawing two more blanks next to "go" and two more next to "stay" is helpful. It should be indicated on the diagram that these two blanks are not fixed:

GO: ____ ____ (____) (____)

STAY: ____ ____ (____) (____)

Next, focus on the rules, which tell us what certain volunteer(s) will do based on what other volunteer(s) do. Listing these six volunteers twice is advantageous, once next to "go" and once next to "stay":

GO: ____ ____ (____) (____)   M   Z   J   K   S

STAY: ____ ____ (____) (____)   M   Z   J   K   S

The first rule states, "If Malcolm goes to register voters, Zoe stays at the campaign office." This can be represented with an arrow from "M" next to "GO" to the "Z" next to "STAY":

GO: M ____ (____) (____) J K   S B

                      ↓

STAY: Z ____ (____) (____)   J K   S B

Note: It is critically important that the arrow goes *from* Malcolm in the top row *to* Zoe in the bottom row, signifying that *if* Malcolm goes, *then* Zoe stays. If an arrow is drawn going the wrong way, the diagram will be wrong, and answers most likely will be incorrect as well.

The second rule states, "If Zoe goes to register, then Jayne does too." It's important to pay attention to which part is the "if" and which part is the "then." Here, *if* Zoe goes, *then* Jayne does, so we draw an arrow from Zoe on the top to Jayne on the top:

GO: Z → J (____) (____) M K S B

STAY: ____ ____ (____) (____)   M K S B

The third rule states, "If Zoe stays at the campaign office, Simon does too." This is a third *if/then*, and will be treated just like the first two by drawing an arrow from Zoe on the bottom to Simon on the bottom:

GO: ____ ____ (____) (____)   M   K   J   B

STAY: Z ➜ S (____) (____)   M   K   J   B

The fourth rule states, "Jayne and Kaylee don't both go or both stay." This means that if Jayne stays, Kaylee goes, and vice versa. It also means that one spot on each team will always be for either Jayne or Kaylee. This can be represented by two-headed arrows from Jayne at the bottom to Kaylee at the top, and vice versa, and also by writing "J/K" into the first slot on both the top and bottom:

GO: J/K ____ (____) (____) M   Z   S   B

STAY: J/K ____ (____) (____) M   Z   S   B

This is an ideal diagram that encompasses all of the given information. When a diagram can be tied together this well, it should be expected that answers to questions will come relatively quickly.

13. D: The question asks which *could* be a list of all volunteers who go. Comparing each choice to the diagram, it's important to see which one isn't barred by one of the rules that's been sketched. Choice *A* has neither Jayne nor Kaylee, so it is wrong. Choice *B* has Zoe but not Jayne, so it is wrong. Choice *C* has Jayne and Kaylee, so it is wrong. Choice *D* violates no rules, so it is correct. Choice *E* also has neither Jayne nor Kaylee, so it is wrong.

14. E: The question asks which pairs of volunteers *could* both go register voters with or without others. Looking at the diagram, Choice *A* is wrong because if Malcolm goes, Zoe stays. Choice *B* is wrong because if Zoe goes, Jayne goes, and Kaylee would stay. Choice *C* is wrong because if Malcolm goes, Zoe stays, and Simon would also stay. Choice *D* is wrong because Jayne and Kaylee can't both go. Choice *E*, which violates no rules, is correct. In this case, we know Jayne will also go since Zoe is going. Therefore, at least three of the volunteers would go together in this case: Zoe, Bridget, and Jayne.

15. B: If Zoe goes to register voters, the diagram shows that Jayne also goes, which means that Kaylee stays. Also, if Malcolm were going, the diagram shows that Zoe would stay, so Malcolm must also be staying along with Kaylee. Here are the choices:

Choice *A* has Jayne, Malcolm, and Simon staying, but it's known that Kaylee must stay and Jayne must go, so this choice is incorrect. Choice *B* has only Kaylee and Malcolm staying, but those are the only two people who must stay. Therefore, Choice *B* should be kept in mind while checking the other choices. Choice *C* has Bridget, Kaylee, Malcolm, and Zoe staying, but Zoe must go, so it is incorrect. Choice *D* has Bridget, Jayne, and Zoe staying, which would be a valid list of volunteers who go, rather than stay like the question asks. Choices *C* and *D* could also be ruled out since the question prompt states that Zoe is going, so she cannot be on the complete list of volunteers who stay put. Lastly, Choice *E* lists Bridget, Jayne, Malcolm, and Simon as the volunteers who stay, but Jayne must go (Z ➜ J GO rule), so Kaylee must stay (K/J rule). Thus, Choice *E* is incorrect as well.

16. D: In this case, the answer choice that cannot be true needs to be found, so the process of elimination is used to check each choice against the diagram. Choice *A* would have Kaylee, Simon, and Zoe stay, implying that Bridget, Jayne, and Malcolm go. After checking both sets of volunteers with the diagram, there are no contradictions, so Choice *A* could be a complete list and is therefore not the

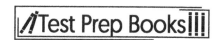

correct answer. Choice *B* would have Kaylee and Malcolm stay, while Bridget, Jayne, Simon, and Zoe go. Again, there are no contradictions, so Choice *B* is not correct. Choice *C* would have Bridget, Kaylee, Simon, and Zoe stay, while Jayne and Malcolm go. Again, there are no contradictions, and Choice *C* is wrong. Choice *D* would have Bridget, Kaylee, and Zoe stay, while Jayne, Malcolm, and Simon go. However, the diagram shows that if Zoe stays, then Simon must also stay, so there is a contradiction. Thus, Choice *D* is correct. Finally, Choice *E* would have Bridget, Kaylee, Malcolm, and Simon stay, while Jayne and Zoe go, which also does not contradict any rule in the setup.

17. B: This question provides a great opportunity to save time by scanning the answers before evaluating them. Note, the question asks, "Which *could* be true?" and provides both "Malcolm goes" and "Malcolm stays" as answers. Obviously, one of these two things must be true, or Malcolm could not be listed. It must be determined which of these two scenarios is true.

According to the diagram, if Malcolm goes, then both Zoe and Simon stay. Additionally, either Jayne or Kaylee must stay, since those two must be separated. If Malcolm goes, then there would be more than two volunteers who stay. Thus, Malcolm cannot go if there are exactly two volunteers who remain in the office, leaving Choice *B* as the correct answer.

18. C: The question adds a rule that states, "Simon and Malcolm get the same assignment." Looking at the diagram, if Malcolm goes, then Zoe stays, which forces Simon to stay as well. Thus, Malcolm must stay if he and Simon are to get the same assignment. It's also known that either Jayne or Kaylee must stay, but not both, as well.

Choices *A*, *B*, and *E* can immediately be ruled out, since Malcolm and Simon must stay. Choice *D* cannot be correct, since Jayne and Kaylee cannot get the same assignment. Thus, Choice *C* is the correct answer.

Problem 4

This problem is tricky for a couple of reasons. First, it doesn't fit neatly into any of the categories. It looks like it might be an ordering problem, since it involves time slots. But when it's studied further, it's really about figuring out the order that the companies received to make their choices. The fact that they were choosing between time slots, rather than anything else, is a "red herring" meant to distract and confuse test takers.

Don't panic. Problems occasionally don't fit neatly into one of the categories. If it happens, continue to start with a diagram. Here, the test writer basically provided the diagram, but it can be simplified a bit:

T:	2	11	4	9
U:	11	4	9	2
V:	2	4	11	9
W:	11	2	4	9

A second reason this problem is unusual is that it doesn't provide a list of rules. As a result, it's not going to be possible to "solve" everything with a diagram before turning to the questions. Instead, jumping right into the questions is the best approach.

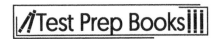

19. B: The question asks which choice *could* be true. Choice *A* states, "Exactly three companies get their second choice." Of course, whichever company goes first gets their first choice; therefore, look for a scenario with one first choice and three second choices.

Looking at the diagram, it shows that no company chose 9 a.m. first or second. So, Choice *A* cannot be right. Eliminate it. Choice *B* states, "Exactly two companies get their third choice." At first glance, this seems possible, but it is hard to prove one way or the other. Set aside this choice and see if it can be ruled out later. Choice *C* states, "Exactly three companies get their third choice." This is plainly impossible, since the company picking second would get, at worst, its second. Eliminate it.

Choice *D* states, "Exactly two companies get their fourth choice." There are only two fourth choices in the diagram: 9 a.m. and 2 p.m. Only U chose 2 p.m. as their 4th preference, so this would mean U definitely picked last and got 2 p.m. But that would mean 9 a.m., 11 a.m., and 4 p.m. were all off the board by the time U picked. No company would've chosen to pick 9 a.m. if 2 p.m. were available, so this cannot be correct. Choice *E* states, "Exactly three companies get their fourth choice." This is impossible for the same reason as Choice *D*. With the rest ruled out, Choice *B* is correct.

Check the answer just to be sure. If W picked first, then it would select 11 a.m. (their #1 choice). If V picked second, then it would select 2 p.m. (their #1 choice). If T picked third, then it would select 4 p.m. (their #3 choice). If U picked fourth, then it would select 9 a.m. (their #3 choice). Thus, it is possible for exactly two companies to receive their third choices. Remember, the more questions practiced, the faster the identification of patterns can be made.

20. E: The question asks which order is *possible*. There's not much to do with this problem other than applying trial and error. Compare each choice to the diagram and see what is determined. Choice *A* is composed of W, V, T, U. Circling the appropriate time slots in the diagram shows that T got its first choice, U its second choice, V its third choice, and W its fourth choice. But if U was picking second with only T's first choice of 2 p.m. off of the board, it would've taken its first choice, 11 a.m. Accordingly, Choice *A* cannot be correct.

An additional diagram for Choice *B* is needed. A diagram from Choice *B* can be reused, or if things get too cluttered, a new one can be drawn. Choice *B* is composed of U, V, T, W. U, V, and W all got their third choices, but whichever one picked second should have gotten their second choice at worst. Choice *B* is wrong.

Choice *C* is composed of U, T, W, V, but our diagram shows that nobody gets their first choice in that situation. Clearly Choice *C* is wrong. Choice *D* is composed of V, W, U, T. Circling these four slots in the diagram, it's apparent that W got its first choice, but nobody else got their first or second choice, so Choice *D* must be wrong.

Choice *E* should be correct by elimination, but it should still be reviewed. U got its first choice of 11 a.m. V and W got their second choices of 4 p.m. and 2 p.m., respectively. And that left only 9 a.m. for T. Choice *E* is correct.

21. D: The question gives a new rule, stating that Company V's presentation takes place before lunch. It then asks which of the five choices *cannot* be true. It's apparent that V has gotten either 11 a.m., its third choice, or 9 a.m., its fourth choice. This is a question where it pays to skim the choices for an obviously correct answer.

The only choice involving V is Choice *D*, which says that V picks second. If V picked second, then V would have at least one of its first two options—2 p.m. and 4 p.m.—still on the board. Thus, V cannot both pick second and give the presentation before lunch (9 a.m. or 11 a.m. slots), so Choice *D* must be the correct answer.

22. B: This question also gives a new rule, stating that Company V goes first, i.e., at 9 a.m., and asks which choice could be true. The critical inference is that V must have picked last if its presentation is at 9 a.m. Let's look at the choices.

Choice *A* has T getting its second choice at 11 a.m. That would mean 2 p.m. was chosen first. However, V is the only other company that has 2 p.m. listed as their first preference, and it's known that V picked last, so *A* cannot be correct.

Choice *B* has U getting its second choice at 4 p.m. This means that the 11 a.m. time slot was off the board when V chose, so W must have picked first. Company T's first choice of 2 p.m. is still available as the third pick. Thus, Company U could conceivably present at 4 p.m., so Choice *B* is the correct answer. The other answers can be quickly ruled out.

Choice *C* has three companies getting their first choice, but there are only two first choices (11 a.m. and 2 p.m.) between the four companies, so Choice *C* cannot be correct.

Choice *D* has exactly two companies getting their second choice. With V picking last, there are three ways this could be true: T picks first and leaves U and W with their second choice, U picks first and leaves T and W with their second choice, or W picks first and leaves T and U with their second choice. Circling these possibilities in the diagram shows that all three lead to contradictions, so Choice *D* cannot be correct.

Choice *E* has exactly two companies getting their third choice. But since it's known that V picked last, that would leave only one company left to pick first (and get their first choice), which would leave no company to get their second choice. Choice *E* cannot be correct, so Choice *B* remains as the correct choice.

23. E: This is a relatively complicated problem. It's always a good idea to scan the choices for an obviously correct answer, but that's especially true on a hard problem. If that's done, Choice *E* appears to be the correct answer: "At least one company gets their first choice." Of course, this is true, so Choice *E* is correct.

24. A: Finally, one more "brute force" question, asking which choice *cannot* be true. For this, the diagram should be reproduced, and the choices should be considered.

Choice *A* states that V goes at 11 a.m., which is the company's third choice. This means that both 2 p.m. and 4 p.m. must have already been taken. After consulting the diagram, this turns out to be impossible, since no company would have picked 4 p.m. if 11 a.m. were still available. However, Company V is the only company that ranks 4 p.m. higher than 11 a.m. This is the type of inference that will become more natural as practice is repeated.

The remaining answer choices then can be ruled out. Choice *B* has T at 11 a.m., which is possible if V picks first and takes 2 p.m. Choice *C* has W at 2 p.m., which is possible if U picks first and takes 11 a.m. Choice *D* has U at 4 p.m., which is possible if W picks first and takes 11 a.m. And Choice *E* has W at 11 a.m., which is possible if W picks first.

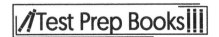

Section III: Logical Reasoning

1. D: Choice *A* is ambiguous. The argument states that Roman society did not consider slavery to be immoral. However, this is not the same as claiming that slavery is generally not immoral. Eliminate this choice.

Choice *B* is unsupported by the historian's argument. Eliminate this choice.

Choice *C* contains the right idea, but it fails to be specific. The historian would definitely agree that slavery was integral in sustaining the Roman Empire. However, *necessary evil* is much stronger. The phrase implies that slavery was needed for a greater good. The historian does not make this argument.

Choice *D* fits within the historian's line of reasoning. The historian concludes that slavery was integral to sustaining the Roman Empire. Therefore, the historian would certainly agree that if not for slavery, the Empire would have collapsed earlier.

Choice *E* is clearly incorrect. The historian does not address conquered peoples' opinions on their enslavement. Eliminate this choice.

Therefore, Choice *D* is the correct answer.

2. B: This question entails determining which answer choice is a necessary assumption upon which the conclusion logically depends. Essentially, the correct answer will be an assumption that is required to bridge the gap between the given evidence and the stated conclusion. The administrator's conclusion is that students receiving scholarships earn higher grades because they avoid the financial stress of needing to pay for school and time-related burden of holding a job to do so. The evidence states that scholarships lead to higher grades, but the conclusion takes this correlation further by stating a cause and effect.

Therefore, the correct answer—the necessary assumption—will likely strengthen the causation by eliminating a viable alternative explanation. This is achieved in Choice *B* because if having a high grade point average was a central and necessary precursor to receiving a scholarship in the first place, then it's not a surprising finding that in general, students on scholarships are earning higher grades than non-scholarship students. This answer option removes the potential alternative that the students in both groups (scholarship earners and non-scholarship students) were not equal in terms of grade point average at baseline. Therefore, Choice *B* identifies the necessary assumption on which the administrator's conclusion depends.

3. D: Choice *A* is clearly incorrect. The argument is drawing an analogy between the end of a decade and the end of lives. The correct answer will complete the analogy. It doesn't make sense that people will reminisce about their lives at decade's end. Eliminate this choice.

Choice *B* is also clearly incorrect. At the end of the decade, people do not fear they're about to die. This might be true for the end of people's lives, but not for the end of a decade. Eliminate this choice.

Choice *C* is misleading. In reality, people often focus on what the next decade will bring. However, the argument is analogizing decades with lives. People do not focus on what their next life will bring at the end of their lives. Eliminate this choice.

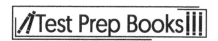

Choice *D* is a strong answer. The first clause of the sentence states that people in their twilight years start to look back on the events of their lives, so it's logical that at decade's end people become very interested in evaluating the events of the last decade. This logically completes the analogy.

Choice *E* is nonsensical. It does not complete the analogy to say that people throw a big party at decade's end. Eliminate this choice.

Therefore, Choice *D* is the correct answer.

4. E: Choice *A* is clearly incorrect. Jorge walked out of the room and avoided violence in adherence with the Sixth Commandment. According to the Religious Scholar, acting morally solely because of religion is not truly moral. Therefore, Jorge did not adhere to this moral code. Eliminate this choice.

Choice *B* is clearly incorrect. Elizabeth only babysat for her sister to earn karma points. This is not moral according to the Religious Scholar's code. Eliminate this choice.

Choice *C* is clearly incorrect. Tyler only tips people to accrue some divine benefit. This is not moral according to the Religious Scholar's code. Eliminate this choice.

Choice *D* is clearly incorrect. Carlos only visited his grandmother in adherence with his religion. Eliminate this choice.

Choice *E* looks tricky, but it is definitely the best answer. Although Arianna volunteers at a soup kitchen run by her church, she is not volunteering her time or donating money to garner some divine benefit or avoid cosmic retribution. Her actions are not based on religious texts. Arianna is moral in accordance with the Religious Scholar's code.

Therefore, Choice *E* is the correct answer.

5. D: Choice *A* is irrelevant. The profitability of nearby businesses does not impact whether foot traffic is the sole reason for the success of Angela's Hair Salon. Eliminate this choice.

Choice *B* does not weaken the argument. Even if foot traffic is greater across the street, it does not mean that the lesser foot traffic can't be the only reason for Angela's success. Eliminate this choice.

Choice *C* actually strengthens the argument. If Angela's Hair Salon had not been successful at the old location but is successful now, then the location is likely the difference. Eliminate this choice.

Choice *D* provides an alternative reason for the success of Angela's Hair Salon. If Angela's employs a hairdresser renowned for her skills, then that could be the reason for the business' success rather than the foot traffic. It definitely weakens the argument.

Choice *E* is not as strong as Choice *D*. Although the sign could be the reason for customers walking into Angela's Hair Salon, it is still somewhat related to foot traffic. If there were minimal foot traffic, then it wouldn't matter how big the sign was. In contrast, Choice *D* provides an alternative reason completely unrelated to foot traffic. Eliminate this choice.

Therefore, Choice *D* is the correct answer.

6. D: Choice *A* is clearly incorrect. Buying a new leather jacket does not sacrifice the musician's health. Eliminate this choice.

Choice *B* looks like a strong answer choice. The model is definitely prioritizing her perceived beauty by undergoing an elective cosmetic procedure. However, it is unclear whether the cosmetic procedure negatively affects her health. Leave this choice for now.

Choice *C* is incorrect. The actress is applying the make-up to increase her perceived beauty. However, she's not prioritizing the beauty over health. Eliminate this choice.

Choice *D* looks extremely promising. The actor is prioritizing perceived beauty over health. The perceived improvement to his smile comes at the cost of exposing himself to several known carcinogens. Unlike Choice *B*, the health risk is clear, so Choice *D* is the better answer.

Choice *E* is clearly incorrect. There's no health drawback from joining the gym. In fact, joining the gym would prioritize both health and beauty. Eliminate this choice.

Therefore, Choice *D* is the correct answer.

7. C: Choice *A* explains the paradox. Jacob became sick after visiting the doctor for the first time in a decade due to the vaccines' effect on his immune system. Eliminate this choice.

Choice *B* explains the paradox. According to this answer choice, Jacob was actually sick prior to his doctor's visit. He just didn't realize it. Eliminate this choice.

Choice *C* does not explain the apparent paradox. The paradox is that Jacob was healthy for years despite never visiting the doctor but fell ill after his first visit in a decade. Whether his immune system remained the same does not explain why this occurred.

Choice *D* explains the paradox. The cold weather and poor wardrobe choice decisions resulted in Jacob's illness. Eliminate this choice.

Choice *E* explains the paradox. Jacob's wife was sick before the appointment, so he seemingly caught the same illness. Therefore, his illness was unrelated to the doctor's visit.

Therefore, Choice *C* is the correct answer.

8. C: Choice *A* misses the point. The argument's conclusion is that companies are foolish to throw parties to market their products. Whether the new tech companies would throw the parties or not for Orange's example does not impact the reasonableness of those parties. Eliminate this choice.

Choice *B* does not make any sense. It is not a valid criticism. Eliminate this choice.

Choice *C* looks extremely promising. This answer choice addresses the possibility that smaller and more affordable parties could still offer some benefit. Therefore, the new tech companies would not be foolish in throwing parties they could afford. This is a valid criticism of the argument's reasoning.

Choice *D* is irrelevant. The argument does not address whether the lavish parties are comparable to the price of national marketing campaigns. This is not a valid criticism. Eliminate this choice.

Choice *E* does not address the argument's contention. The argument is not claiming that throwing lavish parties results in the new companies matching Orange's profitability. Eliminate this choice.

Therefore, Choice *C* is the correct answer.

9. A: Choice *A* is a strong answer choice. The businessman concludes that the company should eliminate every department except the sales team since the sales team is the most important. Choice *A* strengthens the businessman's argument because it eliminates the potential interaction of the other departments' contributions to the sales team's success. Examine the other answer choices before deciding on an answer.

Choice *B* is irrelevant. Does it impact the salesman's conclusion if other companies separate their departments into separate teams? No. It is inconsequential how other companies organize themselves. Eliminate this choice.

Choice *C* restates the argument's conclusion. Therefore, it is not a required assumption. Eliminate this choice.

Choice *D* is irrelevant. Would it matter if businesses have other departments besides marketing, communications, and sales? No, so this is not a necessary assumption. Eliminate this choice.

Choice *E* states a premise. This is not a required assumption. Eliminate this choice.

Therefore, Choice *A* is the correct answer.

10. C: Choice *A* is incorrect. The Conservative Politician definitely believes that spending on social welfare programs increases the national debt. However, the Liberal Politician does not address the cost of those programs. It's possible that the Liberal Politician would agree that the programs increase the national debt, but the country should spend the money anyway. Eliminate this choice.

Choice *B* is a strong answer choice. The Liberal Politician explicitly agrees that certain classes of people rely on social welfare programs. The Conservative Politician actually agrees that people rely on the programs, but thinks this reliance is detrimental. This answer choice is slightly off base. Eliminate this choice.

Choice *C* improves on Choice *B*. The Liberal Politician definitely believes that certain classes of people would be irreparably harmed. In contrast, the Conservative Politician asserts that the programs are actually harmful since people become dependent on the programs. The Conservative Politician concludes that people don't need the assistance and would be better off if left to fend for themselves. This is definitely the main point of disagreement.

Choice *D* is not the main point of dispute. Neither of the politicians discusses whether *all* of the nation's leaders have bootstrapped their way to the top. Eliminate this choice.

Choice *E* is also not the main point of dispute. The Liberal Politician mentions this point, but there's nothing in the Conservative Politician's argument that suggests he would disagree with it. Eliminate this choice.

Therefore, Choice *C* is the correct answer.

11. E: Choice *A* is incorrect. Geoffrey sometimes orders popcorn during movies so it's not definitely true that he ate popcorn during the *Boy Wizard Chronicles*. Eliminate this choice.

Choice *B* is incorrect since he doesn't always read the reviews before seeing a movie. Eliminate this choice.

Choice *C* is only half true. According to the argument, he definitely watched the *Boy Wizard Chronicles'* trailer, but he doesn't always buy popcorn. Eliminate this choice.

Choice *D* is also partially true. Geoffrey always buys a bottle of water, but he only reads the movie reviews some of the time. Thus, this answer choice does not necessarily need to be true. Eliminate this choice.

Choice *E* must be true. As previously discussed, Geoffrey always buys a bottle of water and always watches the trailer before seeing a movie.

Therefore, Choice *E* is the correct answer.

12. B: Choice *A* restates a premise. It serves as a general description of the role advertising serves in marketing. Eliminate this choice.

Choice *B* is correct. Although this sentence is sandwiched between two premises, it is still the conclusion. The argument is working towards proving that advertising works best when companies are experiencing a negative backlash. The first sentence is a general descriptor, while the third sentence also supports the conclusion. This is probably the correct answer.

Choice *C* restates a premise. Don't be fooled into thinking that this is the conclusion just because it's the final sentence in the argument. The importance of advertising in situations where customers have a neutral or negative attitude toward the product supports the conclusion. Eliminate this choice.

Choice *D* is incorrect. This answer choice is too vague. The argument would probably agree that advertising is important, but it can't be said that it's the conclusion. Eliminate this choice.

Choice *E* is also incorrect. *Manipulative* has a stronger connotation than what appears in the argument. This answer choice is more intense than the passage. Eliminate this choice.

Therefore, Choice *B* is the correct answer.

13. E: Choice *A* is nonsensical. The professor is saying that extremism caused by regional instability leads to terrorism. It doesn't make any sense to say that extremism is more dangerous than terrorism. According to the argument, extremism is the base of terrorism, so they're one and the same. Eliminate this choice.

Choice *B* is unsupported by the professor's argument. Don't be trapped by extraneous information. The test developers hope that the test takers will attribute blame. The argument does not address the cause of instability. Eliminate this choice.

Choice *C* is also unsupported by the professor's argument. The argument does not mention democracy and whether a democratic government would increase stability. This is another example of the answer choice pulling in outside information. Eliminate this choice.

Choice *D* lacks specificity. The professor states that the United States should be proactive in protecting itself and its allies. However, the argument does not mention an invasion, particularly enacting a preemptive one. It's quite a leap to say that the professor would agree with this statement. Eliminate this choice.

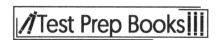

Choice *E* is an extremely strong answer choice. This answer choice paraphrases the professor's last sentence, which states that the United States should be proactive in protecting itself and its allies.

Therefore, Choice *E* is the correct answer.

14. C: Choice *A* is not present in the teacher's argument. There is no discussion of a common rule, so this cannot be the answer. Eliminate this choice.

Choice *B* is inaccurate. The teacher justifies his argument by pointing to the two highest achieving students in his class. It's not a perfect argument, but it's untrue to say that the argument is totally unjustified.

Choice *C* looks much more promising than the other options. The teacher's conclusion is that it's *always* the case that students can overcome parental indifference. He supports this notion by pointing to the two best students in a class of twenty people. The conclusion is too broad when considering the evidence. This is probably the answer, but look at the other choices to make sure.

Choice *D* does not correspond with anything in the teacher's argument. Although the teacher doesn't present any counter arguments, the existence of a competing theory is unclear. Eliminate this choice.

Choice *E* is clearly incorrect. The argument does not show any bias. Eliminate this choice.

Therefore, Choice *C* is the correct answer.

15. C: Choice *A* restates a premise and does not resolve the paradox. Whether Trent's SWAT team is the best police unit does not answer why unsolved crimes are increasing every year despite historic rates of crime solving. Eliminate this choice.

Choice *B* also does not resolve the paradox. It attempts to dismiss the increase in unsolved crimes by characterizing those crimes as petty drug offenses. Even if true, this does not resolve the paradox.

Choice *C* is a strong answer choice. If the raw number of crimes increases every year, then it makes sense that crimes are increasing despite the historic rates of crime solving. This explains the paradox. In questions involving percentages, always pay special attention to answer choices that involve raw numbers.

Choice *D* is irrelevant. The competence of the police department does not explain the paradox. Additionally, the police department is apparently not incompetent since it's solving a higher percentage of crimes than ever before in its history. Eliminate this choice.

Choice *E* is similar to Choice *B*. It attempts to dismiss the increasing number of unsolved crimes by claiming that the police are solving the most important crimes. This does not explain the paradox.

Therefore, Choice *C* is the correct answer.

16. E: Choice *A* is unrelated to the argument's main point. This choice is misleading with extraneous information because the FDA is often criticized for this very reason. However, the argument does not address this point. There's no way it's the main point. Eliminate this choice.

Choice *B* is a very strong answer. The argument is definitely trending in this direction, especially since the argument points out the lack of tar in electronic cigarettes. Choice *B*'s use of *probably* fits with the argument's tone. Leave this option for now.

Choice C goes too far. The scientist's argument is more informational than directional. Choice C fails to match this tone. Eliminate this choice.

Choice D accurately restates one of the argument's premises, but it is not the main point. Eliminate this choice.

Choice E is an excellent balance of information and speculation, like the argument. The answer choice's first phrase identifies the concerns highlighted by the scientist, and the second phrase expresses why the scientist believes that electronic cigarettes are a promising alternative. Choice B is extremely similar, but Choice E better expresses the argument's main point.

Therefore, Choice E is the correct answer.

17. B: Choice A does not necessarily follow from the argument. Although Brittany's dog loves playing fetch, there's nothing in the argument that makes this definitely true. Eliminate this choice.

Choice B follows logically from the argument: *Only German shepherds love protecting their homes.* In other words, no other dogs love protecting their homes. Therefore, if Brittany's dog loves protecting her home, then it must be a German shepherd.

Choice C is clearly incorrect. Just because some dogs are easy to train does not mean that Brittany's dog is easy to train. Eliminate this choice.

Choice D is tricky but incorrect. Although the last sentence references both qualities attributed to Labrador retrievers and German shepherds, there is no information concerning a mix of the two. Eliminate this choice.

Choice E references all of the information included in the argument, but it doesn't follow logically. There is nothing in the argument that suggests that Choice E must be true. Eliminate this choice.

Therefore, Choice B is the correct answer.

18. E: Choice A supports the argument. The argument concludes that poverty is the number one cause of crime. It would make sense that criminals are less wealthy than the average person. Keep this choice for now.

Choice B is irrelevant for the purposes of this argument. Even if redistributing wealth is indeed the best way to lessen poverty, it does not support the connection between poverty and crime. Eliminate this choice.

Choice C is tangentially related to the argument. If substance abuse is the second largest cause of crime and those abusers are poor, then it makes sense that criminals are poor. However, this answer choice is worse than Choice A, which explicitly states the same thing. Eliminate this choice.

Choice D is irrelevant. The argument makes no mention of morality or how moral societies would treat the poor. Eliminate this choice.

Choice E is a very strong answer. If the majority of crimes involve food theft and trespassing, then it supports the notion that people commit crimes to meet their basic needs. Choice E strengthens the conclusion that if these people's basic needs were met then the majority of crime would not be committed. This offers more support than Choice A.

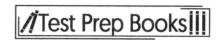

Therefore, Choice *E* is the correct answer.

19. A: Choice *A* is a strong answer choice. Negate the choice to see if it's a necessary assumption: *Strength and size gains are NOT indicators of good health.* This destroys the argument. If strength and size are not indicators of good health, then regular weightlifting is not necessary for good health. This is probably the correct answer, but work through the remaining options.

Choice *B* is not a necessary assumption. The argument is no worse off if there are other ways to increase strength and size besides compound movements. Eliminate this choice.

Choice *C* is not a contention made by the argument. The argument merely states that compound movements are an especially effective type of heavy resistance weightlifting. This is definitely not a necessary assumption. Eliminate this choice.

Choice *D* is also clearly incorrect. Don't be fooled by the parallels with Choice *C*. This choice is wrong for the same reason as Choice *C*. Eliminate this choice.

Choice *E* restates the conclusion, so it is not a necessary assumption. It is an explicit conclusion. Eliminate this choice.

Therefore, Choice *A* is the correct answer.

20. C: Choice *A* definitely strengthens the argument by highlighting a benefit of an autocratic government. Eliminate this choice.

Choice *B* seems to strengthen the argument. This answer choice connects the start of the autocratic despot's reign with the start of economic growth. Eliminate this choice.

Choice *C* appears to weaken the argument. This answer choice provides an alternate explanation for the economic growth. According to Choice *C*, West Korea experienced economic growth as a result of the oil reserve. This hurts the argument's contention that West Korea's economy benefits from limiting civil liberties. This is a very strong answer choice.

Choice *D* clearly strengthens the argument. If political protest harms economic growth, then there's additional support for West Korea's curtailment of civil liberties. Eliminate this choice.

Choice *E* also strengthens the argument. The despot is able to devote all of his time to solving economic problems since there are no civil liberties. Eliminate this choice.

Therefore, Choice *C* is the correct answer.

21. E: Choice *A* is too extreme. The sociologist definitely believes that the abolition of marriage would harm society, but collapse goes too far. Eliminate this choice.

Choice *B* is tricky since the previous sentence references how children born out of wedlock are more likely to work at lower paying jobs. However, this answer choice also goes too far. According to the argument, unmarried people are less likely to be homeowners or save for retirement. But if marriage rates decline, it is not necessarily true that everyone would have less money. Eliminate this choice.

Choice *C* is tricky but also incorrect. Unmarried people are less likely to own homes. If marriage rates decline, fewer people would be homeowners. This is not the same as arguing that nobody would own homes. Eliminate this choice.

Choice *D* is irrelevant to the argument. The argument makes no reference to happiness. There is no way that such new information would logically complete the passage. Eliminate this choice.

Choice *E* looks much more promising than the other choices. If unmarried people are less likely to attend college and marriage rates decline, then it is reasonable to say that college attendance would probably decrease. Choice *E* also matches the argument's tone through the use of *probably*, unlike many of the other answer choices.

Therefore, Choice *E* is the correct answer.

22. B: Choice *A* is not a necessary assumption. This answer choice provides additional support to the argument, but it is not dependent on this fact. The test developers hope the test takers will mistake this for a strengthening question. Don't be fooled. Eliminate this choice.

Choice *B* looks very promising. Negate this answer choice to see if the argument falls apart: *Consumers' disposable income is NOT directly related to their ability to purchase goods and services.* This hurts the argument. If disposable income is unrelated to purchasing goods and services, then tax rates don't matter. Definitely keep this answer.

Choice *C* is irrelevant to the argument. The argument does not depend on consumers' preferences. Eliminate this choice.

Choice *D* is a strong answer choice. Negate this answer choice to see if the argument falls apart: *Increasing disposable income is NOT the only way to ensure economic growth.* The argument is definitely worse off, but it is not destroyed. Therefore, this is not a necessary assumption. Eliminate this choice.

Choice *E* is irrelevant to the argument. The argument discusses how tax rates impact economic growth. It does not mention social welfare programs. Always be careful of new information, like the role social welfare programs play in this choice. Eliminate this choice.

Therefore, Choice *B* is the correct answer.

23. B: Choice *A* is similar to the argument in that it makes a prediction based on past events; however, Choice *A*'s argument is much more reasonable than the argument. If Ted has eaten an apple pie every day for the last decade, then it's reasonable to assume that he will do so again tomorrow. Eliminate this choice.

Choice *B* is a very strong answer choice. Like the argument, it takes past events and speculates that conditions will not change. Just as any number of factors could alter the United States' economic growth, it is similarly unreasonable to say that Alexandra will be the top salesperson based on one year's data. This answer choice also uses extremely strong language in its speculation (*guaranteed* and *undoubtedly*). Definitely keep this answer choice as an option.

Choice *C* is similar to the argument, but its conclusion is much more reasonable. If George has brushed his teeth right before bed for twenty years, then it is not unreasonable to speculate that he will do the same tonight. This is not the same as predicting that past economic conditions will continue into the future. George has much more control over brushing his teeth than the United States has over its economy. Eliminate this choice.

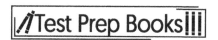

Choice *D* mirrors the language as the argument, but it draws a very different conclusion. In contrast to the argument, Choice *D*'s conclusion gives a reason why Germany's economy is on the rise. It does not make a guarantee of future growth. This is not the same as the argument. Eliminate this choice.

Choice *E* does not rely on flawed reasoning, so it must be incorrect. If Tito is the top ranked surfer in the world and listed as a clear favorite, then it's true that he's the most likely to win the tournament. Eliminate this choice.

Therefore, Choice *B* is the correct answer.

24. B: Choice *A* weakens one of the argument's premises. If big cats don't try to escape because they can't figure out their enclosures, then never attempting to escape is not a sign of intelligence. This definitely weakens the argument by negating one of its premises. Keep it for now.

Choice *B* looks extremely promising. This answer choice tells us that experts disagree that adjusting to captivity is a measure of intelligence. If big cats' adjustment to captivity does not correspond to intelligence, then the zookeeper's entire argument is flawed. This destroys the argument.

Choice *C* weakens the argument, but it's less powerful than Choice *B*. If bears share similarities with big cats, then there might be some doubt as to which animal is the smartest land mammal. This weakens the argument, but not as much as Choice *B*, which completely disrupts the argument's logic. Eliminate this choice.

Choice *D* actually strengthens the zookeeper's argument. The brain scans support the zookeeper's conclusion that big cats are the smartest land mammals. Eliminate this choice.

Choice *E* is a strong answer choice. If the zoo is devoting significantly more resources to caring for big cats, then the difference in resources could be the reason for their adaptability. However, Choice *B* spoils the argument's entire logical thrust. Eliminate Choice *E*.

Therefore, Choice *B* is the correct answer.

25. C: Choice *A* is incorrect. The argument states that nearly all lawyers dutifully represent their clients' best interest. *Nearly all* is not the same as *all*. It can't be definitively said that it must be true that Tanya represents her clients' best interests. Eliminate this choice.

Choice *B* is incorrect. The argument states that only some lawyers charge exorbitant and fraudulent fees. Thus, Tanya is not necessarily one of these bad apple attorneys. Eliminate it.

Choice *C* follows the argument's reasoning. The argument states that all lawyers are bound by extensive ethical codes. Therefore, if Tanya is a lawyer, then she must be bound by extensive ethical codes. This is the correct answer.

Choice *D* is incorrect. The argument states that only some lawyers become millionaires. Therefore, it's not necessarily true that Tanya is a millionaire. She could be, but it doesn't have to be true. Eliminate this choice.

Choice *E* is incorrect. Similar to Choice *D*, the argument states that only some lawyers work in the public sector. Therefore, it's not necessarily true. Eliminate this choice.

Therefore, Choice *C* is the correct answer.

Section IV: Reading Comprehension

1. C: The author contrasts two different viewpoints, then builds a case showing preference for one over the other. Choice *A* is incorrect because the introduction does not contain an impartial definition, but rather another's opinion. Choice *B* is incorrect. There is no puzzling phenomenon given, as the author doesn't mention any peculiar cause or effect that is in question regarding poetry. Choice *D* does contain another's viewpoint at the beginning of the passage; however, to say that the author has no stake in this argument is incorrect; the author uses personal experiences to build their case. Finally, Choice *E* is incorrect because there is no description of the history of poetry offered within the passage.

2. B: Choice *B* accurately describes the author's argument in the text—that poetry is not irrelevant. While the author does praise—and even value—Buddy Wakefield as a poet, he or she never heralds Wakefield as a genius. Eliminate Choice *A*, as it is an exaggeration. Not only is Choice *C* an exaggerated statement, but the author never mentions spoken word poetry in the text. Choice *D* is incorrect because this statement contradicts the writer's argument. Choice *E* can also be eliminated, because the author mentions how performance actually *enhances* poetry and that modern technology is one way poetry remains vital.

3. D: *Exiguously* means not occurring often, or occurring rarely, so Choice *D* would LEAST change the meaning of the sentence. Choice *A*, *indolently*, means unhurriedly, or slow, and does not fit the context of the sentence. Choice *B*, *inaudibly*, means quietly or silently. Choice *C*, *interminably*, means endlessly, or all the time, and is the opposite of the word *exiguously*. Choice *E*, *impecunious,* means impoverished or destitute, and does not fit within the context of the sentence.

4. E: The author of the passage tries to insist that performance poetry is a subset of modern poetry, and therefore prove that modern poetry is not "dying," but thriving on social media for the masses. Choice *A* is incorrect, as the author is not refusing any kind of validation. Choice *B* is incorrect; the author's insistence is that poetry will *not* lose popularity. Choice *C* mimics the topic but compares two different genres, while the author makes no comparison in this passage. Choice *D* is incorrect as well; again, there is no cause or effect the author is trying to prove.

5. B: The author's purpose is to disprove Gioia's article claiming that poetry is a dying art form that only survives in academic settings. In order to prove his argument, the author educates the reader about new developments in poetry (Choice *A*) and describes the brilliance of a specific modern poet (Choice *C*), but these are used to serve as examples of a growing poetry trend that counters Gioia's argument. Choice *D* is incorrect because it contradicts the author's argument. Choice *E* is incorrect because the passage uses the performance as a way to convey the author's point; it's not the focus of the piece. It's also unclear if the author was actually present at the live performance.

6. D: This question is difficult because four out of the five choices offer real reasons as to why the author includes the quote. However, the question specifically asks for the *main reason* for including the quote. First off, eliminate Choice *A*. "Speaking meter" doesn't exist and isn't mentioned in the passage. The quote from a recently written poem shows that people are indeed writing, publishing, and performing poetry (Choice *B*). The quote also shows that people are still listening to poetry (Choice *C*). These things are true and, by their nature, serve to disprove Gioia's views (Choice *E*), which is the author's goal. However, Choice *D* is the most direct reason for including the quote, because the article analyzes the quote for its "complex themes" that "draws listeners and appreciation" right after it's given.

7. E: *Extraneous* most nearly means *superfluous*, or *trivial*. Choice *A*, *indispensable*, is incorrect because it means the opposite of *extraneous*. Choice *B, bewildering*, means *confusing* and is not relevant to the context of the sentence. Choice *C* is incorrect because *fallacious* means *false* or *wrong*. Finally, Choice *D* is incorrect because although the prefix of the word is the same, ex-, the word exuberant means elated or enthusiastic, and is irrelevant to the context of the sentence.

8. A: This is a challenging question because the author's purpose is somewhat open-ended. The author concludes by stating that the questions regarding human perception and observation can be approached from many angles. Thus, the author does not seem to be attempting to prove one thing or another. Choice B is incorrect because we cannot know for certain whether the electron experiment is the latest discovery in astroparticle physics because no date is given. Choice C is a broad generalization that does not reflect accurately on the writer's views. While the author does appear to reflect on opposing views of human understanding (Choice D), the best answer is Choice A. Choice E is also wrong because the author never says that classical philosophy is wrong or directly attempts to debunk it.

9. C: It presents a problem, explains the details of that problem, and then ends with more inquiry. The beginning of this paragraph literally "presents a conundrum," explains the problem of partial understanding, and then ends with more questions, or inquiry. There is no solution offered in this paragraph, making Choices A, B, and E incorrect. Choice D is incorrect because the paragraph does not begin with a definition.

10. D: Looking back in the text, the author describes that classical philosophy holds that understanding can be reached by careful observation. This will not work if they are overly invested or biased in their pursuit. Choices A, B, and C are in no way related and are completely unnecessary. A specific theory is not necessary to understanding, according to classical philosophy mentioned by the author. Again, the key to understanding is observing the phenomena outside of it, without bias or predisposition. Thus, Choice E is wrong.

11. B: The electrons passed through both holes and then onto the plate. Choices A, C, and E are wrong because such movement is not mentioned at all in the text. In the passage, the author says that electrons that were physically observed appeared to pass through one hole or another. Remember, the electrons that were observed doing this were described as acting like particles. Therefore, Choice D is incorrect. Recall that the plate actually recorded electrons passing through both holes simultaneously and hitting the plate. This behavior—the electron activity that wasn't seen by humans—was characteristic of waves. Thus, Choice B is the right answer.

12. C: The author uses "gravity" to demonstrate an example of natural phenomena humans discovered and understood without the use of tools or machines. Choice A mirrors the language in the beginning of the paragraph but is incorrect in its intent. Choice B is incorrect; the paragraph mentions nothing of "not knowing the true nature of gravity." Choices D and E are both incorrect as well. There is no mention of an "alternative solution" or "looking forward" to new technology in this paragraph.

13. E: The important thing to keep in mind is that we must choose a scenario that best parallels, or is most similar to, the discovery of the experiment mentioned in the passage. The important aspects of the experiment can be summed up like so: humans directly observed one behavior of electrons and then through analyzing a tool (the plate that recorded electron hits), discovered that there was another electron behavior that could not be physically seen by human eyes. This best parallels the scenario in Choice E. Like Feynman, the colorblind person is able to observe one aspect of the world but through the special goggles (a tool) he is able to see a natural phenomenon that he could not physically see on his own. While Choice *D* is compelling because an x-ray helps humans see the broken bone, it is not necessarily revealing that the bone is broken in the first place. The other choices do not parallel the scenario in question. Therefore, Choice *E* is the best choice.

14. B: The author would not agree that technology renders human observation irrelevant. Choice *A* is incorrect because much of the passage discusses how technology helps humans observe what cannot be seen with the naked eye; therefore, the author would agree with this statement. This line of reasoning is also why the author would agree with Choice *D*, making it incorrect as well. As indicated in the second paragraph, the author seems to think that humans create inventions and tools with the goal of studying phenomena more precisely. This indicates increased understanding as people recognize limitations and develop items to help bypass the limitations and learn. Therefore, Choice *C* is incorrect as well. Again, the author doesn't attempt to disprove or dismiss classical philosophy. He or she actually offers examples of how classical understanding is still used in the world, such as the gravity example. Therefore, the author would agree with Choice *E*.

15. E: The author explains that Boethianism is a Medieval theological philosophy that attributes sin to temporary pleasure and righteousness with virtue and God's providence. Besides Choice *E,* the choices listed are all physical things. While these could still be divine rewards, Boethianism holds that the true reward for being virtuous is in God's favor. It is also stressed in the article that physical pleasures cannot be taken into the afterlife. Therefore, the best choice is *E*, God's favor.

16. C: *The Canterbury Tales* presents a manuscript written in the medieval period that can help illustrate Boethianism through stories and show how people of the time might have responded to the idea. Choices *A* and *B* are generalized statements, and we have no evidence to support Choice *B*. There is also no evidence that Chaucer was a devoted Boethianist, so Choice *E* is wrong. Choice *D* is very compelling, but it looks at Boethianism in a way that the author does not. The author does not mention "different levels of Boethianism" when discussing the tales, only that the concept appears differently in different tales. Boethianism also doesn't focus on enlightenment.

17. D: The author is referring to the principle that a desire for material goods leads to moral malfeasance punishable by a higher being. Choice *A* is incorrect; while the text does mention thieves ravaging others' possessions, it is only meant as an example and not as the principle itself. Choice *B* is incorrect for the same reason as Choice *A*. Choice *C* is mentioned in the text and is part of the example that proves the principle, and also not the principle itself. Choice *E* might be something the author holds to be true; however, it is not the main principle laid out in the two examples.

18. C: The word *avarice* most nearly means *covetousness*, or extremely desirous of money or wealth. Choice *A* means *evil* or *mischief* and does not relate to the context of the sentence. Choice *B* is also incorrect, because *pithiness* means *shortness* or *conciseness*. Choice *D*, *pompousness*, means someone is arrogant, which is also irrelevant to the context of the sentence. Choice *E* is close because *capriciousness* means erratic or unstable, which goes well with the context. However, we are told of the summoner's specific characteristic of greed, which makes Choice *C* the best answer.

19. D: Desire for pleasure can lead toward sin. Boethianism acknowledges desire as something that leads out of holiness, so Choice *A* is incorrect. Choice *B* is incorrect because in the passage, Boethianism is depicted as being wary of desire and anything that binds people to the physical world. Choices *C* and *E* can be eliminated because the author never says that desire indicates demonic possession or that it is the result of original sin.

20. A: The purpose is to inform the reader about what assault is and how it is committed. Choice *B* is incorrect because the passage does not state that assault is a lesser form of lethal force, only that an assault can use lethal force, or alternatively, lethal force can be utilized to counter a dangerous assault. Choices *C* and *D* are incorrect because the passage is informative and does not have a set agenda. Finally, Choice *E* is incorrect because although the author uses an example in order to explain assault, it is not indicated that this is the author's personal account.

21. C: The situation of the man who is attacked in an alley by another man with a knife would most merit the use of lethal force. If the man being attacked used self-defense by lethal force, it would not be considered illegal. The presence of a deadly weapon indicates mal-intent and because the individual is isolated in an alley, lethal force in self-defense may be the only way to preserve his life. Choices *A* and *B* can be ruled out because in these situations, no one is in danger of immediate death or bodily harm by someone else. Choice *D* is an assault that does exhibit intent to harm, but this situation isn't severe enough to merit lethal force; there is no intent to kill. Choice *E* is incorrect because this is a vehicular accident, and the driver did not intend to hit and injure the other driver.

22. B: As discussed in the second passage, there are several forms of assault, like assault with a deadly weapon, verbal assault, or threatening posture or language. Choice *A* is incorrect because lethal force and assault are separate as indicated by the passages. Choice *C* is incorrect because anyone is capable of assault; the author does not state that one group of people cannot commit assault. Choice *D* is incorrect because assault is never justified. Self-defense resulting in lethal force can be justified. Choice *E* is incorrect because the author does mention what the charges are on assaults; therefore, we cannot assume that they are more or less than unnecessary use of force charges.

23. D: The use of lethal force is not evaluated on the intent of the user but rather the severity of the primary attack that warranted self-defense. This statement most undermines the last part of the passage because it directly contradicts how the law evaluates the use of lethal force. Choices *A*, *B*, and *E* are stated in the paragraph, and therefore do not undermine the explanation from the author. Choice *C* does not necessarily undermine the passage, but it does not support the passage either. It is more of an opinion that does not strengthen or weaken the explanation.

24. C: An assault with deadly intent can lead to an individual using lethal force to preserve their well-being. Choice *C* is correct because it clearly establishes what both assault and lethal force are and gives the specific way in which the two concepts meet. Choice *A* is incorrect because lethal force doesn't necessarily result in an assault. This is also why Choice *B* is incorrect. Not all assaults would necessarily be life-threatening to the point where lethal force is needed for self-defense. Choice *D* is compelling but ultimately too vague; the statement touches on aspects of the two ideas but fails to present the concrete way in which the two are connected to each other. Choice *E* is incorrect because it contradicts the information in the passage (that assault with deadly intent can lead to an individual using lethal force).

25. A: Both passages open by defining a legal concept and then describing situations in order to further explain the concept. Choice *D* is incorrect because while the passages utilize examples to help explain the concepts discussed, the author doesn't indicate that they are specific court cases. It's also clear that the passages don't open with examples, but instead, begin by defining the terms addressed in each passage. This eliminates Choice *B* and ultimately reveals Choice *A* to be the correct answer. Choice *A* accurately outlines the way both passages are structured. Because the passages follow a near identical structure, the rest of the choices can easily be ruled out.

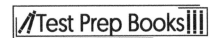

26. E: Intent is very important for determining both lethal force and assault; intent is examined by both parties and helps determine the severity of the issue. Choices *A*, *B*, and *C* are incorrect because it is clear in both passages that intent is a prevailing theme in both lethal force and assault. Choice *D* is compelling, but if a person uses lethal force to defend themselves, the intent of the defender is also examined in order to help determine if there was excessive force used. Choice *E* is correct because it states that intent is important for determining both lethal force and assault, and that intent is used to gauge the severity of the issues. Remember, just as lethal force can escalate to excessive use of force, there are different kinds of assault. Intent dictates several different forms of assault.

27. B: The example is used to demonstrate a single example of two different types of assault, then adds in a third type of assault to the example's conclusion. The example mainly serves to show an instance of "threatening body language" and "provocative language" with the homeowner gesturing threats to his neighbor. It ends the example by adding a third type of assault: physical strikes. This example is used to show the variant nature of assaults. Choice *A* is incorrect because it doesn't mention the "physical strike" assault at the end and is not specific enough. Choice *C* is incorrect because the example does not say anything about the definition of lethal force or how it might be altered. Choice *D* is incorrect, as the example mentions nothing of cause and effect. Choice *E* is also incorrect; the example proves that threatening body language is considered a type of assault in and of itself.

LSAT Practice Test #2

Section I: Logical Reasoning

Time – 35 minutes

25 Questions

1. President Abraham Lincoln presided over a divided nation that would soon be engulfed in the bloodiest war in American history. After Lincoln's election as President, but prior to his inauguration, seven Southern states seceded, and four more states seceded after the battle of Fort Sumter on April 12, 1861. Later that month, President Lincoln grew concerned that Washington D.C. could not be defended, particularly due to rebel riots in Baltimore. As a result, President Lincoln suspended the right of *habeas corpus* for the first time in American history. Although President Lincoln took an unprecedented step, his decision was...

Which of the following best completes the argument?
   a. necessary to end the Civil War quickly.
   b. necessary to stop the South from seceding.
   c. unprecedented in American history.
   d. justified in light of the unprecedented national emergency.
   e. illegal under the Constitution of the United States.

2. Politician: The principle of net neutrality requires Internet service providers to provide access to all content without any discrimination. Repealing net neutrality would allow Internet service providers to slow down speeds or charge additional fees for certain content at will. The largest Internet service providers also own the most popular news networks. Consequently, the removal of net neutrality would threaten the integrity of American democracy.

The strength of the argument depends on which one of the following being true?
   a. American democracy is dependent on universal access to the Internet.
   b. American democracy is dependent on repealing net neutrality.
   c. American democracy is dependent on prohibiting Internet service providers from owning news networks.
   d. American democracy is dependent on fast Internet connections.
   e. American democracy is dependent on news networks free from content discrimination.

3. Dwight is the manager of a mid-sized regional paper company. The company's sales have declined for seven consecutive quarters. All of the paper company's regional and national competitors have experienced a similar loss in revenue. Dwight instituted a mass layoff and successfully kept his company out of bankruptcy.

Which one of the following is most strongly supported by the passage?
   a. Mass layoffs were the only way to keep the company out of bankruptcy.
   b. The paper industry is experiencing a fundamental change in demand.
   c. Mid-sized regional paper companies will no longer exist in ten years.
   d. National paper companies poached Dwight's customers, causing the decline in sales.
   e. The paper industry's decline is due to the digitalization of business records.

4. The dead-ball era of baseball occurred between 1900 and 1919. Baseball historians refer to the period as the dead-ball era due to a decrease in scoring and lack of home runs. In the 1920 season, Ray Chapman died after getting hit in the head with a dirty baseball while batting. In response, Major League Baseball required that more baseballs be used per game. Scoring increased dramatically as a result of more baseballs being used per game, ending the dead-ball era.

Which one of the following statements, if true, most weakens the argument?
   a. Baseballs soften with continued use, and it is more difficult to hit home runs with soft baseballs.
   b. Hitters have a more difficult time seeing dirty baseballs, as opposed to new ones.
   c. Major League Baseball outlawed the extremely effective spitball in 1920.
   d. Using more baseballs raised the operating expense for Major League Baseball teams.
   e. Dirty baseballs move unnaturally and erratically, rendering them more difficult to hit.

5. Recycling is the best possible way for people to preserve the environment. Recycling conserves finite natural resources, protects forests, and reduces fossil fuel. If recycling achieves a 75% conversion rate, it would be the equivalent of removing 55 million cars from the road per year.

Which one of the following statements, if true, most strengthens the argument?
   a. The unreleased energy in the average trash could power a television for 5,000 hours.
   b. Recycling prevents waste from entering the oceans—the leading producer of oxygen.
   c. Recycling reduces carbon emissions more than green energy programs.
   d. Recycling benefits the economy, as manufacturers can reuse materials at lower costs.
   e. Recycling one aluminum can saves the equivalent amount of energy needed to power a television for three hours.

6. An advertising firm creates campaigns for both television and Internet platforms, and both campaigns are comparable in size. The audience for television advertisements is one thousand times the size of the Internet audiences, but the firm generates two-thirds of its revenue from Internet advertisements.

Which one of the following statements, if true, would resolve the apparent paradox?
   a. Internet advertisements allow the firm to more accurately target audiences.
   b. The firm has considerably more experience with television advertising.
   c. The Internet and television advertisements are identical.
   d. There is more competition for advertising time on the Internet.
   e. The firm pays more for Internet advertising than for television advertising.

7. Politician: The bill under current consideration is deeply flawed. If passed, the bill would undermine our great state's commitment to women's rights. Passing such a flawed piece of legislation would be like building a house with warped wood. My esteemed colleague who proposed this legislation plays fast and loose with the truth, obscuring his true purpose—re-election. As we've heard from our police chief, this bill will guarantee that fewer women will report incidents of assault.

What is a flaw in the argument's reasoning?
   a. It appeals to an inappropriate authority.
   b. It attacks the source of an argument.
   c. It offers an irrelevant analogy.
   d. It confuses causation with correlation.
   e. It relies on a hasty generalization.

8. All police officers carry guns, and all soldiers carry guns; therefore, police officers and soldiers are similar.

Which one of the following most closely parallels the argument?
    a. All apples have seeds and all grapefruits have seeds.
    b. Some professional football players lift weights every day, and all bodybuilders lift weights every day; therefore, football players and bodybuilders are similar.
    c. All dogs have fur, and all mammals have fur; therefore, all dogs are mammals.
    d. Some video games depict violence and everything depicting violence harms society in some way. As a result, all video games should be banned.
    e. Farms and fisheries are similar. All farms produce food, and all fisheries produce food.

9. Alexandra and Ronan work for a widget manufacturer. Both Alexandra and Ronan received raises based on their annual performance review. Alexandra received a 25% raise, while Ronan received a 10% raise. Therefore, Alexandra now makes more money than Ronan.

The flawed reasoning in which of the following is most similar to that in the argument?
    a. Two test tubes contain the same amount of potassium cyanide. A scientist adds some amount of potassium cyanide to one test tube, so that test tube now contains more potassium cyanide.
    b. A school holds chorus recitals and plays in the auditorium. Ticket sales for the chorus recitals have risen by 15%, while tickets for the plays have dropped by 30%. More people now attend the chorus than plays.
    c. A widget company has increased production by at least 10% every year for the last five years. Next year, the company will increase production by 10%.
    d. A company starts every new employee with the same salary. Tyrone and Samantha are new hires, and both recently received their first raise. Tyrone's raise was 25%, while Samantha received a 10% raise. Therefore, Tyrone now makes more money than Samantha.
    e. A salesman's salary is entirely dependent on commission from sales. This year, he set a record for sales, so he will make more money than ever before.

10. All smart people read more than six books per year, and the smartest people read more than twelve books per year. John is not a smart person.

If the statements above are correct, which one of the following must be true?
    a. John reads fewer than seven books per year.
    b. John reads more than six books per year.
    c. John reads twelve books per year.
    d. John reads more than twelve books per year.
    e. John reads six books per year.

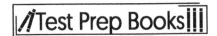

11. Economist: Markets work most efficiently without any government interference, since competition increases in free markets. Government regulation will never achieve its intended goal, since the most sophisticated corporations will always be able to game the system at the expense of the start-ups that are necessary to spur growth. Competition between corporations also forces those entities to self-regulate and it protects the interests of consumers.

Politician: Unregulated markets are ripe for abuse. Under the current regulatory scheme, a handful of corporations dominate the marketplace. Vertical integration, under the umbrella of a larger corporation, expands a single corporation's power across multiple economic sectors. We need to increase regulations to disrupt this integration and allow start-ups to compete on a level playing field.

What is the main issue in dispute between the economist and politician?
    a. Competition is important for a nation's economic health.
    b. The current regulatory scheme is adequate.
    c. Increasing regulations will increase competitiveness.
    d. Consolidating economic power in a handful of corporations is healthy.
    e. Corporations cannot be trusted to act in consumers' best interest.

12. Direct democracy is the best system of government for every society. No other system of government maximizes individual freedom more than democracy. In direct democracies, the people's will is manifested in the state's policies, as they can directly vote on every political issue. All of the politicians who killed the most people, like Adolf Hitler and Joseph Stalin, led dictatorships. Direct democracy is obviously better than a dictatorship, so it is the best form of government.

Which one of the following most accurately describes how the argument proceeds?
    a. The argument leads with a conclusion then provides several illustrative examples.
    b. The argument leads with a conclusion, offers several premises, and then sets up a false dichotomy to support its conclusion.
    c. The argument starts and finishes with contradictory conclusions.
    d. The argument offers several premises and then creates a false dichotomy to support its conclusion.
    e. The argument leads with a generalization, offers some examples, and then finishes with a conclusion.

13. Some rich people cheat on their taxes, but no one pays zero taxes, except those who do not own land. Jacob is a rich landowner.

Assuming all of the statements above are correct, which one of the following must be true?
    a. Jacob cheats on his taxes.
    b. Jacob pays more taxes than the average person.
    c. Jacob does not cheat on his taxes.
    d. Jacob pays taxes.
    e. Jacob does not pay taxes.

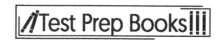

14. CEO: Our company raises chickens and adheres to the most stringent ethical standards known to man. All of the chickens live in cage-free environments with more than enough room to stretch their wings. The chicken feed consists of corn and soybean meal supplemented with essential vitamins. Hormones and steroids are strictly prohibited. In addition, the chickens receive regular attention from professional veterinarians.

Activist: Your company's chicken farm may meet the existing ethical standards, but those standards fail to adequately protect the chickens. Cage-free is misleading, given the fact that chickens basically live in a closed facility. At no point in their lives do chickens see the sun and breathe fresh air. Chicken feed might not include hormones and steroids, but it is genetically-modified. Professional veterinarians treat the chickens, yet more than half of the flock does not survive before meeting maturity.

The CEO and activist would most likely agree on which one of the following statements?
   a. Ethical standards are important.
   b. The current ethical standards are adequate.
   c. Chickens need time outside to lead happy lives.
   d. Genetic modification is comparable to adding hormones and steroids to chicken's food.
   e. The ethical standards can be improved.

15. Studies show that the moderate consumption of alcohol, particularly red wine, offers some health benefits. In addition, even if deemed appropriate, prohibition would be impossible since the demand is so high. However, the heavy consumption of alcohol can be addictive and deadly.

Which one of the following conclusions most logically follows from the argument?
   a. Excessive consumption of alcohol is harmful.
   b. Prohibition of alcohol is ill-conceived.
   c. Regulation of alcohol would work better than prohibition.
   d. Black markets would frustrate any prohibition efforts.
   e. The benefits of alcohol outweigh the costs.

16. Farmer: A report has just been released that criticizes our corn, alleging that the genetically-modified seed we use is harmful to consumers. However, the report was commissioned by our main competition—a large-scale corporate farm. The conflict of interest is so obvious that consumers can continue to eat our corn without worry.

Which one of the following best explains why the farmer's argument is vulnerable to criticism?
   a. The farmer fails to elaborate on the corporate farm's conflict of interest.
   b. The farmer draws a conclusion without considering alternative motivations for the commissioning of the report by the corporate farm.
   c. The farmer wrongly assumes that a conflict of interest automatically negates the validity of the report's conclusion.
   d. The farmer does not provide any evidence as to why their corn is safe for consumption.
   e. The farmer is biased against the corporate farm.

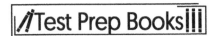

17. A graduate degree in policymaking is necessary to serve in the presidential cabinet. In addition, every member of the cabinet must pass a security clearance. No person with a felony can pass a security clearance. Rick holds a graduate degree in policymaking, but he has a conviction for driving under the influence. Therefore, Rick cannot serve in the cabinet.

The argument's conclusion follows logically if which one of the following is assumed?
   a. Rick's conviction for drunk driving calls his character in question.
   b. Anyone without a felony conviction can pass a security clearance.
   c. Holding a graduate degree is less important than having a felony conviction.
   d. Driving under the influence is a felony.
   e. If Rick did not have the felony conviction, then he could serve in the cabinet.

18. Philosopher: The most moral actions provide the most benefits to the most people at the lowest costs without any regard for intentions.

Which one of the following exhibits the most moral action, as described by the philosopher?
   a. Tyree quits smoking cigarettes, and as a result, he will live longer and save taxpayers' money.
   b. Leroy develops a vaccine for malaria, but the cure decimates the mosquito population, destroying the local ecosystem, and causing famine across an entire continent.
   c. Isabella founds a non-profit organization that teaches sustainable farming on a small island in the Pacific Ocean, but the island's villages adopt a different farming practice
   d. Trevor starts a website that provides people with the best solutions for reforming his nation's corrupt government, but nobody ever reads it.
   e. Becky joins the military to help overthrow a corrupt government, but the new government is comparable to the one that has been toppled.

19. Terrorism aims to instill fear in the target population, disrupting all daily activities and forcing an irrational backlash. More people die in car accidents in a day than terrorists have killed in two decades. Our country spends more money on fighting terrorism than any other single initiative, including healthcare. As such, our country should...

Which one of the following most logically completes the argument?
   a. spend less on military responses but more on criminal investigations.
   b. spend more money on reducing car accidents.
   c. spend money in proportion to terrorism's threat.
   d. spend more money on healthcare.
   e. spend money in proportion to the fear terrorism inspires.

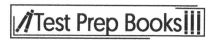

20. Scientist: a new vaccine will soon completely eradicate all types of influenza. The vaccine works on the cellular level, but it will only be effective if applied to the most high-risk individuals during the upcoming flu season. All people over sixty-five years of age are considered high-risk. Without vaccinating the entire high-risk group, the influenza virus will permanently mutate by the next flu season, rendering the vaccine completely ineffective. However, if the high-risk group of people is vaccinated in time, nobody will suffer from influenza ever again. As such, the government should force every high-risk individual to receive the vaccination, even by force, if they refuse to participate.

The scientist would most likely concur with which one of the following?
    a. Public health concerns should always trump individual rights.
    b. Fighting influenza is the most important objective for the government.
    c. High-risk individuals who refuse the vaccine should face severe punishment.
    d. The government should never intervene with individuals' healthcare decisions.
    e. Science will be able to create a new vaccine next year.

21. Employer: In the current economic climate, the best way to run a business is to pay employees the least amount possible to do the job. The supply of labor is far outpacing demand since the number of college graduates increases every year and the average age of retirement is also increasing. Applicants will typically take the first job offer on the table, and any employee who demands a raise can be easily replaced from the labor pool. Even if the employee is unhappy, he or she will often remain on the job due to the competition in the job market. Keeping payroll costs low allows more resources to be devoted to innovation, delivering a higher quality product to customers.

Each of the following, if true, weakens the employer's argument EXCEPT:
    a. Unhappy employees work less efficiently than happy workers.
    b. Paying employees the minimum will hurt the company's image amongst customers.
    c. Dissatisfied employees lead to labor unrest, and the resulting protests disrupt business.
    d. Automation is the leading cause of unemployment.
    e. Training new employees costs more than giving existing employees a raise.

22. A recent study conducted near the southwestern border of the San Joaquin Valley found no traces of the giant kangaroo rat, an endangered species. The researchers laid traps baited with oats and left them for several weeks during the summer, monitoring the traps on a daily basis. Two years ago, the researchers conducted the same study and caught more than one thousand giant kangaroo rats. If any of the animals had been present, the researchers would have surely caught at least one, so this is conclusive evidence that the giant kangaroo rat must be extinct.

Which one of the following assumptions does the author most rely upon?
    a. The researchers used the same type of traps as the study conducted two years ago.
    b. The giant kangaroo rats eat oats.
    c. The giant kangaroo rat forages during the summer months.
    d. The researchers did not make any mistakes during the study.
    e. The giant kangaroo rat does not live anywhere outside of the San Joaquin Valley.

23. Psychologist: While there are certain therapy techniques generally applicable to all patients, some patients require a specific technique for helping them overcome a particular challenge. However, specific techniques will not have the same effects or deliver the same insights for all patients. As a result, the best practice is to keep in mind all of the generally applicable techniques and then tailor the specifics to each individual.

Which one of the following propositions does the psychologist's reasoning most closely conform to?
a. Although generally applicable techniques exist for treating patients, therapists must be responsive to each individuals' needs and circumstances.
b. Individual patients always require the same combination of techniques.
c. The best practice always includes the generally applicable techniques.
d. Some patients can be treated with only the generally applicable techniques, while others do not require any technique at all.
e. Applying the wrong specific technique can cause severe harm to patients.

24. Historian: In the antebellum period before the American Civil War, the Northern states opposed the expansion of slavery in the recently acquired Western territories. The South's agrarian economy depended on its four million African slaves, and the South worried that failing to expand slavery into the new territories would lead to an abolitionist controlled Congress. The abolition of slavery would have entirely upended the South's political and economic power. Tensions between the North and South erupted in Kansas in the 1850s, commonly referred to as Bleeding Kansas. Less than two years before the start of the Civil War, John Brown attempted to launch a slave insurrection at Harper's Ferry, further solidifying Southern fears that the North intended to abolish slavery. Other historians claim that the cause of the Civil War involved principles of federalism, like states' rights, but the only right truly in dispute was slavery. Every other right implicated slavery whether directly or indirectly

Which one of the following most accurately represents the author's conclusion?
a. The dispute over slavery contributed to the American Civil War.
b. The Southern economy relied on slavery.
c. Bleeding Kansas and John Brown's slave insurrection foreshadowed the eventual war.
d. The role of slavery in causing the American Civil War cannot be overstated.
e. The dispute over states' rights did not cause the American Civil War.

25. Climate change is caused by an increase in carbon dioxide in the Earth's atmosphere. Carbon dioxide traps heat and remains in the atmosphere longer than other heat-trapping gases. Between 2000 and 2012, 890,000 square miles of trees around the world were cut down—more than one-eighth of the original forest covering Earth. Overall, deforestation has led to the loss of half the world's trees. Unless the rapid pace of deforestation is halted, the Earth's climate will change drastically in the near future.

The argument relies on which one of the following assumptions being true?
a. Trees produce carbon dioxide, releasing the gas into the atmosphere.
b. Deforestation is a manmade phenomenon.
c. Climate change negatively impacts the Earth.
d. Trees cannot be grown to replace the trees lost to deforestation.
e. Trees lower the amount of carbon dioxide in the atmosphere.

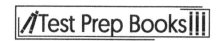

Section II: Analytical Reasoning

Time – 35 minutes

25 Questions

Directions: Each group of questions in this section is based on a set of conditions. It may be helpful to make diagrams as you read the questions. Choose the answer that most accurately and completely answers each question.

Questions 1 – 5

There are six students, John, Sofia, Tristan, Patricia, Tommy, and Claire, all competing to earn two available scholarships. John has a 3.6 GPA and perfect attendance. Tommy has a 3.7 GPA and one absence. Patricia has a 3.4 GPA and perfect attendance. The selection committee for the scholarships has set the following criteria:

- The winners cannot both be male or both be female. John, Tristan, and Tommy are male. Sofia, Patricia, and Claire are female.
- The winners must have a 3.5 or higher GPA.
- The winners must have perfect attendance.
- John can only win if Claire wins.

1. If Sofia wins one of the scholarships, then who could win the other one?
    a. John
    b. Tristan
    c. Tommy
    d. Claire
    e. Patricia

2. Which students are automatically disqualified?
    a. John and Patricia
    b. John and Tommy
    c. Tommy and Tristan
    d. Tommy and Patricia
    e. Patricia and Claire

3. Which of the following is an acceptable combination to win?
    a. John and Sofia
    b. Tommy and Sofia
    c. Tommy and Claire
    d. Patricia and Tristan
    e. John and Claire

4. If neither John nor Sofia wins, then who must win?
    a. Tommy and Claire
    b. Tristan and Patricia
    c. Tristan and Claire
    d. Claire and Patricia
    e. Tommy and Patricia

5. If it is determined that Claire has multiple absences, then who must win?
    a. Sofia and Tristan
    b. John and Sofia
    c. Patricia and John
    d. Tommy and Sofia
    e. John and Patricia

Questions 6 – 10

A construction worker is given the following list of jobs to complete and the estimated time needed to complete them.

- Paint a bedroom – 5 hours
- Install a vanity in the bathroom – 2 hours
- Install cabinet hardware throughout the house – 2 hours
- Frame out two doors – 4 hours
- Texture the walls in a bedroom – 4 hours
- Lay tile in a bathroom – 3 hours
- Install gutters – 4 hours

There are also the following conditions:

- He will only work up to 8 hours in a day, but does not have to work all 8.
- All jobs must be completed on the day they are started.
- The texture must be done before painting and they cannot be done on the same day.
- He must frame out the doors first.
- The vanity must be done last.

6. If he only works for 7 hours on his first two days combined, then what is the fewest number of days that he has left?
    a. 1
    b. 2
    c. 3
    d. 4
    e. 5

7. Which of the following would be an acceptable day of work, if done in the order listed?
    a. Lay tile, install cabinet hardware, and install vanity
    b. Texture the walls, lay tile, and install cabinet hardware
    c. Install gutters and frame out two doors
    d. Lay tile, install gutters, and texture the walls
    e. Texture the walls and paint a bedroom

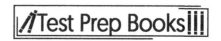

8. If he starts his day by installing cabinet hardware then which of the following could he also do that day?

    a. Frame out two doors and install vanity

    b. Lay tile and install gutters

    c. Install gutters and install vanity

    d. Paint a bedroom and install vanity

    e. Texture the walls and lay tile

9. On the 2nd day of the job, his boss tells him that he can work 10 hours that day. Which combination of day 1 and 2 work allows him to work all 10 hours on day 2?

    a. Day 1: Frame out two doors and install gutters. Day 2: Lay tile, paint a bedroom, and install a vanity

    b. Day 1: Frame out two doors and install gutters. Day 2: Texture walls, lay tile, and install gutters

    c. Day 1: Frame out two doors and texture walls. Day 2: Paint a bedroom, lay tile, and install cabinet hardware.

    d. Day 1: Frame out two doors and texture walls. Day 2: Paint a bedroom and install gutters

    e. Day 1: Frame out two doors and install gutters. Day 2: Paint a bedroom, lay tile, and install cabinet hardware.

10. Which one of the following could not happen?

    a. He textured the walls then took a one-hour lunch before laying the tile.

    b. During his 2nd and 3rd day of work, he completed the texturing of the walls, the painting, installing the gutters and laying the tile.

    c. It took him 5 days to complete all of the jobs.

    d. On day 2 he decided to only paint the walls and still completed all of the jobs in 4 days

    e. He painted a bedroom and installed the gutters on the same day.

Questions 11-15

A new restaurant has just opened. They have the following items on their menu:

- Turkey Club
- Philly Cheesesteak
- Hot Dog
- Patty Melt
- Salad
- Pizza
- French Fries
- Onion Rings

There are also the following conditions when ordering:

- Patty Melts are only served on Wednesdays-Fridays.
- French Fries and Onion Rings can only be purchased with a sandwich.
- A Salad can only be purchased if you also purchase something else.
- A Philly Cheesesteak and Turkey Club cannot be purchased together.
- Hot Dogs are only served Monday-Thursday.
- Pizza is only served on Thursday-Sunday.

11. If you visit the restaurant on a Tuesday, then which of the following is an acceptable order?
    a. Patty Melt and Onion Rings
    b. Pizza and French Fries
    c. Turkey Club, Salad, and Onion Rings
    d. Philly Cheesesteak, Turkey Club, and a Hot Dog
    e. Hot Dog and French Fries

12. If someone orders a Pizza, Patty Melt, Hot Dog and Salad then which day did they visit the restaurant?
    a. Monday
    b. Tuesday
    c. Wednesday
    d. Thursday
    e. Friday

13. Which of the following could be true?
    a. A Turkey Club and Patty Melt were purchased on Monday.
    b. A Hot Dog and Pizza were purchased on Friday.
    c. A Salad and French Fries were purchased on Thursday
    d. A Turkey Club, Philly Cheesesteak, and Hot Dog were purchased on Monday
    e. A Philly Cheesesteak, Pizza, and Onion Rings were purchased on Saturday

14. Which of the following would be an acceptable order on any day of the week?
    a. Patty Melt and Onion Rings
    b. Turkey Club, French Fries, and Onion Rings
    c. Hot Dog, Pizza, and French Fries
    d. Salad and Onion Rings
    e. Turkey Club, Onion Rings, and a Hot Dog

15. If a customer wanted to purchase a single item on a Friday, how many different menu items would be available to him or her?
    a. 4
    b. 5
    c. 6
    d. 7
    e. 8

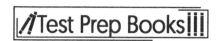

Questions 16-20

A professor is setting up advising meetings with her students John, Dan, Emily, Ashley, Ben, and Eli. She can meet with exactly one student per day at lunch, except Fridays, when she can meet with two students after school instead. The following conditions apply:

- Ashley's appointment is before Ben's but after Eli's
- The professor will meet with a male student on Wednesday
- John is one of the students who meets on Friday
- Dan cannot meet on Fridays
- Emily's appointment is after the student who meets on Wednesday

16. Which of the following is a possible order for the students' appointments?
   a. Eli, Ashley, Dan, Ben, Emily, John
   b. Dan, Eli, Ashley, Ben, Emily, John
   c. Eli, Ashley, Ben, Emily, Dan, John
   d. Dan, Ashley, Eli, Ben, Emily, John
   e. Eli, Dan, Ashley, Ben, Emily, John

17. How many of the students can be assigned to Monday?
   a. One
   b. Two
   c. Three
   d. Four
   e. Five

18. If Emily is NOT on Thursday, who could be?
   a. John or Dan
   b. Ben or Dan
   c. Eli or Ben
   d. Eli or Ashley
   e. Dan or Eli

19. Ashley's appointment could be on which of the following days?
   a. Monday
   b. Tuesday
   c. Wednesday
   d. Thursday
   e. Friday

20. If Ben's appointment is Thursday, which of the following could be true?
   a. Eli's appointment is Friday
   b. Two male students meet with the professor on Friday
   c. Emily's appointment is Tuesday
   d. Ashley's appointment is Wednesday
   e. Dan's appointment is Wednesday

Questions 21-25

A meal subscription service must load each customer's weekly box with at least one meal from each of the meal categories: breakfast, lunch, or dinner. This week, the breakfast choices are French toast, Omelets, or Waffles. Lunch selections include Chili, Paninis, or a Chopped Salad. Dinner options are Steak, Chicken Parmesan, and Pad Thai.

When the company packs the boxes, the following conditions must be met:

- An equal number of choices from each meal type must be packed in the box.
- Paninis and Steak cannot be packed together
- If a customer gets a Chopped Salad, Chicken Parmesan must also be supplied
- Chili must be packed if the box includes French Toast
- Chopped Salads are not included if Paninis are

21. If two dinner options are packed in the box, which of the following is definitely NOT true?
    a. Steak and Chicken Parmesan are in the box
    b. Chili and Chopped Salad are in the box
    c. Paninis and Chili are in the box
    d. Omelets and French Toast are in the box
    e. Steak and Pad Thai are added to the box

22. If Paninis are packed as the only lunch item in the box, how many possible combinations of meals can be added to that box?
    a. 2
    b. 3
    c. 4
    d. 5
    e. 6

23. If the condition that requires that an equal number of food items from each meal type must be selected is lifted but all of the other conditions remain, what is the greatest number of different foods that can be included in a box?
    a. 4
    b. 5
    c. 6
    d. 7
    e. 8

24. Which one of the following is a possible subscription box to mail to a new customer?
    a. Omelets, Waffles, and Steak
    b. French Toast, Chicken Parmesan, and Panini
    c. French Toast, Omelets, Chili, Steak, and Pad Thai
    d. Omelets, Waffle, Chili, Panini, Chicken Parmesan, and Pad Thai
    e. French Toast, Omelets, Chili, Chopped Salad, Steak, and Pad Thai

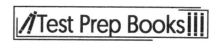

25. If Pad Thai and a Chopped Salad are both in a box, then which of the following foods MUST also be included?

    a. French toast
    b. Omelets
    c. Chili
    d. Waffles
    e. Steak

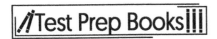

Section III: Logical Reasoning

Time – 35 minutes

25 Questions

1. Surgeon General: Smoking causes more deaths than the combined causes of HIV, illegal drug use, alcohol consumption, motor vehicle accidents, and firearms, killing more than 480,000 Americans each year. As opposed to nonsmokers, smokers are two-to-four times more likely to suffer from heart disease and twenty-five times more likely to develop lung cancer. Nevertheless, the United States is founded on the principle of liberty and free market business. If Americans want to smoke, they should be free to do so, and if a market exists, businesses should be able to meet that demand. The most we can possibly do is educate Americans about the risks of smoking.

Which of the following is most strongly suggested by the Surgeon General's statement above?
   a. Without big businesses marketing cigarettes, no Americans would smoke.
   b. Protecting some principles is more important than health.
   c. Americans should be able to do whatever they want with their bodies.
   d. Education will eventually end smoking.
   e. The United States should ban smoking.

2. Trainer: I recently developed an exercise routine that can get anybody to meet their goals. The routine combines cardio and bodybuilding during each session for the purpose of losing weight. Every person I've trained has lost weight on the program.

The strength of the argument depends on which one of the following?
   a. Every client the trainer has worked with has prior experience lifting weights.
   b. Every client the trainer has worked with has also adopted a healthy diet.
   c. Every client the trainer has worked with has weight loss as a goal.
   d. The exercise routine combines cardio and bodybuilding in equal amounts.
   e. Losing weight is always a healthy outcome.

3. The news exclusively covers important current events. Reality television stars are never covered on the news, except when they become pregnant.

Which one of the following must be true?
   a. Reality television stars never qualify as an important current event.
   b. All current events involve reality television stars.
   c. Some pregnancies are important current events.
   d. All pregnancies are important current events.
   e. The news always covers pregnancies.

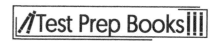

Use the following passage to answer questions 4 and 5.

The United States deploys two types of submarines—attack submarines and ballistic submarines. Attack submarines carry cruise missiles to attack specific locations on land, and they are also used to spy on foreign countries. Ballistic submarines carry intercontinental ballistic missiles that deliver nuclear missiles at a minimum range of 3,400 miles. Consequently, there is little advantage to placing a ballistic submarine near the coast of any country. Both submarines are nuclear-powered, but only the ballistic submarines carry nuclear weapons. The United States believes that a foreign country is plotting to attack her homeland, but more intelligence must be collected. The United States plans to deploy a submarine off the coast of the foreign country.

4. Which one of the following would be a reasonable conclusion based on the passage?
    a. The United States should deploy a ballistic submarine off the coast of the foreign country.
    b. The United States should develop a new type of submarine to gather the evidence.
    c. The United States should plant an agent in the foreign country's intelligence service.
    d. The United States should pre-emptively attack the foreign country to best defend itself.
    e. The United States should deploy an attack submarine off the coast of the foreign country.

5. Which one of the following CANNOT be inferred from the passage?
    a. The ballistic submarine is more useful if located in the open sea.
    b. The United States should not attack a foreign country based on unverified intelligence.
    c. Some attack submarines can carry intercontinental ballistic missiles as well as cruise missiles.
    d. Spying on foreign countries is part of the United States' military defense strategy.
    e. Submarines are the best way to collect intelligence in this specific situation.

6. Big-game trophy hunting is the hunting of large terrestrial mammals, typically in reference to Africa's "Big Five" game—lions, African elephants, Cape buffalos, leopards, and rhinoceroses. Despite widespread criticism and vocal public protest, big-game trophy hunting is entirely defensible. The controversial practice places a monetary value on the "Big Five" game. Hunters spend millions of dollars in Africa, which allows the participating countries to better care for the animals.

Which one of the following, if true, most strengthens the argument?
    a. The hunters are only allowed to hunt sick or elderly animals.
    b. African countries would otherwise not be able to afford to protect the animals.
    c. None of the "Big Five" animals are endangered.
    d. The widespread criticism and vocal public protest are misguided.
    e. Placing monetary value on the lives of animals is moral.

7. Cities now suffer from unprecedented levels of air pollution. Urban residents need to wear surgical masks whenever they go outside. Nuclear power is fully in compliance with the Clean Air Act of 1970, which imposes standards on air quality, unlike the current source of power—coal. Surprisingly, no city has seriously considered transitioning to a nuclear power source. Rural areas use exclusively nuclear power, and they do not suffer from any air pollution.

All of the following explains the discrepancy EXCEPT:
    a. It is impossible to discard nuclear waste in a safe manner.
    b. Terrorists would target a nuclear power plant in a heavily populated area.
    c. A nuclear accident would be catastrophic in an area of high population density.
    d. Transitioning to nuclear power is significantly more expensive than continuing to use coal.
    e. Urban populations have vigorously protested the introduction of nuclear power.

8. On the first day of the course, a philosophy professor told the class that no student has ever earned an A without reading all of the mandatory books. Jorge read all of the mandatory books and suggested course materials for his philosophy course. Therefore, Jorge will earn an A in his philosophy course.

What mistake does the argument commit in its reasoning?
    a. It confuses correlation and causation.
    b. It confuses a necessary and sufficient condition.
    c. It confuses probability and certainty.
    d. It confuses is and ought.
    e. It confuses relative and absolute solutions.

9. If a President is elected, then he or she won the nomination of a major party and received at least 270 Electoral College votes, even if he or she did not win the popular vote.

Which one of the following must be true?
    a. No President has received less than 270 Electoral College votes.
    b. Some Presidents have received less than 270 Electoral College votes.
    c. No President who won the nomination of a major party received 270 Electoral College votes.
    d. Some Presidents have won the popular vote.
    e. All Presidents have won the popular vote.

10. Brick and Mortar Bookstore Owner: Bookstores are the backbone of our country. Democracies depend on a literate population, and reading fosters the creativity necessary to drive innovation. Brick and mortar bookstores introduce people to new books and entice people to expand their literary preferences. Without brick and mortar bookstores, the demand for books would collapse, killing the publishing industry.

Digital Bookstore Owner: There is no denying the importance of reading for any democracy. However, digital books are the future. People can easily access our enormous catalogue of books, which is far greater than any brick and mortar bookstore. We provide synopses and reviews that allow people to discover new interests. In addition, digital books are cheaper than paper books.

What is the main point of dispute in the two arguments?
    a. Digital books will someday replace paper books altogether.
    b. Reading is the backbone of the country.
    c. Digital books are cheaper than paper books.
    d. Digital bookstores depend on the existence of brick and mortar bookstores.
    e. Customers prefer paper books.

11. Americans democracy is under fire. Voter turnout is at a record low, particularly for local elections. Some municipal elections have less than thirty percent voter participation. Congressional approval ratings have not surpassed 30 percent since 2009, but incumbents win reelection campaigns at a rate of 90 percent. Rank choice voting is the answer. Under this system, voters rank candidates in order of choice, and when their preferred candidate is eliminated in an instantaneous runoff, their vote is transferred to their next most-preferred candidate. As a result, voter participation will increase, since there will be more candidates and competition, leading to more effective representation.

Which one of the following most accurately identifies the argument's primary purpose?

    a. To express Americans' dissatisfaction with the status quo.

    b. To present a solution to an apparent problem.

    c. To explain rank choice voting.

    d. To criticize the current congressional representatives, especially incumbents.

    e. To support the need for greater competition in elections.

12. Livestock is a major contributor to climate change, accounting for 18 percent of the greenhouse gas released every year. In addition, livestock accounts for eight percent of global water use, and as much as 70 percent of deforestation is driven by the need for more pastures and feed crops. Dietary changes can dramatically decrease humanity's environmental footprint, such as adopting a vegan or vegetarian lifestyle.

Which one of the following most accurately represents the author's conclusion?

    a. The Earth will be destroyed unless everyone stops eating meat.

    b. Dietary changes are the only way to decrease humanity's environmental footprint.

    c. Deforestation contributes to climate change.

    d. Livestock is a major contributor to climate change.

    e. People can reduce their environmental impact by adopting dietary changes.

13. Communism is the greatest source of evil on the planet. In the twentieth century, communism was the leading cause of death, killing more than 90 million people in the Soviet Union, China, North Korea, Afghanistan, and Eastern Europe. The death toll even surpasses the number of people who died during either World War. The leading cause of death in communist countries was famine, which did not occur in any country that was not communist. Despite this hard evidence to the contrary, more than ten percent of Americans believe communism would be better than our current system.

The author would be most likely to agree with which one of the following?

    a. Communism would be an acceptable form of government if it did not cause famine.

    b. Every country should adopt capitalism.

    c. Communism failed in the twentieth century only because countries failed to follow it properly.

    d. Some people cannot be trusted to decide what system their government should adopt.

    e. Communism caused both World Wars.

14. People often pay more taxes than necessary, due to their failure to take advantage of the numerous deductibles offered by the government. If more people filed their taxes online, they would save more money.

The strength of the argument depends on which one of the following?
- a. Saving money on taxes is beneficial.
- b. It is easier to take advantage of deductibles by filing taxes online.
- c. Taking advantage of deductibles will not hurt the government's revenue.
- d. The government makes it difficult to take advantage of deductibles.
- e. Most people want to save money.

15. Electronic cigarettes should not be subject to the same regulation as other products that contain nicotine. Recent studies indicate that electronic cigarettes help people quit smoking by providing nicotine without the harmful tar and additive chemicals. Although electronic cigarettes also contain their own additives, they are much less harmful in the short-term than traditional cigarettes. People who smoke electronic cigarettes are ten times less likely to die from cancer than smokers of traditional cigarettes.

Which one of the following most weakens the argument?
- a. The current regulations are designed to prevent children from using nicotine.
- b. Electronic cigarettes are difficult to quit.
- c. More smokers die from heart disease than cancer.
- d. The recent studies are not conclusive.
- e. The additives in electronic cigarettes have not been tested as thoroughly as those in traditional cigarettes.

16. Michael hit a pedestrian, Meredith, with his car, and as a result, Meredith broke her hip in three places. Obviously, Michael is the cause of Meredith's injury. In cases of a broken hip, 100 percent of people make a full recovery, as long as the injured party is younger than sixty. Meredith is 52 years old. Thus, Meredith will make a full recovery. Michael's friend, Jim, a widget salesman, told Michael not to settle since Jim believes that Meredith was negligently crossing the street. Thus, Michael has chosen to fight Meredith in a protracted legal battle.

The argument above is most vulnerable to criticism on the grounds that:
- a. it mistakes probability for certainty.
- b. it confuses causation with correlation.
- c. it relies on an inappropriate authority.
- d. it makes a hasty generalization.
- e. it uses a term unclearly.

17. An advertising agency employs ten times the number of employees relative to its competitors. Thus, any company should hire that advertising agency.

Which one of the following arguments contains the most similar reasoning to the argument above?
    a. A tree produces more apples than any other tree. Thus, that tree is the best tree for growing apples.
    b. A widget company produces more products per year than its competitors and sells each widget for the highest price in the industry. Thus, that widget company earns more revenue than any other widget company.
    c. A blog produces ten times the amount of content relative to its competitors. Thus, that blog produces more content than its competitors.
    d. A tiger needs to eat three rabbits every day. Thus, that tiger needs to eat twenty-one rabbits per week.
    e. A building is twice as tall as any other building on the city's skyline. Thus, that building is the tallest building on the city's skyline.

18. Social media websites rely on user engagement. Increasing the number of users and those users' activity means more advertising revenue. Most social media websites offer the service at no cost in order to attract more users, relying exclusively on advertising revenue to make a profit. The most popular articles shared on social media websites involve sensationalized stories of dubious value, including misleading titles and incorrect factual information. However, many users will stop using a social media website when the sensational stories become too overwhelming. As a result, social media companies would be best served by...

Which one of the following best completes the argument?
    a. prohibiting sensationalized articles.
    b. monitoring the ratio of sensationalized and factual articles.
    c. surveying their users to determine what type of content they most prefer.
    d. searching for alternative sources of revenue.
    e. lying to advertisers about their user engagement.

19. High schools should only teach abstinence. Students who practice abstinence will never experience an unplanned pregnancy or contract a sexually-transmitted disease.

Each of the following weakens the argument EXCEPT:
    a. Students are less likely to follow teaching about abstinence than safe sex.
    b. The percentage of students engaging in abstinence is lowest in school districts that only teach abstinence.
    c. Religious organizations support the teaching of abstinence.
    d. Failing to teach about contraceptives increases the spread of sexually-transmitted diseases.
    e. Contraceptive use is the cause of the nation's declining unintended pregnancy rate.

20. Bill is capable of reading two pages per minute, typing one hundred words per minute, and speaking twenty words per minute. All lawyers can read two pages per minute, and some philosophers can read two pages per minute. Only secretaries can type one hundred words per minute. Many chief executive officers can speak twenty words per minute, and few doctors can speak more than twenty words per minute.

Which one of the following statements can be deduced from the argument?
   a. Bill is a lawyer.
   b. Bill is a philosopher.
   c. Bill is a doctor.
   d. Bill is a chief executive officer.
   e. Bill is a secretary.

21. Editorialist: The national media is composed of private companies that depend on ratings to increase advertising revenue, which depends on how many people watch. People are only going to watch topics they find interesting. In much the same way that the local news focuses on violent crimes, the national media focuses on political scandals. Topics such as election reform are rarely covered.

The argument most strongly supports which one of the following assertions?
   a. The national media covers violent crimes.
   b. The national media only covers political scandals.
   c. The local news focuses on political scandals as well as violent crimes.
   d. The current coverage is problematic for the country.
   e. Election reform is not interesting to people.

22. Most politicians are liars. Timothy is a politician, but he never lies. As a result, Timothy is the best politician in the country.

Which one of the following best describes how the argument proceeds?
   a. It starts with a generalization and then applies the generalization to a specific situation.
   b. It starts with a hard rule and then applies the rule to a specific situation.
   c. It starts with a generalization, provides additional evidence, and then draws an unsupported conclusion.
   d. It starts with a generalization and then identifies an exception, which is the basis for its conclusion.
   e. It starts with a hard rule and then identifies an exception, which is the basis for its conclusion.

23. If it is not raining, then Andy is singing. Andy always dances on Wednesdays, but if it is any other day, then Andy is miming. It is Tuesday, and Andy is singing.

According to the argument above, which of the following must follow?
   a. It is raining.
   b. Andy is miming, and it is not raining.
   c. Andy is not miming, and it is raining.
   d. Andy is miming, and it is raining.
   e. Andy is miming.

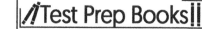

24. College is increasingly unaffordable for everyone that is not independently wealthy, outpacing inflation every year since the early 1970s. This year the average cost of tuition at a private, four-year university is more than $31,000 per year. In 1971, tuition cost less than $2,000, even after adjusting for inflation. The trend is similar at public, four-year institutions. Fortunately, with the advent of the Internet, independent learning is easier than ever before. Students can learn hard skills online for relatively minimal costs, like coding and web design. Online courses can also replicate a traditional college education, with options such as math, science, and liberal arts courses. As a result, high school students would be wise to weigh their options before choosing to attend a traditional four-year college.

Which one of the following strengthens the argument?
   a. Students who do not attend traditional college miss out on important life experiences.
   b. The average earning potential for a traditional college graduate is higher than for any alternative.
   c. The government should have capped tuition at traditional four-year colleges.
   d. Employers increasingly value work experience and self-starters more than formal education.
   e. The independently wealthy should still attend traditional college programs.

25. The first publicly available fantasy football league was launched in 1997, and within three years, every major football media website had launched their own sites. From 2000 until 2015, viewership for the National Football League rose by 27 percent, and it is currently the most popular televised sport in the United States. Fantasy football heavily contributed to the increased viewership since fantasy players had a vested interest in nearly every game.

Upon which one of the following assumptions does the author's argument rely?
   a. Fantasy football increased the players' knowledge of the National Football League.
   b. The National Football League earns a large portion of its revenue from high television ratings.
   c. Fantasy football increased at a similar rate as National Football League viewership.
   d. Some fantasy players watch National Football League games.
   e. Football was the least popular sport in the United States before 2000.

Section IV: Reading Comprehension

Time – 35 minutes

26 Questions

Questions 1 – 5 are based on the following two passages:

Passage A

Excerpt from Thomas Henry Huxley, "Science and Culture"

The representatives of the humanists in the nineteenth century take their stand upon classical education as the sole avenue to culture, as firmly as if we were still in the age of Renaissance. Yet, surely, the present intellectual relations of the modern and the ancient worlds are profoundly different from those which obtained three centuries ago. Leaving aside the existence of a great and characteristically modern literature, of modern painting, and, especially, of modern music, there is one feature of the present state of the civilized world which separates it more widely from the Renaissance than the Renaissance was separated from the Middle Ages.

This distinctive character of our own times lies in the vast and constantly increasing part which is played by natural knowledge. Not only is our daily life shaped by it, not only does the prosperity of millions of men depend upon it, but our whole theory of life has long been influenced, consciously or unconsciously, by the general conceptions of the universe, which have been forced upon us by physical science.

In fact, the most elementary acquaintance with the results of scientific investigation shows us that they offer a broad and striking contradiction to the opinions so implicitly credited and taught in the Middle Ages.

Passage B

Excerpt from Matthew Arnold, "Literature and Science"

When I speak of knowing Greek and Roman antiquity, therefore, as a help to knowing ourselves and the world, I mean more than a knowledge of so much vocabulary, so much grammar, so many portions of authors in the Greek and Latin languages. I mean knowing the Greeks and Romans, and their life and genius, and what they were and did in the world; what we get from them, and what is its value. That, at least, is the ideal; and when we talk of endeavoring to know Greek and Roman antiquity, as a help to knowing ourselves and the world, we mean endeavoring so to know them as to satisfy this ideal, however much we may still fall short of it.

The same also as to knowing our own and other modern nations with the like aim of getting to understand ourselves and the world. To know the best that has been thought and said by the modern nations, is to know, says Professor Huxley, "only what modern *literatures* have to tell us; it is the criticism of life contained in modern literature." And yet "the distinctive character of our times," he urges, "lies in the vast and constantly increasing part which is played by natural knowledge." And how, therefore, can a man, devoid of knowledge of what physical science has done in the last century enter hopefully upon a criticism of modern life?

1. The authors of the passages differ in their attitudes toward humanities in that the author of passage B is:

    a. an advocate of the study of science as it relates to classical text only, namely the writings of Greek and Roman text.

    b. an advocate of the study of science as it relates to natural knowledge only, namely the importance of it and how we are shaped by it.

    c. a defender of the study of humanities in "modern" schooling as it relates to both literature and science.

    d. a defender of the study of humanities in "modern" schooling as it relates to the study of literature only, namely Greek and Roman texts.

    e. a defender of the study of humanities in "modern" schooling as it relates to the axioms of Professor Huxley.

2. Which one of the following most accurately characterizes the relationship between the two passages?

    a. Passage B is written in response to passage A; passage B uses textual evidence from passage A to contradict passage A's argument.

    b. Passage B is written in response to passage A; passage B uses textual evidence from passage A to enthusiastically agree with its argument.

    c. Passage A is written in response to passage B; passage A offers a critique of passage B's views on classical literature in relation to the study of science, or natural knowledge.

    d. Passage A is written in response to passage B; passage A offers a concession of passage B's argument by showing that Greek and Roman literature can be studied alongside natural knowledge.

    e. Passage A is written in response to passage B; passage A is supportive of the argument of passage B with a few exceptions.

3. The authors of the passages would be most likely to disagree over whether:

    a. the process of evolution is considered an area of science or not.

    b. Eastern literature is more formidable than Western literature.

    c. science should be given a place in academia within this time period.

    d. whether art should be used for its intrinsic nature or for political purposes.

    e. classical literature lends itself to the progression of future generations.

4. The author of passage B thinks that knowing Greek and Roman culture is valuable because:

    a. scholars consider Greek and Roman literature the best in the world.

    b. it is a culture that offers foundation and experience on an array of subjects that we can learn from in the present.

    c. Latin is an important language to study in order to have a firm understanding of the natural sciences.

    d. Greek and Roman culture were far superior to the culture of the authors' time period.

    e. the Greeks and Romans placed more importance on the humanities than on science, which is what the author of passage B is arguing for.

5. What does the author of passage A mean by the last paragraph?

a. That the Middle Ages was a formidable period of scientific progress and that modern science would do well to follow after it.

b. That those with little acquaintance of scientific investigation are synonymous with those who lived during the Middle Ages.

c. That an elementary knowledge of the Middle Ages is not conducive to the knowledge of scientific investigation.

d. That what was studied and valued in the Middle Ages is in stark contrast to the scientific process valued in the author's period.

e. That the opinions taught in the Middle Ages are superior to those opinions taught centuries later.

Questions 6 – 9 refer to the following passage, titled "Education is Essential to Civilization."

Early in my career, a master teacher shared this thought with me, "Education is the last bastion of civility." While I did not completely understand the scope of those words at the time, I have since come to realize the depth, breadth, truth, and significance of what he said. Education provides society with a vehicle for raising its children to be civil, decent, human beings with something valuable to contribute to the world. It is really what makes us human and what distinguishes us as civilized creatures.

Being "civilized" humans means being "whole" humans. Education must address the mind, body, and soul of students. It would be detrimental to society if our schools were myopic in their focus, only meeting the needs of the mind. As humans, we are multi-dimensional, multi-faceted beings who need more than head knowledge to survive. The human heart and psyche have to be fed in order for the mind to develop properly, and the body must be maintained and exercised to help fuel the working of the brain.

Education is a basic human right, and it allows us to sustain a democratic society in which participation is fundamental to its success. It should inspire students to seek better solutions to world problems and to dream of a more equitable society. Education should never discriminate on any basis, and it should create individuals who are self-sufficient, patriotic, and tolerant of other's ideas.

All children can learn, although not all children learn in the same manner. All children learn best, however, when their basic physical needs are met and they feel safe, secure, and loved. Students are much more responsive to a teacher who values them and shows them respect as individual people. Teachers must model at all times the way they expect students to treat them and their peers. If teachers set high expectations for their students, the students will rise to that high level. Teachers must make the well-being of their students their primary focus and must not be afraid to let their students learn from their own mistakes.

In the modern age of technology, a teacher's focus is no longer the "what" of the content, but more importantly, the "why." Students are bombarded with information and have access to ANY information they need right at their fingertips. Teachers have to work harder than ever before to help students identify salient information and to think critically about the information they encounter. Students have to read between the lines, identify bias, and determine who they can trust in the milieu of ads, data, and texts presented to them.

Schools must work in consort with families in this important mission. While children spend most of their time in school, they are dramatically and indelibly shaped by the influences of their family and culture. Teachers must not only respect this fact, but must strive to include parents in the education of their

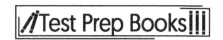

children and must work to keep parents informed of progress and problems. Communication between classroom and home is essential for a child's success.

Humans have always aspired to be more, do more, and to better ourselves and our communities. This is where education lies, right at the heart of humanity's desire to be all that we can be. Education helps us strive for higher goals and better treatment of ourselves and others. I shudder to think what would become of us if education ceased to be the "last bastion of civility." We must be unapologetic about expecting excellence from our students—our very existence depends upon it.

6. Which of the following best summarizes the author's main point?
    a. Education as we know it is over-valued in modern society, and we should find alternative solutions.
    b. The survival of the human race depends on the educational system, and it is worth fighting for to make it better.
    c. The government should do away with all public schools and require parents to home school their children instead.
    d. While education is important, some children simply are not capable of succeeding in a traditional classroom.
    e. All children must be given equal opportunity to participate in the education system without fear of discrimination.

7. Based on this passage, which of the following can be inferred about the author?
    a. The author feels passionately about education.
    b. The author does not feel strongly about his point.
    c. The author is angry at the educational system.
    d. The author is unsure about the importance of education.
    e. The author is against the use of technology in schools.

8. Based on this passage, which of the following conclusions could be drawn about the author?
    a. The author would not support raising taxes to help fund much needed reforms in education.
    b. The author would support raising taxes to help fund much needed reforms in education, as long as those reforms were implemented in higher socio-economic areas first.
    c. The author would support raising taxes to help fund much needed reforms in education for all children in all schools.
    d. The author would support raising taxes only in certain states to help fund much needed reforms in education.
    e. The author would support raising taxes to fund much needed reforms only for minority students who may lack certain advantages.

9. According to the passage, which of the following is not mentioned as an important factor in education today?
    a. Parent involvement
    b. Communication between parents and teachers
    c. Impact of technology
    d. Cost of textbooks
    e. High teacher expectations

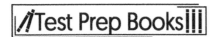

Questions 10 – 13 refer to the following passage.

Although many Missourians know that Harry S. Truman and Walt Disney hailed from their great state, probably far fewer know that it was also home to the remarkable George Washington Carver. At the end of the Civil War, Moses Carver, the slave owner who owned George's parents, decided to keep George and his brother and raise them on his farm. As a child, George was driven to learn and he loved painting. He even went on to study art while in college but was encouraged to pursue botany instead. He spent much of his life helping others by showing them better ways to farm; his ideas improved agricultural productivity in many countries. One of his most notable contributions to the newly emerging class of Black farmers was to teach them the negative effects of agricultural monoculture, i.e. growing the same crops in the same fields year after year, depleting the soil of much needed nutrients and resulting in a lesser yielding crop. Carver was an innovator, always thinking of new and better ways to do things, and is most famous for his over three hundred uses for the peanut. Toward the end of his career, Carver returned to his first love of art. Through his artwork, he hoped to inspire people to see the beauty around them and to do great things themselves. When Carver died, he left his money to help fund ongoing agricultural research. Today, people still visit and study at the George Washington Carver Foundation at Tuskegee Institute.

10. Which of the following describes the kind of writing used in the above passage?
    a. narrative
    b. persuasive
    c. technical
    d. expository
    e. descriptive

11. According to the passage, what was George Washington Carver's first love?
    a. plants
    b. peanuts
    c. animals
    d. soil
    e. art

12. According to the passage, what is the best definition for agricultural monoculture?
    a. The practice of producing or growing a single crop or plant species over a wide area and for a large number of consecutive years
    b. The practice of growing a diversity of crops and rotating them from year to year
    c. The practice of growing crops organically to avoid the use of pesticides
    d. The practice of charging an inflated price for cheap crops to obtain a greater profit margin
    e. The practice of planting the same crop at several farms to establish a monopoly on that crop

13. Which of the following is the best summary of this passage?
    a. George Washington Carver was born at a time when scientific discovery was at a virtual standstill.
    b. Because he was African American, there were not many opportunities for George Washington Carver.
    c. George Washington Carver was an intelligent man whose research and discoveries had an impact worldwide.
    d. George Washington Carver was far more successful as an artist than he was as a scientist.
    e. George Washington Carver was the person who first discovered peanuts.

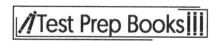

Questions 14 – 16 are based on the following passage.

Smoking is Terrible

Smoking tobacco products is terribly destructive. A single cigarette contains over 4,000 chemicals, including 43 known carcinogens and 400 deadly toxins. Some of the most dangerous ingredients include tar, carbon monoxide, formaldehyde, ammonia, arsenic, and DDT. Smoking can cause numerous types of cancer including throat, mouth, nasal cavity, esophageal, gastric, pancreatic, renal, bladder, and cervical cancer.

Cigarettes contain a drug called nicotine, one of the most addictive substances known to man. Addiction is defined as a compulsion to seek the substance despite negative consequences. According to the National Institute of Drug Abuse, nearly 35 million smokers expressed a desire to quit smoking in 2015; however, more than 85 percent of those who struggle with addiction will not achieve their goal. Almost all smokers regret picking up that first cigarette. You would be wise to learn from their mistake if you have not yet started smoking.

According to the U.S. Department of Health and Human Services, 16 million people in the United States presently suffer from a smoking-related condition and nearly nine million suffer from a serious smoking-related illness. According to the Centers for Disease Control and Prevention (CDC), tobacco products cause nearly six million deaths per year. This number is projected to rise to over eight million deaths by 2030. Smokers, on average, die ten years earlier than their nonsmoking peers.

In the United States, local, state, and federal governments typically tax tobacco products, which leads to high prices. Nicotine users who struggle with addiction sometimes pay more for a pack of cigarettes than for a few gallons of gas. Additionally, smokers tend to stink. The smell of smoke is all-consuming and creates a pervasive nastiness. Smokers also risk staining their teeth and fingers with yellow residue from the tar.

Smoking is deadly, expensive, and socially unappealing. Clearly, smoking is not worth the risks.

14. Which of the following statements most accurately summarizes the passage?
   a. Tobacco is less healthy than many alternatives.
   b. Tobacco is deadly, expensive, and socially unappealing, and smokers would be much better off kicking the addiction.
   c. In the United States, local, state, and federal governments typically tax tobacco products, which leads to high prices.
   d. Tobacco products shorten smokers' lives by ten years and kill more than six million people per year.
   e. Tobacco products are addictive, and smokers find it very difficult to quit.

15. The author would be most likely to agree with which of the following statements?
   a. Smokers should only quit cold turkey and avoid all nicotine cessation devices.
   b. Other substances are more addictive than tobacco.
   c. Smokers should quit for whatever reason that gets them to stop smoking.
   d. People who want to continue smoking should advocate for a reduction in tobacco product taxes.
   e. Most smokers begin smoking early in life.

LSAT Practice Test #2 | Section IV: Reading Comprehension

16. Which of the following represents an opinion statement on the part of the author?
    a. According to the Centers for Disease Control and Prevention (CDC), tobacco products cause nearly six million deaths per year.
    b. Nicotine users who struggle with addiction sometimes pay more for a pack of cigarettes than a few gallons of gas.
    c. They also risk staining their teeth and fingers with yellow residue from the tar.
    d. Smokers, on average, die ten years earlier than their nonsmoking peers.
    e. Additionally, smokers tend to stink. The smell of smoke is all-consuming and creates a pervasive nastiness.

Questions 17 – 19 are based on the following passage.

Christopher Columbus is often credited for discovering America. This is incorrect. First, it is impossible to "discover" something where people already live; however, Christopher Columbus did explore places in the New World that were previously untouched by Europe, so the term "explorer" would be more accurate. Another correction must be made, as well: Christopher Columbus was not the first European explorer to reach the present day Americas! Rather, it was Leif Erikson who first came to the New World and contacted the natives, nearly five hundred years before Christopher Columbus.

Leif Erikson, the son of Erik the Red (a famous Viking outlaw and explorer in his own right), was born in either 970 or 980, depending on which historian you read. His own family, though, did not raise Leif, which was a Viking tradition. Instead, one of Erik's prisoners taught Leif reading and writing, languages, sailing, and weaponry. At age 12, Leif was considered a man and returned to his family. He killed a man during a dispute shortly after his return, and the council banished the Erikson clan to Greenland.

In 999, Leif left Greenland and traveled to Norway where he would serve as a guard to King Olaf Tryggvason. It was there that he became a convert to Christianity. Leif later tried to return home with the intention of taking supplies and spreading Christianity to Greenland, however his ship was blown off course and he arrived in a strange new land: present day Newfoundland, Canada.

When he finally returned to his adopted homeland Greenland, Leif consulted with a merchant who had also seen the shores of this previously unknown land we now know as Canada. The son of the legendary Viking explorer then gathered a crew of 35 men and set sail. Leif became the first European to touch foot in the New World as he explored present-day Baffin Island and Labrador, Canada. His crew called the land Vinland since it was plentiful with grapes.

During their time in present-day Newfoundland, Leif's expedition made contact with the natives whom they referred to as Skraelings (which translates to "wretched ones" in Norse). There are several secondhand accounts of their meetings. Some contemporaries described trade between the peoples. Other accounts describe clashes where the Skraelings defeated the Viking explorers with long spears, while still others claim the Vikings dominated the natives. Regardless of the circumstances, it seems that the Vikings made contact of some kind. This happened around 1000, nearly five hundred years before Columbus famously sailed the ocean blue.

Eventually, in 1003, Leif set sail for home and arrived at Greenland with a ship full of timber. In 1020, seventeen years later, the legendary Viking died. Many believe that Leif Erikson should receive more credit for his contributions in exploring the New World.

174

17. Which of the following is an opinion, rather than historical fact, expressed by the author?
    a. Leif Erikson was definitely the son of Erik the Red; however, historians debate the year of his birth.
    b. Leif Erikson's crew called the land Vinland since it was plentiful with grapes.
    c. Leif Erikson deserves more credit for his contributions in exploring the New World.
    d. Leif Erikson explored the Americas nearly five hundred years before Christopher Columbus.
    e. Leif Erikson was converted to Christianity in Norway.

18. Which of the following most accurately describes the author's main conclusion?
    a. Leif Erikson is a legendary Viking explorer.
    b. Leif Erikson deserves more credit for exploring America hundreds of years before Columbus.
    c. Spreading Christianity motivated Leif Erikson's expeditions more than any other factor.
    d. Leif Erikson contacted the natives nearly five hundred years before Columbus.
    e. Leif Erikson and his crew made contact with the local natives whom they called Skraelings.

19. Which of the following can be logically inferred from the passage?
    a. The Vikings disliked exploring the New World.
    b. Leif Erikson's banishment from Iceland led to his exploration of present-day Canada.
    c. Leif Erikson never shared his stories of exploration with the King of Norway.
    d. Historians have difficulty definitively pinpointing events in the Vikings' history.
    e. Leif Erikson chose to revisit the New World because he was no longer welcome in Greenland.

This article discusses the famous poet and playwright William Shakespeare. Read it and answer questions 20 – 23.

People who argue that William Shakespeare is not responsible for the plays attributed to his name are known as anti-Stratfordians (from the name of Shakespeare's birthplace, Stratford-upon-Avon). The most common anti-Stratfordian claim is that William Shakespeare simply was not educated enough or from a high enough social class to have written plays overflowing with references to such a wide range of subjects like history, the classics, religion, and international culture. William Shakespeare was the son of a glove-maker, he only had a basic grade school education, and he never set foot outside of England—so how could he have produced plays of such sophistication and imagination? How could he have written in such detail about historical figures and events, or about different cultures and locations around Europe? According to anti-Stratfordians, the depth of knowledge contained in Shakespeare's plays suggests a well-traveled writer from a wealthy background with a university education, not a countryside writer like Shakespeare. But in fact, there is not much substance to such speculation, and most anti-Stratfordian arguments can be refuted with a little background about Shakespeare's time and upbringing.

First of all, those who doubt Shakespeare's authorship often point to his common birth and brief education as stumbling blocks to his writerly genius. Although it is true that Shakespeare did not come from a noble class, his father was a very *successful* glove-maker and his mother was from a very wealthy landowning family—so while Shakespeare may have had a country upbringing, he was certainly from a well-off family and would have been educated accordingly. Also, even though he did not attend university, grade school education in Shakespeare's time was actually quite rigorous and exposed students to classic drama through writers like Seneca and Ovid. It is not unreasonable to believe that Shakespeare received a very solid foundation in poetry and literature from his early schooling.

Next, anti-Stratfordians tend to question how Shakespeare could write so extensively about countries and cultures he had never visited before (for instance, several of his most famous works like *Romeo and Juliet* and *The Merchant of Venice* were set in Italy, on the opposite side of Europe!). But again, this criticism does not hold up under scrutiny. For one thing, Shakespeare was living in London, a bustling metropolis of international trade, the most populous city in England, and a political and cultural hub of Europe. In the daily crowds of people, Shakespeare would certainly have been able to meet travelers from other countries and hear firsthand accounts of life in their home country. And, in addition to the influx of information from world travelers, this was also the age of the printing press, a jump in technology that made it possible to print and circulate books much more easily than in the past. This also allowed for a freer flow of information across different countries, allowing people to read about life and ideas from throughout Europe. One needn't travel the continent in order to learn and write about its culture.

20. Which sentence contains the author's thesis?
    a. People who argue that William Shakespeare is not responsible for the plays attributed to his name are known as anti-Stratfordians.
    b. First of all, those who doubt Shakespeare's authorship often point to his common birth and brief education as stumbling blocks to his writerly genius.
    c. It is not unreasonable to believe that Shakespeare received a very solid foundation in poetry and literature from his early schooling.
    d. Next, anti-Stratfordians tend to question how Shakespeare could write so extensively about countries and cultures he had never visited before.
    e. But in fact, there is not much substance to such speculation, and most anti-Stratfordian arguments can be refuted with a little background about Shakespeare's time and upbringing.

21. In the first paragraph, "How could he have written in such detail about historical figures and events, or about different cultures and locations around Europe?" is an example of which of the following?
    a. Hyperbole
    b. Onomatopoeia
    c. Rhetorical question
    d. Appeal to authority
    e. Figurative language

22. How does the author respond to the claim that Shakespeare was not well-educated because he did not attend university?
    a. By insisting upon Shakespeare's natural genius.
    b. By explaining grade school curriculum in Shakespeare's time.
    c. By comparing Shakespeare with other uneducated writers of his time.
    d. By pointing out that Shakespeare's wealthy parents probably paid for private tutors.
    e. By discussing Shakespeare's upbringing in London which was a political and cultural hub of Europe.

23. The word "bustling" in the third paragraph most nearly means which of the following?
    a. Busy
    b. Foreign
    c. Expensive
    d. Undeveloped
    e. Quiet

Questions 24-26 are based on the following article.

The Myth of Head Heat Loss

It has recently been brought to my attention that most people believe that 75% of your body heat is lost through your head. I had certainly heard this before, and am not going to attempt to say I didn't believe it when I first heard it. It is natural to be gullible to anything said with enough authority. But the "fact" that the majority of your body heat is lost through your head is a lie.

Let me explain. Heat loss is proportional to surface area exposed. An elephant loses a great deal more heat than an anteater because it has a much greater surface area than an anteater. Each cell has mitochondria that produce energy in the form of heat, and it takes a lot more energy to run an elephant than an anteater.

So, each part of your body loses its proportional amount of heat in accordance with its surface area. The human torso probably loses the most heat, though the legs lose a significant amount as well. Some people have asked, "Why does it feel so much warmer when you cover your head than when you don't?" Well, that's because your head, because it is not clothed, is losing a lot of heat while the clothing on the rest of your body provides insulation. If you went outside with a hat and pants but no shirt, not only would you look silly, but your heat loss would be significantly greater because so much more of you would be exposed. So, if given the choice to cover your chest or your head in the cold, choose the chest. It could save your life.

24. Why does the author compare elephants and anteaters?
   a. To express an opinion.
   b. To give an example that helps clarify the main point.
   c. To show the differences between them.
   d. To persuade why one is better than the other.
   e. To educate about animals.

25. Which of the following best describes the tone of the passage?
   a. Harsh
   b. Angry
   c. Casual
   d. Indifferent
   e. Comical

26. The author appeals to which branch of rhetoric to prove their case?
   a. Factual evidence
   b. Emotion
   c. Ethics and morals
   d. Author qualification
   e. Expert testimony

Answer Explanations #2

Section I: Logical Reasoning

1. D: The last sentence will complete the conclusion. The author is arguing that the extreme action—suspending *habeas corpus*—is justified in light of the unprecedented national emergency—the Civil War. Thus, Choice *D* is the correct answer. Choice *A* is unsupported by the rest of the argument. We do not know that the Civil War ended quickly after the suspension of *habeas corpus*. Choice *B* is contradicted by the preceding information since we know the South seceded before Lincoln's action. Choice *C* is true, but it is circular reasoning, merely repeating the first clause in the sentence, so it is not a strong conclusion. Choice *E* is irrelevant to the passage. The argument does not discuss the legality of the suspension under the Constitution.

2. E: The argument depends on American democracy being free from content discrimination. The argument tells us that repealing net neutrality will allow Internet service providers to discriminate content by slowing down speeds or charging additional fees. The threat of content discrimination is particularly severe, since many Internet service providers also own the most popular news networks. Consequently, without net neutrality, Internet service providers would favor their own news content. Choice *E* connects this threat with American democracy, so it is the correct answer. If you negate Choice *E*, then the argument unravels, since repealing net neutrality would no longer implicate the integrity of American democracy. Choices *A* and *D* are irrelevant and unmentioned in the argument. Choice *B* states the opposite of what is asserted in the passage. Choice *C* is the second-best answer, but it does not address the conclusion's connection between net neutrality and the integrity of American democracy.

3. B: The passage is clear that it is not only Dwight's mid-sized regional paper company that is struggling, but all of its regional and national competitors are as well. The paper industry is clearly undergoing a massive downturn, and Choice *B* provides an explanation—a fundamental change in demand. Thus, Choice *B* is the correct answer. Choice *A* is incorrect, because it is unclear whether mass layoffs were the *only* way to keep the company out of bankruptcy. Choice *C* speculates without any justification. Choice *D* is unsupported by the passage, and in addition, it is unlikely since the national paper companies are experiencing similar struggles. Choice *E* is the next best answer, but it is too specific to be supported by the passage.

4. C: The argument attributes the end of the dead-ball era to the increase in baseballs used per game. Choices *A*, *B*, and *E* all strengthen the argument since they explain why using more baseballs would increase scoring. Choice *D* is irrelevant to how scoring changed. Choice *C* is correct, because it weakens the argument. According to Choice *C*, Major League Baseball outlawed the spitball at the same time that the dead-ball era ended, so that could have been an alternative cause for the change.

5. C: The argument's conclusion is that recycling is the best possible way for people to preserve the environment, so the correct answer will show how recycling is more effective than other policy initiatives. Choice *C* is correct, because it states that recycling is more effective than green energy programs. Choices *B* and *E* are the next best answers, but they are not as strong as Choice *C*, which directly supports the supremacy of recycling. Choice *A* only touches on the potential for additional recycling. Choice *D* is irrelevant since it references recycling's economic benefits, rather than its environmental benefits.

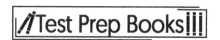

6. A: The paradox is that the advertising firm is running comparable advertising campaigns on the Internet and on television, but the firm makes two-thirds of its revenue from the Internet campaign despite the smaller audience size. Choice *A* states that the Internet advertisements more accurately target audiences. As such, the advertising is more profitable since it connects to audiences more likely to buy the goods or services, resolving the paradox. Thus, Choice *A* is the correct answer. Choice *C* does not explain the paradox since the advertisements are identical. Choices *B* and *D* would explain why the television advertising is more profitable, but that is the opposite of what we need. Choice *E* is irrelevant.

7. B: Choices *A* and *C* reference reasoning from the argument, but the politician does not do so incorrectly. The argument references an authority—a police chief—but that is an appropriate authority to attest to how the bill will impact the reporting of crime. Likewise, the analogy offers a relevant analogy since a flawed bill would undermine a government like warped wood would destabilize a house. Choices *D* and *E* are not part of the politician's reasoning. Choice *B* is correct, because the politician attacks another politician's character and motivation, rather than the strength of their argument.

8. E: The argument names two things that share a characteristic and then concludes that those things are similar. Although the order of the premises and conclusions is reversed, Choice *E* is correct since it follows the same reasoning. Choice *A* is nearly correct, but it does not contain the conclusion. Choice *B* is incorrect, because only some of the professional football players lift weights. Choice *C* is a logically-sound argument, but it has a different conclusion than the reasoning in the prompt. Choice *D* does not follow logically, and more importantly, it does not correctly parallel the argument.

9. B: The flawed reasoning is the drawing of a conclusion from percentages without knowing the underlying quantities. Choices *A, D,* and *E* are all logically sound and do not contain flaws. In Choice *A*, the test tubes contain the same amount of potassium cyanide, so any increase would make one more full than the other. Choice *D* appears superficially similar to the argument, but it adds the premise that Tyrone and Samantha started at the same salary and were receiving their first raise; therefore, the quantity is not a mystery, so a conclusion can be drawn based on the percentage increase. In Choice *E*, the salesman's salary entirely depends on commissions and set a record for sales this year, so his salary must be the highest ever. Choice *C* is flawed since it projects specific levels of future production based on past performance, but that is a very different flaw than that presented in the argument. Choice *B* is the correct answer since the initial attendance of the recitals and plays are unknown, like the initial salaries of Alexandra and Ronan, so a conclusion cannot be drawn from percentage changes.

10. A: Smart people read more than six books per year, and John is not a smart person; therefore, John must read fewer than seven books per year. Thus, Choice *A* is the correct answer. Choice *E could* be true, but it is too specific. We only know that John reads fewer than seven books per year. The rest of the answer choices draw incorrect conclusions from the statements.

11. C: The economist and politician disagree over the impact of government regulation, especially in regard to fostering competition. The economist believes that competition is highest in a free market since sophisticated corporations will be able to navigate complex regulations, unlike start-ups, which lack the necessary resources. In contrast, the politician believes that implementing more regulations would increase competition since it disrupts vertical integration, which consolidates resources at the expense of start-ups. Thus, Choice *C* is the correct answer. Both parties would agree with Choice *A*, so it must be incorrect. The politician would disagree with Choices *B* and *D*, but it is unclear how the economist views the existing regulatory scheme or consolidation of economic power. The economist would disagree with Choice *E*, but it is less clear how the politician feels about it. Although the politician would likely disagree, their argument only addresses abuses related to vertical integration and competition.

12. B: The argument proceeds by first stating a conclusion. Next, the argument offers two supporting premises—increasing individual freedom and the benefit of direct participation. Lastly, the argument finishes by setting up a false dichotomy between dictatorships and direct democracy, which assumes there are no alternative systems of government. Choice *B* accurately describes this process, and therefore, it is the correct answer. Choice *D* is the second-best answer, but it does not include how the argument begins with a conclusion. The remaining three answer choices incorrectly describe how the argument proceeds.

13. D: Jacob is a rich landowner, so we know for certain that he must pays taxes. Thus, Choice *D* is the correct answer. Choices *A* and *C* could be true since Jacob is rich and *some* rich people cheat on their taxes, but it is not necessarily true. Choice *B* is not supported anywhere in the argument. Choice *E* is incorrect since Jacob is a landowner and all landowners pay taxes.

14. A: The CEO believes that the current ethical standards are adequate, even going as far to describe the standards as the most stringent known to man. In contrast, the activist finds flaws in all of the current ethical standards. However, the CEO and activist both agree that some ethical standards are important; they just disagree as to what those ethical standards should be. Thus, Choice *A* is the correct answer. Of the remaining answer choices, the activist would agree with Choices *C, D,* and *E*, while the CEO would only agree with Choice *B*.

15. C: The question is asking for a conclusion to complete the argument. The premises state that alcohol holds some identifiable health benefits, prohibition would be impossible, and heavy consumption can be harmful. Choice *C* would be the best conclusion. Regulation would retain alcohol's health benefits, while limiting the harm, and prohibition would be impossible. Choices *A* and *B* restate the second and third premises, respectively. Choice *D* explains why the second premise is true, but it is not a conclusion. The premises are not strong enough to support Choice *E*.

16. C: The farmer is rejecting the conclusion of a report, because the farmer's main competition commissioned the report. Although the farmer's competition could definitely be biased, that does not justify rejecting the conclusion without offering any substantive counterargument. Thus, Choice *C* is the correct answer. Choice *D* is the next best answer, but Choice *C* more accurately states the problem with the farmer's argument.

17. D: According to the argument, serving in the presidential cabinet requires holding a graduate degree and passing a security clearance, and a felony prevents an applicant from receiving a security clearance. Rick cannot serve in the cabinet since he was convicted for driving under the influence. The correct answer will provide the assumption that fills a hole in the argument. So, for the argument to be logically sound, driving under the influence must be a felony, and that is why Rick cannot serve in the cabinet, since he has such a felony. Otherwise, if driving under the influence was a misdemeanor, then he could serve in the cabinet. Thus, Choice *D* is the correct answer. None of the other answer choices must be true for the argument to follow logically.

18. A: The correct answer will be an action with benefits that outweigh the costs. In Choice *A*, Tyree will be healthier, and the taxpayers will save money. There is no cost identified. Choices *B* and *E* involve enormous benefits, but the costs are likewise enormous. Choices *C* and *D* provide strong potential benefits, but the benefits are never actually realized. Thus, Choice *A* is the correct answer.

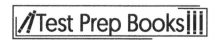

19. C: The argument is criticizing the country's current approach to fighting terrorism. The government is spending more money on fighting terrorism than any other initiative, even though terrorists kill a relatively small number of people. Thus, Choice *C* is the correct answer since it completes the conclusion with a principle requiring more proportional spending. The argument would support the first half of Choice *A* but reject the second half. Choices *B* and *D* are irrelevant for the argument's conclusion about terrorism. Choice *E* sounds similar to Choice *C*, but Choice *E* misstates the argument's first sentence. The argument is saying that addressing the fear inspired by terrorism—rather than the actual harm—is irrational.

20. A: The scientist's conclusion is that the government should force high-risk individuals to get vaccinated, even if against their wishes, before the vaccination becomes obsolete. Therefore, Choice *A* is the statement most applicable to this situation. Even though it's more broad, the scientist is likely to agree that the government should take drastic actions for other public health concerns. Choice *B* speculates without justification. The scientist does not mention other government objectives, let alone announce fighting influenza as the most important objective. The scientist also does not mention punishments for non-compliance, so Choice *C* is incorrect. Choices *D* and *E* are the opposite of what the argument implies. If Choice *E* was true, for example, the scientist would not be advocating for forced vaccinations.

21. D: The employer is arguing for paying employees the lowest possible wages, so we need the only answer that does not weaken that argument. Choice *A* weakens the argument since happy workers would be more efficient, completing more work than their lower-paid counterparts. Choice *B* hurts the company's image amongst customers who might stop patronizing the business. Choice *C* states that protests will disrupt business, which could result in decreased revenue. Choice *E* justifies giving employees raises, since it is cheaper than hiring and training new employees. In contrast, Choice *D* does not weaken the argument; it is merely irrelevant. Thus, Choice *D* is the correct answer.

22. E: The argument concludes that the giant kangaroo rat must be extinct since the study did not catch any. As the question is asking for a necessary assumption, the correct answer will unravel this argument. Choice *E* states that the giant kangaroo rat is only found in the San Joaquin Valley. If the giant kangaroo rat can be found somewhere other than the San Joaquin Valley, then the rat is not necessarily extinct. The population could have simply left the area where the study was conducted, or the giant kangaroo rat could be indigenous to an alternative or additional location, so just because the study found no rats does not mean the species is extinct. Thus, Choice *E* is the correct answer. None of the other answer choices are necessary assumptions.

23. A: The psychologist describes how treatment requires some nuance. There are some generally applicable techniques, while some patients require a specific technique tailored to their circumstances. Choice *A* best describes this proposition. Choice *B* contradicts the psychologist's argument. Choice *C* is the next strongest answer, but it does not include the need to tailor some of the techniques to specific circumstances. The psychologist does not mention patients that require no techniques at all or any possible harm caused to patients, so Choices *D* and *E* are both incorrect.

24. D: The historian argues that slavery is the primary cause of the Civil War, citing numerous examples and dismissing the second most common explanation—states' rights. Choice *D* best captures the historian's heavy emphasis on slavery, asserting that the role cannot be overstated. Thus, Choice *D* is the correct answer. Choice *A* is the second-best answer, but it is not nearly as strong as Choice *D*. The historian is making the claim that slavery was the primary cause of the Civil War, not merely a contributor. The other three answer choices are premises in the historian's argument.

25. E: The argument concludes that Earth's climate will change drastically in the near future unless deforestation is halted. We are looking for an assumption that would undermine this argument if it were not true. Choice *E* states that trees lower the amount of carbon dioxide in the atmosphere. If trees did not lower the amount of carbon dioxide in the atmosphere, then stopping deforestation would not impact climate change, which is caused by an increase in carbon dioxide. This completely undermines the argument. Choice *A* is contradictory to the entire argument. Choices *B* and *C* are irrelevant to the argument. Choice *D* is the second-best answer, but even if the trees could be replaced, the time to grow new trees could still be quite extensive, so deforestation would still need to be addressed.

Section II: Analytical Reasoning

1. B: If Sofia wins one of them, then a male must win the other one. This means that Choices *D* and *E* are incorrect. John can only win if Claire wins, so he can't win in this case. This means that Choice *A* is also incorrect. Tommy has one absence so he is not able to win, and Choice *C* is incorrect. This leaves Tristan, who is a male and has no other criteria that would disqualify him. This means Choice *B* is the correct answer.

2. D: Students can be automatically disqualified based on GPA and attendance. John has a high enough GPA and perfect attendance, so is not disqualified. This means that Choices *A* and *B* are incorrect. Tommy has a high enough GPA but he has one absence, therefore he can be disqualified. There is no additional information about Tristan though. So, he is not immediately disqualified. This means that Choice *C* is also incorrect. Patricia would be disqualified because of her GPA, however there is no additional information about Claire. So, Choice *E* is incorrect.

3. E: To be an acceptable combination they must meet all of the criteria. Tommy is disqualified because of his one absence. That makes Choices *B* and *C* incorrect. Patricia is disqualified because of her GPA. This makes Choice *D* incorrect. John, Sofia, and Claire are all eligible to win. However, John may only win if Claire wins. That makes Choice *A* incorrect and means that Choice *E* is correct.

4. C: Tommy and Patricia are both disqualified due to either GPA or absences. So, if neither John nor Sofia wins then that must mean that Tristan and Claire win. That means that Choice *C* is the correct answer.

5. A: If it is determined that Claire has multiple absences then that would disqualify her. Since, Tommy and Patricia are both disqualified as well that makes Choices *C, D,* and *E* all incorrect. Also, John can only win if Claire wins, which means he cannot win in this case. That makes Choice *B* incorrect. This means that Sofia and Tristan must win and Choice *A* is the correct answer.

6. C: 3. If he only works 7 hours between the first two days combined then he will have 17 hours of work left. This means that it will take him at least 3 more days since he can't work over 8 hours a day.

7. A: Choices *B* and *D* would not work because they add up to more than 8 hours. Choice *C* would not work because he does not frame out the two doors first. Choice *E* does not work because he cannot texture and paint on the same day.

8. C: If he starts his day by installing the cabinet hardware then that means it can't be his first day, and he can't frame out the two doors. So, Choice *A* is incorrect. If he laid tile and installed the gutters then he would work a total of 9 hours which he can't do, so Choice *B* is incorrect. Choices *D* and *E* are also incorrect because they require him to work too many hours. This leaves Choice *C* which does not violate any of the conditions assuming that this would be his last day so that he installs the vanity last.

9. C: Choice *A* is incorrect because he has to install the vanity last. This is only day 2 and he will still have more work after today. Choice *B* requires him to work 11 hours, so it is incorrect. Choice *D* is also incorrect because it only allows him to work 9 hours on day 2. At first Choice *E* may seem to work because it adds up to 10 hours, but he did not texture the walls on day 1. This means he can't paint on day 2. So, Choice *E* is also incorrect. This leaves Choice *C* which adds up to 10 hours and does not violate any other conditions.

10. E: Each of these options is possible other than Choice *E* which would require him to work 9 hours in one day. Choice *A* is 7 hours worth of work and a 1 hour lunch. Even if the lunch counted as 1 of his 8 hours he is still fine. Choice *B* adds up to 16 hours and can be broken into two 8 hour days. Also the texture can be done on day 2 and the painting on day 3. So, it is possible for this to happen. It is also possible for him to stretch this out to 5 days. So it is possible for Choice *C* to happen. If he uses one day to just paint then that leaves him 3 full days, or 24 hours, to complete everything else. There are only 19 more hours of work so it is possible for him to do this.

11. C: A Turkey Club, Salad, and Onion Rings may all be purchased together and on a Tuesday. Choice *A* is incorrect because a Patty Melt may not be purchased on a Tuesday. Choices *B* and *E* are incorrect because French Fries may only be purchased with a sandwich. A Philly Cheesesteak and a Turkey Club may never be purchased together which makes Choice *D* incorrect.

12. D: This question looks at the restriction of certain items on certain days. It may help to make a table like the one below and list each item that can be purchased on that day. Saturday and Sunday can be left off because they were not answer choices.

Monday	Tuesday	Wednesday	Thursday	Friday
Hot Dog	Hot Dog	Patty Melt	Patty Melt	Patty Melt
Salad	Salad	Hot Dog	Pizza	Pizza
		Salad	Hot Dog	Salad
			Salad	

Once the table is complete we see that Thursday is the only day that all four of these items may be purchased.

13. E: This question asks about which choice could be true. So, start by looking for something that would make each choice false and then eliminate that choice. Choice *A* is false because Patty Melts are not available on Mondays. Choice *B* is false because Hot Dogs are not available on a Friday. Choices *C* and *D* are incorrect because the items that were purchased can't be purchased together. This leaves Choice *E* which doesn't break any of the restrictions.

14. B: For this question, anything that has a restriction on days it can be purchased can be immediately eliminated. This makes choices *A, C,* and *E* incorrect. Choice *D* is incorrect because the Onion Rings can't be purchased without a sandwich. This leaves Choice *B* which doesn't break any of the restrictions.

15. A: There are a total of 8 items that the restaurant sells. The only item that is not available for sale on Friday is Hot Dogs. While it is true that a Philly Cheesesteak and Turkey Club cannot be purchased together, the customer is just selecting a single item, so either a Philly Cheesesteak or a Turkey Club would be viable menu options along with Pizza or a Patty Melt. Salad is not an option since it requires purchasing another item, and Onions Rings and French Fries also require a sandwich. This means that 4 different single items may be purchased on Friday.

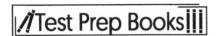

16. A: A possible order is Eli (Monday), Ashley (Tuesday), Dan (Wednesday), Ben (Thursday), Emily and John (Friday). The best method is to try a sketch out a grid to fill out which student might meet each day. After that, the answer choices provided can be examined and then ruled out using a process of elimination where contradictions exist with the provided details. Choices *B* and *E* can be eliminated because it lists Ashley as the Wednesday student, but one of the given criteria is that Wednesday's student is not a female. For example, Choices *C* can be eliminated because it lists Dan as the Friday student, but one of the given criteria is that Dan cannot meet on Fridays. Finally, Choice *D* can be eliminated because Eli is after Ashley but he needs to meet before her.

17. A: This question is also best solved through making a grid of the knowns and trying to see which student may fall on which day. We have six students. We know it's not John, since he is Friday, so that leaves 5. It can't be Emily, Ashley, or Ben since they all fall after other people or days (Emily is after Wednesday, while Ashley is after Eli, and Ben is after Ashley). That leaves two students, Eli or Dan. However, if we put Dan in for Monday, then Eli would need to be Tuesday so that Ashley could be Thursday (she's female so she can't be Wednesday) and Ben would be on Friday with John. But this would force Emily to be on Wednesday and she can't be Wednesday, because she's female, so Dan cannot be Monday, which just leaves Eli.

18. B: If Emily is not on Thursday, she has to be on Friday since she is after Wednesday. We know it can't be John (he's Friday). It cannot be Eli (he's before two people). This eliminates Choices *A, C, D,* and *E.* This leaves Ben or Dan.

19. B: This problem can be solved through process of elimination and seeing which days violate the stipulations of the conditions. We know that Ashley cannot be on Monday, Wednesday, or Friday based on the conditions because the Wednesday appointment is with a male student, and Ashley has people before and after her, so she can't be on Monday or Friday. If Ashley were to meet Thursday, Ben must meet Friday, but since John also must Friday, that would violate the rule that Emily must meet after Wednesday. Therefore, Choice *B* is correct; Ashley can only meet Tuesday.

20. E: Again, let's look at each of these choices one by one to determine which can be eliminated. Choice *A* can be eliminated because Eli can't be last, since it would violate the first condition. Choices *B* and *C* can be eliminated because if Ben is Thursday, Emily has to be Friday since she is after Wednesday according to the fifth condition. Choice *D* can be eliminated because a female student cannot be in Wednesday as this would violate the second condition. This leaves Choice *E,* which satisfies the provided stipulations.

21. E: Let's consider each choice. Choices *A* and *B* could work if Omelets, Waffles, Chili, Chopped Salad, Steak, and Chicken Parmesan are selected. Choice *C* could be true as long as Pad Thai and Chicken Parmesan are selected. Because there are no restrictions stated for Omelets or Waffles, Choice *D* can be true. Choice *E* violates some of the conditions. When Steak and Pad Thai are added to the box, then Paninis can't be. This means that the Chopped Salad and the Chili would have to be added to get two lunches. But this is problematic because when Chopped Salads are added, Chicken Parmesan needs to be.

22. C: Since there is only one lunch item, then a total of three foods are selected because we need an equal number of foods per meal type. Since Paninis are the only lunch food, Chili and Chopped Salads are not included. When Chili isn't included, French Toast cannot be added, but Waffles or Omelets can be. When Paninis are included, Steak cannot be added but Pad Thai or Chicken Parmesan could work for the dinner option. Therefore, there are four possible combinations.

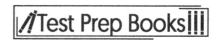

23. E: All we need to do is identify and examine the mutually exclusive foods and then analyze their restrictions. Based on the stated conditions, the maximum number of foods can be added is 8. Paninis would be excluded because they can't be packed with Steak or Chopped Salad. This leaves 8 other foods that could be packed.

24. D: This problem presents an interesting scenario because the packed boxes do not have a fixed number of items. They need to have at least three (one from each meal type) and they must contain a multiple of three since there must be an equal number of choices per meal selected. This makes six a valid choice. All items cannot be selected (nine) without violating rules, so we know it's either three or six. This allows us to rule out Choice *C*. Choices *A* can be eliminated because it doesn't contain an option for each meal. Choice *B* can be eliminated because French Toast cannot be included without Chili. Choice *E* can be eliminated because Chicken Parmesan must be included if Chopped Salad is. This leaves choice *D*, which does satisfy the conditions.

25. C: When Chopped Salads are selected, Chicken Parmesan must also be selected. Since Chicken Parmesan and Pad Thai are two dinners we know we need at least two of each meal. Of the lunch foods, when Chopped Salads are added, Paninis cannot be, so Chili must be. Lastly, any of the breakfast options have an equal choice of being added since they don't have restrictions so we don't have one choice that *must* be added for breakfast so we can rule out Choices *A, B,* and *D.* Choice *E* does not work because Steak does not have to be selected since Pad Thai fills the first dinner slot and Chicken Parmesan takes the second.

Section III: Logical Reasoning

1. B: The argument admits the serious health risks associated with smoking, but it concludes that the United States should not ban smoking due to the principles of liberty and free market business. The Surgeon General is prioritizing principles over health risks. Thus, Choice *B* is the correct answer. The argument does not mention marketing campaigns and never attributes any blame to big business, so Choice *A* is incorrect. Choice *C* is the second strongest answer. The Surgeon General heavily emphasizes the importance of freedom; however, Choice *C* is too broad, as it asserts that Americans can do *whatever* they want with their bodies. Choice *D* is incorrect since the argument does not mention the power of education, and Choice *E* contradicts the main point of the argument.

2. C: The correct answer will be a dependent assumption, so if it were not true, then the argument would no longer be logically coherent. Thus, Choice *C* is the correct answer. Every client who the trainer has worked with loses weight. If nobody the trainer has worked with has weight loss as a goal, then the trainer's exercise routine is allowing anybody to meet their goal. This directly undermines the conclusion. Choice E is the second-best answer, but the argument does not mention desirable outcomes, only goals. Losing weight could be an unhealthy outcome, while still being the goal of those clients working with the trainer. The other three answer choices appear reasonable at face-value, but they are not dependent assumptions.

3. C: The correct answer must necessarily be true. The second sentence of the argument says that reality television stars are never covered on the news, except when they become pregnant; therefore, pregnant reality television stars are covered on the news. The first sentence of the argument says that the news exclusively covers important current events. As a result, pregnant reality television stars must be important current events. Choice *C* is the correct answer, because *some* pregnancies are important current events. Choice *D* is too broad since the exception for pregnant reality television stars only allows for the possibility of the news covering the event. In addition, the argument does not mention pregnancies of non-reality television stars. Choice *E* is incorrect for the same reason. Choices *A* and *B* are contradicted by the argument's second sentence.

4. E: The passage describes two different types of submarines that play different roles in the American military. The last sentence states that the United States plans to deploy a submarine off the coast of the foreign country to gather intelligence. The most accurate conclusion is that the United States should deploy an attack submarine. The attack submarine is capable of spying. Thus, Choice *E* is the correct answer. The ballistic submarine carries nuclear weapons and provides little utility when located on the coast, so Choice *A* is incorrect. The other answers cannot be correct since the passage never mentions developing new submarines, spying through foreign intelligence services, or pre-emptive attacks.

5. C: The correct answer will be something that the passage does not infer. Choice *A* is a correct inference. The passage states that ballistic submarine's minimum range is 3,400 miles, and as a result, there is little advantage to placing a ballistic submarine off the coast. Thus, ballistic submarines are more useful if located in the open sea. Choice *B* is also a correct inference since the United States is seeking to collect more intelligence, rather than launch a pre-emptive attack, even though the United States believes it is under threat. Choice *D* is inferred from the capabilities of attack submarines. Choice *E* is inferred since the United States needs intelligence, and the passage only discusses using submarines. The passage never mentions whether an attack submarine can carry intercontinental ballistic missiles. Thus, Choice *C* is the correct answer.

6. B: The argument justifies big-game trophy hunting under financial reasoning, so the correct answer will likely address the role of money in some way. Choice *B* states that the African countries could not otherwise afford to protect the animals. So, big-game trophy hunting should be allowed since it actually helps more animals than it hurts. Thus, Choice *B* is the correct answer. Choice *E* is the second-best answer, but morality is less important than how the money is used to help animals. Choices *A* and *C* are unsupported by the passage. The author would agree with Choice *D*, but it does not strengthen the argument.

7. A: The discrepancy is that cities suffer from air pollution yet they are not considering a proven method of reducing air pollution. Choice *A* fails to explain the discrepancy since it is contradicted by the passage. Rural areas use nuclear power, so the waste cannot be *impossible* to discard in a safe manner. Thus, Choice A is the correct answer. Choices *B*, *C*, and *E* explain the discrepancy by offering reasons why urban areas would be less likely than rural areas to adopt nuclear power. Choice *D* explains the discrepancy by asserting that nuclear power is cost-prohibitive for urban areas.

8. B: In this argument, the author sets a necessary condition. If students do not read all of the mandatory books, they cannot earn an A. However, this is not the same as claiming that reading all of the mandatory books guarantees an A, as the conclusion incorrectly asserts. That would be a sufficient condition. Thus, Choice *B* is correct since the author is confusing a necessary and sufficient condition. The other four answer choices do not apply to the argument.

9. A: The argument establishes two necessary conditions for getting elected as President. Failing to win the popular vote is addressed as not being a requirement. Thus, Choice *A* is the correct answer, because receiving more than 270 Electoral College votes is a necessary condition, so it is impossible to become President without meeting the condition. Choices *B* and *C* contradict a necessary condition. Choices *D* and *E* are unsupported by the passage.

10. D: The two owners are arguing over whether digital bookstores can survive without brick and mortar bookstores. The brick and mortar bookstore owner contends that his store is a place to introduce people

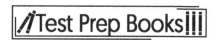

to new books and expand their preferences, creating demand for books that keeps the publishing industry alive. In contrast, the digital bookstore owner argues that his store serves the same function due to its enormous catalogue and readily-available synopses and reviews. Thus, Choice *D* is the correct answer. The brick and mortar bookstore owner would disagree with Choice *A*, but the digital bookstore owner never makes that assertion. Both owners explicitly agree with Choice *B*. The brick and mortar bookstore owner does not dispute Choice *C*. Although both owners would likely dispute Choice *E*, neither owner explicitly discusses customers' preferences.

11. B: The argument identifies a problem—inadequate voter participation and dissatisfaction with representatives—and concludes that adopting rank choice voting would solve the problem. Thus, Choice *B* is the correct answer. The argument does more than merely express Americans' dissatisfaction with the status quo, since half of the argument is devoted to the potential of rank choice voting, so Choice *A* is incorrect. The argument does explain rank choice voting, as suggested by Choice *C*, but the argument is more than merely informative. Choices *D* and *E* are premises in the argument and not the primary purpose.

12. E: The author provides evidence as to how livestock is harming the environment and then proposes dietary changes as a potential solution. Choice *E* best expresses the logical conclusion—people can reduce their environmental impact by adopting dietary changes. Choice *A* is too extreme, speculating that environmental harm will destroy the Earth. Similarly, Choice *B* goes too far. The author states that dietary changes can have a dramatic impact, but the author does not claim that this is the only solution. Choices *C* and *D* are premises, and therefore, not the conclusion.

13. D: The author is claiming that communism is the greatest source of evil on the planet due to the death toll the author attributes to communism. The last sentence states that ten percent of Americans support communism despite its apparent ugly history. As a result, the author would agree that some people should not be trusted to decide what system their government should adopt. Thus, Choice *D* is the correct answer. Choice *A* is unsupported by the argument. Famine is cited as the leading cause of death, but even if famine did not occur, the author would still likely oppose communism based on the remaining deaths. Choice *B* is the second-best answer, but the author does not directly address the merits of capitalism. The author would disagree with Choice *C*. The author does not mention what caused both World Wars, let alone attribute the cause to communism, so Choice *E* cannot be correct.

14. B: The correct answer will be a dependent assumption. As such, if the correct answer is negated, then the argument will fall apart. Choice *B* is the correct answer. If it were not easier to take advantages of deductibles by filing taxes online, then taxpayers would not save more money. The other answer choices do not undermine the argument in a similar way.

15. A: The argument's conclusion is that electronic cigarettes should not be subject to the same regulations as other products that contain nicotine. Less harmful additives and lower mortality rates are the reasons why the author believes electronic cigarettes should be exempt from the regulation. The correct answer will explain why the regulations should still apply, even if electronic cigarettes are healthier than other nicotine products. According to Choice *A*, the regulations exist to prevent children from using nicotine, presumably under the theory that if children use electronic cigarettes, then they will become addicted to nicotine and use more harmful products in the future. As a result, the relative health benefits are irrelevant, undermining the author's only evidence. Thus, Choice *A* is the correct answer. Choice *C* is irrelevant. Choices *B*, *D*, and *E* weaken the argument but not to the same degree as Choice *A*.

16. C: The argument relies on an inappropriate authority. Michael decided not to settle the case after his friend, Jim, told him that Meredith was negligently crossing the street. Jim is a widget salesman, not a lawyer, so Michael should not be relying on his legal advice. Thus, Choice *C* is the correct answer. Choice *A* is incorrect. The argument does rely on a probability—a 100-percent chance of a recovery—but it is correctly assumed to be certain since it does apply to Meredith's case. Choice *B* is incorrect, because the argument does not confuse causation with correlation. The only causation mentioned is the car accident and Meredith's broken hip, which is correct. Choices *D* and *E* do not appear in the argument.

17. A: The argument is claiming that customers should hire an advertising agency solely due to the fact that it has the most employees, ignoring all other possible factors, like specialization or price. Choice *A* follows the same reasoning, concluding that a certain tree is the best tree for growing apples since it produces the most apples, ignoring other factors, like apple quality or cost of maintaining the tree. Thus, Choice *A* is the correct answer. The other answer choices contain different reasoning and stronger logical cohesiveness.

18. B: The argument states that social media websites are the most profitable when they have the most engaged users, and sensational stories increase user engagement. However, the last complete sentence states that user engagement will decline when the sensational stories become too overwhelming. As a result, the correct answer will involve some type of balance. Choice *B* completes the sentence by stating that the social media company would be best served by monitoring the ratio of sensationalized and factual articles. This strikes the necessary balance. Thus, Choice *B* is the correct answer. Choice *A* goes too far. Although sensationalized stories can harm the social media websites, the argument also emphasizes their importance to user engagement. Choice *C* is the second-best answer since it would be useful for the social media websites to know more about their customers; however, Choice *B* more directly relates to the argument. Choice *D* is not mentioned in the argument, and Choice *E* is not supported by the argument.

19. C: The argument's conclusion is that high schools should only teach abstinence, because students practicing abstinence will not incur an unplanned pregnancy or contract a sexually-transmitted disease. The correct answer will either be irrelevant or strengthen the argument, while the others will weaken it. Choices *A* and *B* weaken the argument by asserting that teaching abstinence does not result in abstinent students. Choices *D* and *E* weaken the argument by emphasizing the benefits of teaching contraceptive use. Thus, Choice *C* is the correct answer. Whether religious organizations support abstinence is irrelevant to whether abstinence lowers the risk or unplanned pregnancy or obtaining a sexually-transmitted disease.

20. E: Bill meets the standards for all of the professions, so he *could* be any of the five professions. However, we need the profession that *must* be true. Only secretaries can type one hundred words per minute, and Bill can type one hundred words per minute; therefore, Bill must be a secretary. If Bill were not a secretary, then he would not be able to type one hundred words per minute. Thus, Choice *E* is the correct answer. All of the other answer choices are only possibilities.

21. E: According to the argument, the national media covers topics people find interesting to increase advertising revenue. Election reform is not covered, so an inference can be drawn that people do not find that topic to be interesting. Thus, Choice *E* is the correct answer. Choice *A* is the second-best answer; the argument draws an analogy between the local news covering violent crime and the national media covering political scandals. However, we do not explicitly know if the local news also depends on advertising revenue and tends to cover topics of interest. The analogy could just be that both overemphasize one specific topic. As such, Choice *E* is more strongly supported. Choice *B* is not

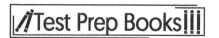

supported by the argument. The national media definitely covers political scandals, but there is no support for that being the only topic. Choices *C* and *D* are similarly unsupported by the argument.

22. D: The argument's first sentence is a generalization since it says *most*, the second sentence identifies an exception, and the third sentence is a conclusion based on the exception. Choice *D* correctly describes how the argument proceeds. Choices *B* and *E* cannot be the correct since the first sentence is not a hard rule. Choice *A* is incorrect, because the generalization is not applied; instead, the second sentence is an exception to the generalization. Similarly, Choice *C* is incorrect, because the argument does not apply any additional evidence.

23. E: The question is asking what *must* be true, rather than *could* be true. If it is Tuesday, then Andy must be miming since he mimes every day that is not Wednesday. Although Andy is singing, we do not know whether it is raining. The contra positive of the first sentence is "If Andy is not singing, then it is raining." The possibility of it raining and Andy singing is still open. Thus, Choice *E* is the correct answer since it is the only answer that *must* be true.

24. D: The argument's conclusion is that high school students should not necessarily decide to attend college since the cost is prohibitive and viable alternatives exist. The correct answer will strengthen the argument, while the others will either weaken the argument or be irrelevant. Choice *D* strengthens the argument. If employers value work experience and self-starters more than formal education, then that is additional reason not to attend increasingly unaffordable traditional colleges. Thus, Choice *D* is the correct answer. Choices *A* and *B* weaken the argument. Although the author would almost certainly agree with Choice *C*, what the government should have done in the past is irrelevant to what high school students should do in the future. Choice *E* is similarly irrelevant.

25. D: The correct answer will be a dependent assumption underlying the conclusion. The conclusion is that fantasy football contributed to the increase in television ratings for National Football League games. In support of that conclusion, the author explains how the start of fantasy football coincided with the increased television ratings and claims that fantasy players now had a vested interest in nearly every game. Choice *D* is the correct answer, because if it were not true, then the argument would not make any sense. If no fantasy players watched National Football League games, then fantasy football could not have contributed to increased television ratings. Choice *A* sounds reasonable, but it does not directly undermine the argument, like Choice *D*. The other three answer choices are irrelevant.

Section IV: Reading Comprehension

1. C: A defender of the study of humanities in "modern" schooling as it relates to both literature and science. Choice *A* is incorrect; the author of passage B isn't advocating for the study of science, but defending the study of humanities. Choice *B* is also incorrect; this position is a characteristic of the author of passage A. Choice *D* is incorrect; a good portion of the argument is focused on the advantages of Greek and Roman antiquity. However, we see in the conclusion of passage B that Matthew Arnold, the author, uses the knowledge of classical texts as a proponent to the knowledge of both literature and science; that classical texts aid in the knowledge of both areas of studies and a broader "criticism of modern life." Finally, Choice *E* is incorrect; passage B uses the quotes from Huxley not as axioms, but to discredit the argument of passage A.

2. A: Passage B is written in response to passage A; passage B uses textual evidence from passage A to contradict passage A's argument. Choice *B* is incorrect; passage B does not enthusiastically agree with passage A. We see passage B use passage A's own rhetoric to contradict itself. Choices *C, D,* and *E* are

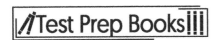

also incorrect; we know that passage B was written in response to passage A because passage B uses quoted phrases from passage A.

3. E: The authors of the passages would be most likely to disagree over whether classical literature lends itself to the progression of future generations. Choice *A* is incorrect; the framework of the two arguments doesn't touch on what areas science consists of. Choice *B* is also incorrect; there is not enough information in the two passages to discern whether the authors would disagree over Eastern and Western literature. Choice *C* is incorrect; the passages seemingly disagree over science and its place in academia; however, passage B only argues for the place of Greek and Roman antiquity in academia, and not against the implementation of science. Choice *D* is incorrect; the authors might possibly disagree over this choice. The author of passage A would be more prone to agree that art should have a justified end, and would perhaps thus argue for political purposes. However, this isn't the *best* choice.

4. B: The author of passage B thinks that knowing Greek and Roman culture is valuable because it is a culture that offers foundation and experience on an array of subjects that we can learn from in the present. The author of passage B begins his second paragraph by saying "The same also as to knowing our own and other modern nations with the like aim of getting to understand ourselves and the world." The author of passage B thinks a key to understanding the building blocks of humanity is to know a wide array of subjects and past that contribute to humanity as a whole.

5. D: That what was studied and valued in the Middle Ages is in stark contrast to the scientific process valued in the author's period. Choices *A* and *E* are incorrect; the author is not saying that the Middle Ages were a "formidable period of scientific progress" or "superior to those opinions taught centuries later." Choices *B* and *C* are also incorrect; they both use the same language as presented in the last paragraph; however, they twist the words around and do not offer a truthful summary of the last paragraph.

6. B: The author clearly states that education is crucial to the survival of the human race, and it can be easily inferred that if this is true, then improvements to our educational system are certainly worth fighting for. Choices *A* and *C* are incorrect because there is nothing in the passage that relates to these statements. Choice *D* is incorrect because it directly contradicts what the author states about all children's ability to learn. Choice *E* is a point made in the passage, but it is not the overall main point.

7. A: Clearly, this author feels passionately about the importance of education. This is evident especially in his word choices. For this reason, all the other answer choices are incorrect.

8. C: Based on the author's passionate stance about the importance of education for all children, this answer choice makes the most sense. For this reason, all the other answer choices are incorrect.

9. D: The author mentions the importance of parent involvement and communication between school and home. He also devotes one full paragraph to the impact of technology on education. The issue of teachers having high expectations for students is also discussed. Nowhere in the passage does the author mention the cost of textbooks, so Choice *D* is correct.

10. D: This is the correct answer choice because expository writing involves straightforward, factual information and analysis. It is unbiased and does not rely on the writer's personal feelings or opinions. Choice *A* is incorrect because narrative writing tells a story. Choice *B* is incorrect because persuasive writing is intended to change the reader's mind or position on a topic. Choice *C* is incorrect because technical writing attempts to outline a complex object or process. Choice *E* is incorrect because descriptive writing appeals to the senses to create a picture for the reader.

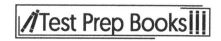

11. E: This is the correct answer choice because the passage begins by describing Carver's childhood fascination with painting and later returns to this point when it states that at the end of his career, "Carver returned to his first love of art." For this reason, all the other answer choices are incorrect.

12. A: This is the correct answer choice because the passage contains a definition of the term, *agricultural monoculture*, which is very similar to this answer; therefore, all the other answer choices are incorrect.

13. C: This is the correct answer choice because there is ample evidence in the passage that refers to Carver's brilliance and the fact that his discoveries had a far-reaching impact both then and now. There is no evidence in the passage to support any of the other answer choices; therefore, they are all incorrect.

14. B: The author is opposed to tobacco. He cites disease and deaths associated with smoking. He points to the monetary expense and aesthetic costs. Choice *A* is incorrect because alternatives to smoking are not addressed in the passage. Choice *C* is incorrect because it does not summarize the passage but rather is just a premise. Choice *D* is incorrect because, while these statistics are a premise in the argument, they do not represent a summary of the piece. Choice *E* is incorrect because addiction is discussed in the passage but is not a summary of the passage. Choice *B* is the correct answer because it states the three critiques offered against tobacco and expresses the author's conclusion.

15. C: We are looking for something the author would agree with, so it should be anti-smoking or an argument in favor of quitting smoking. Choice *A* is incorrect because the author does not speak against means of cessation. Choice *B* is incorrect because the author does not reference other substances but does speak of how addictive nicotine, a drug in tobacco, is. Choice *D* is incorrect because the author would not encourage reducing taxes to encourage a reduction of smoking costs, thereby helping smokers to continue the habit. Choice *E* is incorrect because when smokers start smoking is not mentioned in the article. Choice *C* is correct because the author is attempting to persuade smokers to quit smoking.

16. E: Here, look for an opinion of the authors rather than a fact or statistic. Choice *A* is incorrect because quoting statistics from the Centers of Disease Control and Prevention is stating facts, not opinions. Choice *B* is incorrect because it expresses the fact that cigarettes sometimes cost more than a few gallons of gas. It would be an opinion if the author said that cigarettes were not affordable. Choice *C* is incorrect because yellow stains are a known possible adverse effect of smoking. Choice *D* is incorrect because the average lifespan of a smoker would be a statistic or fact. Choice *E* is correct as an opinion because smell is subjective. Some people might like the smell of smoke, they might not have working olfactory senses, and some people might not find the smell of smoke akin to "pervasive nastiness," so this is the expression of an opinion. Thus, Choice *E* is the correct answer.

17. C: Choice *A* is incorrect because it describes facts: Leif Erikson was the son of Erik the Red and historians debate Leif's date of birth. These are not opinions. Choice *B* is incorrect; that Erikson called the land Vinland is a verifiable fact as is Choice *D* because he did contact the natives almost 500 years before Columbus. Choice *E* is incorrect because Leif Erikson was converted to Christianity in Norway. Choice *C* is the correct answer because it is the author's opinion that Erikson deserves more credit. That, in fact, is his conclusion in the piece, but another person could argue that Columbus or another explorer deserves more credit for opening up the New World to exploration. Rather than being an incontrovertible fact, it is a subjective value claim.

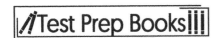

18. B: Choice *A* is incorrect because the author aims to go beyond describing Erikson as merely a legendary Viking. Choice *C* is incorrect because the author does not focus on Erikson's motivations, let alone name the spreading of Christianity as his primary objective. Choice *D* is incorrect because it is a premise that Erikson contacted the natives 500 years before Columbus, which is simply a part of supporting the author's conclusion. Choice *E* is incorrect because Leif Erikson making contact with the natives is discussed, but it is not the author's main conclusion. Choice *B* is correct because, as stated in the previous answer, it accurately identifies the author's statement that Erikson deserves more credit than he has received for being the first European to explore the New World.

19. D: Choice *A* is incorrect because the author never addresses the Vikings' state of mind or emotions. Choice *B* is incorrect because the author does not elaborate on Erikson's exile and whether he would have become an explorer if not for his banishment. Choice *C* is incorrect because there is not enough information to support this premise. It is unclear whether Erikson informed the King of Norway of his finding. Although it is true that the King did not send a follow-up expedition, he could have simply chosen not to expend the resources after receiving Erikson's news. It is not possible to logically infer whether Erikson told him. Choice *E* is incorrect because the passage does not state why Erikson chose to revisit the New World. Choice *D* is correct because there are two examples—Leif Erikson's date of birth and what happened during the encounter with the natives—of historians having trouble pinning down important details in Viking history.

20. E: But in fact, there is not much substance to such speculation, and most anti-Stratfordian arguments can be refuted with a little background about Shakespeare's time and upbringing. The thesis is a statement that contains the author's topic and main idea. The main purpose of this article is to use historical evidence to provide counterarguments to anti-Stratfordians. Choice *A* is simply a definition; Choice *B* states part of the reasoning of the anti-Stratfordians; Choice *C* is a supporting detail, not a main idea; and Choice *D* represents an idea of anti-Stratfordians, not the author's opinion.

21. C: Rhetorical question. This requires readers to be familiar with different types of rhetorical devices. A rhetorical question is a question that is asked not to obtain an answer but to encourage readers to more deeply consider an issue.

22. B: By explaining grade school curriculum in Shakespeare's time. This question asks readers to refer to the organizational structure of the article and demonstrate understanding of how the author provides details to support their argument. This particular detail can be found in the second paragraph: "even though he did not attend university, grade school education in Shakespeare's time was actually quite rigorous."

23. A: Busy. This is a vocabulary question that can be answered using context clues. Other sentences in the paragraph describe London as "the most populous city in England" filled with "crowds of people," giving an image of a busy city full of people. Choice *B* is incorrect because London was in Shakespeare's home country, not a foreign one. Choice *C* is not mentioned in the passage. Choice *D* is not a good answer choice because the passage describes how London was a popular and important city, probably not an undeveloped one. Choice *E* is incorrect because quiet would be the opposite of how the city of London is described.

24. B: Choice *B* is correct because the author is trying to demonstrate the main idea, which is that heat loss is proportional to surface area, and so they compare two animals with different surface areas to clarify the main point. Choice *A* is incorrect because the author uses elephants and anteaters to prove a point, that heat loss is proportional to surface area, not to express an opinion. Choice *C* is incorrect because though the author does use them to show differences, they do so in order to give examples that prove the above points. Choice *D* is incorrect because there is no language to indicate favoritism between the two animals. Choice *E* is incorrect because the passage is not about animals and only uses the elephant and the anteater to make a point.

25. C: Because of the way the author addresses the reader and the colloquial language the author uses (i.e., "let me explain," "so," "well," didn't," "you would look stupid," etc.), Choice *C* is the best answer because it has a much more casual tone than the usual informative article. Choice *A* may be a tempting choice because the author says the "fact" that most of one's heat is lost through their head is a "lie" and that someone who does not wear a shirt in the cold looks stupid. However, this only happens twice within the passage, and the passage does not give an overall tone of harshness. Choice *B* is incorrect because again, while not necessarily nice, the language does not carry an angry charge. The author is clearly not indifferent to the subject because of the passionate language that they use, so Choice *D* is incorrect.

26. A: The author gives logical examples and reasons in order to prove that most of one's heat is not lost through their head, therefore *A* is correct. *B* is incorrect because there is not much emotionally charged language in this selection, and even the small amount present is greatly outnumbered by the facts and evidence. *C* is incorrect because there is no mention of ethics or morals in this selection. *D* is incorrect because the author never qualifies himself as someone who has the authority to be writing on this topic. *E* is incorrect because the author never mentions any specific experts as references.

Practice Test #3

Section I: Logical Reasoning

Time – 35 minutes

25 Questions

1. Professor: Politicians should only be required to abide by the strict letter of the law—not the spirit of the law—since they need flexibility to govern. Trading political favors for a politician's personal financial gain is illegal under an anti-corruption statute. A state governor awarded a contract to a local construction company outside of the usual bidding process. Only the local construction company made any personal financial gain, so...

Which one of the following most logically completes the professor's argument?
 a. the state governor should have followed the usual bidding process.
 b. the state governor is guilty of violating the anti-corruption statute.
 c. the state governor is not guilty of violating the anti-corruption statute.
 d. the state governor wasted the taxpayers' money.
 e. the state governor broke the spirit of the law, while abiding by the strict letter of the law.

2. Zoos provide a space for the public to view wild animals, allowing people to forge a stronger relationship with nature. In addition, zoos save endangered species through breeding programs. A combination of public funds and private donations funds most zoos. More tigers now live in Texas than in the wild, as state law allows tigers to be kept as pets.

The author would most likely agree with which one of the following?
 a. The fact that more tigers live in Texas than the in the wild is a positive development.
 b. Wild animals are appropriate pets.
 c. The government should provide more funding for zoos.
 d. All wild animals should be held in captivity.
 e. Wild animals should sometimes be held in captivity.

3. Nutritionist: The food pyramid was amended to provide the public with a healthier nutrition plan to combat the obesity epidemic. The base of the previous food pyramid—the grains group—advised people to eat six-to-eleven servings of pasta and bread per day. In contrast, the updated pictorial nutrition guide shows a plate, and it reduces the percentage of dietary intake of grains and replaces the difference with lean proteins and vegetables. The updated guide has been wildly successful, as citizens have lost a significant amount of weight.

Which one of the following, if true, most strengthens the nutritionist's conclusion?
 a. Eating six-to-eleven servings of pasta and bread increased citizens' risk of heart disease.
 b. Eating more lean proteins and vegetables contributes to weight loss.
 c. The old food pyramid used horizontal layers, while the updated guide uses vertical layers.
 d. The government published the old pyramid, while private nutritionists devised the updated pictorial guide.
 e. Since the publication of the updated food guide, citizens have started to exercise more.

4. A bodybuilder needs to win a regional contest before competing in the national championship. Arnold just won the West Coast regional contest, so he is eligible to compete in the national championship. The last five winners of the West Coast regional contest have all won the national championship. Arnold's trainer has worked with the last three national champions, and he believes Arnold will win the national championship this year. Thus, Arnold will win the national championship.

The argument above is most vulnerable to criticism on the grounds that:
    a. it confuses a probability with a certainty.
    b. it confuses correlation with causation.
    c. it confuses a necessary and sufficient condition.
    d. it appeals to an inappropriate authority.
    e. it draws a hasty generalization based on a small sample size.

5. If John is not attending medical school, then he is attending business school. John is not attending business school, so he must be attending medical school.

Which one of the following most closely parallels the argument's reasoning?
    a. Hank is the best college basketball player, and therefore, he will play professionally next year.
    b. If Maria attends the ballet, then she will wear a dress. Maria is wearing a dress, so she is at the ballet.
    c. All scientists hold a graduate degree, and Dan is a scientist, so he must hold a graduate degree.
    d. If tomorrow is a holiday, then the museum will not be closed. The museum is not closed tomorrow, so tomorrow is a holiday.
    e. If Eric is eating soup, then he is not eating a sandwich. Eric is eating a sandwich, so he is not eating soup.

6. Journalist: There is no downside to journalists using anonymous sources. National newspapers require journalists to use multiple sources to corroborate anonymous tips, and corroboration removes any possibility of abuse. Any failure to corroborate sources would risk national security through the publication of misleading information.

The strength of the argument depends upon which one of the following?
    a. All journalists work for national newspapers.
    b. The government has never infringed on the freedom of press.
    c. Journalists should only use anonymous sources.
    d. Journalists should only use anonymous sources under extraordinary circumstances.
    e. Abuse by the press is only possible when anonymous sources are used without corroboration.

7. Movie Director: Movies come out the best, in terms of both critical and box office success, when a single person has full creative control over the final product. Studios providing "notes" to the director, writer, producer, or whomever controls that vision, stifle the creative process.

Studio Head: At the end of the day, the film industry is a business. Movies will only be made if they are profitable. The most successful movies focus on subjects that the audience cares about, and the studios spend millions of dollars on test screenings to determine what audiences prefer. Whether the studio transmits its research by "notes" or informal discussion, the studio's input must be considered.

Which one of the following best describes the main point in dispute?
a. Critical acclaim is more important than box office success.
b. Audiences' preference is a critical aspect of making movies.
c. More than one person should be involved in the creative process.
d. The best way for the studio to communicate its feedback is always through "notes."
e. Test screenings are a waste of money.

8. The city depends on supplemental federal funding for its education budget, and the federal money is dependent on the city raising its cumulative high school literacy rate from the previous year. Over the past ten years, the city has received supplemental federal funding every year, but the city has had the highest illiteracy rate in the country for ten years.

Which one of the following would resolve the apparent discrepancy in the passage?
a. The city's manufacturing industry makes it a desirable destination for illiterate immigrants.
b. The city's government is the most corrupt in the country.
c. The city increases the difficulty of the high school test for literacy every year.
d. The high school literacy test is arbitrary and subject to change on a yearly basis.
e. The national literacy rate has fallen over the last ten years.

9. Life on Earth depends on water. Unfortunately, water is the world's most threatened natural resource as a result of unrelenting pollution. In the near future, wars will be fought over clean drinking water, as climate change reduces the amount of potable water and pollution taints the drinking water. However, this trend can be broken. Citizens around the globe can aggressively lobby their governments to invest in sustainable energy sources, cleanup polluted waterways, and implement regulations to prevent commercial dumping. Citizens can also have a lasting impact by recycling and taking other steps to reduce their household's biological footprint. As long as citizens actively respond, then the crisis can be mitigated.

What is the argument's primary purpose?
a. To educate citizens about the water crisis.
b. To spur activism amongst citizens.
c. To inform citizens about the consequences of continued pollution.
d. To promote the benefits of recycling.
e. To criticize the status quo in government.

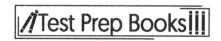

10. If the government institutes criminal justice reform, then the percentage of citizens in prison will decrease. If the government does not institute criminal justice reform during this legislative session, then the government will go bankrupt. All attempts at criminal justice reform require 60 Purple Party politicians to hold office. There are currently 55 Purple Party politicians in office during this legislative session.

According to the passage above, what must follow?
   a. Criminal justice reform will be enacted when five more Purple Party politicians hold office.
   b. The percentage of citizens in prison will increase during this legislative session.
   c. The percentage of citizens in prison will decrease during this legislative session.
   d. The government will go bankrupt during this legislative session.
   e. A bipartisan compromise will prevent the government from going bankrupt during this legislative session.

11. Psychologist: Attention Deficit Hyperactivity Disorder (ADHD) is a brain disorder that prevents people from paying attention and controlling their impulses. Relatively recently, prescription drugs have become the most common treatment for ADHD. In patients suffering from ADHD, the drugs always increase the patients' impulse control and ability to pay attention. However, when prescribed to patients who do not suffer from ADHD, severe side effects and intense dependency can result. Determining whether a teenager is suffering from ADHD or mere teenage angst is difficult, if not impossible, and therefore, ADHD drugs should be banned.

To which one of the following propositions does the psychologist's reasoning most closely conform?
   a. Drugs are an inherently risky treatment option.
   b. More testing should be done before engaging in risky treatments.
   c. Popular wisdom cannot be trusted.
   d. Doctors overprescribe medication due to financial incentives.
   e. Risk prevention should be the guiding priority.

12. Even when invading countries, overthrowing democratically-elected governments, or supporting violent militant groups, Kekistan's foreign policy adheres to strict morality. Every foreign affairs action taken by Kekistan is moral, because Kekistan is the most morally righteous country in the world. Kekistan is truly the shiny city upon the hill, a beacon of hope for the entire world.

What is the most serious mistake committed in the author's reasoning?
   a. The author makes an emotional appeal without supporting evidence.
   b. The author asserts an unjustified metaphor.
   c. The author relies on circular reasoning.
   d. The author fails to define an important term.
   e. The author sets up a false dichotomy.

13. Corruption is the cost of doing business in the context of the modern governmental climate. In some countries, corruption takes the form of campaign donations to politicians for passing favorable legislation, while in other countries, politicians receive kickbacks for the successful completion of a government initiative. As long as humans are involved in government, corruption will never be eliminated.

Which one of the following most accurately describes how the argument proceeds?
a. It begins with a definition, offers a bright-line test, and concludes with speculation.
b. It begins with a bright-line test, offers some examples, and concludes with a definition.
c. It begins with a generalization, offers some examples, and concludes with a definition.
d. It begins with a definition, offers some examples, and concludes with speculation.
e. It begins with a generalization, defines some terms, and concludes with an example.

14. The drinking age should remain at 21 years of age. Prior to reaching the age of 21, the brain is not fully developed. As a result, people cannot make informed decisions about alcohol, and the abuse of alcohol can lead to severe brain damage.

Which one of the following, if true, would most weaken the argument's conclusion?
a. The brain fully develops around 24 years of age.
b. More people over the age of 21 suffer from alcohol-related brain damage than people under the age of 21.
c. Alcohol can cause severe brain damage after the age of 21.
d. Making informed decisions about alcohol reduces the risk of severe brain damage.
e. People over the age of 21 spend more money on alcohol than people under the age of 21.

15. The Founding Fathers created the Electoral College to balance state-based and population-based representation. The Electoral College allows only electors to vote for the President, and the number of electors per state is equal to the state's total number of representatives and senators. Each political party nominates its electors based on their own methods. In the past, some electors have cast ballots for candidates that did not receive the most popular votes.

Which one of the following can be properly inferred from the passage?
a. The number of states' representatives is based on population, while the number of senators is equal for every state.
b. The Founding Fathers considered the majority to be a mob that cannot be trusted.
c. The Electoral College is not a direct election.
d. The winning candidate must receive the majority of the electors' votes.
e. No law requires the electors to vote for the candidate that receives the most ballots.

16. A healthy economy requires a strong financial sector, especially in regards to investment banks. The financial sector organizes and injects capital into the economy, allowing businesses to expand and hire more workers. In order to strengthen the financial sector, regulations must be relaxed to allow capital to flow more freely.

Which one of the following most strengthens the argument?
a. Business growth and decreased unemployment are signs of a strong economy.
b. Investment banks hold the highest market share in the financial sector.
c. More regulation increases competition in the financial sector.
d. No heavily regulated financial sector has ever been strong
e. The financial sector actively lobbies for cutting regulations.

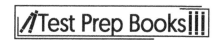

17. Soccer is the most popular sport in the world. Unlike other sports, soccer does not require very much equipment. The field can be any size, goal posts can be makeshift, and anything that can be kicked can serve as the ball. Therefore, it is entirely unsurprising that the most recent FIFA World Cup—the largest international soccer tournament—attracted more than three billion viewers, which was a world record.

The argument depends on which one of the following assumptions?
   a. Soccer is the most popular in South America and Europe.
   b. People who play a sport are likely to be fans of that sport.
   c. Other sports would be similarly popular if they could reduce their economic cost.
   d. Economic cost is the most important factor in determining every sport's popularity.
   e. Soccer is relatively less popular in the United States due to the country's prosperity.

18. No widget factory is located in the Western Time Zone. Some widget factories are employee owned and operated, and nearly all widget factories are publicly owned. Widget factories are the only businesses with more than one thousand employees. A privately-owned factory employs two thousand people.

If the statements above are correct, which one of the following must be true?
   a. The factory is located in the Eastern Time Zone.
   b. The factory is located in the Central Time Zone.
   c. The factory is a widget factory.
   d. The factory is not a widget factory.
   e. The factory is employee-owned and -operated.

19. Tech startups need more than one million dollars in initial investments for product development and marketing to survive. Of course, tech startups also need a compelling product that fills a need in the market. In addition, tech startups need to hit the market within twelve months of development, or else they will risk becoming obsolete. Jason has raised two hundred thousand dollars in initial investments for a video chat application. There are currently six video chat applications on the market, but Jason believes his recently developed application offers a superior product. Following a blind test, participants preferred his video chat application over the competition. Jason's video chat application stands the best chance at surviving if he...

Which one of the following best completes the passage?
   a. spends his existing investment on marketing.
   b. runs another blind test trial to confirm the results.
   c. studies the other six video chat applications.
   d. hires another developer.
   e. seeks a larger initial investment.

20. Samantha recently won a poetry contest at her college, and the poem will be published in a national poetry magazine. Her English professor believes that Samantha is the most talented poet she's ever taught. Samantha attributes her talent for poetry to her high school English teacher, because her high school English teacher was a talented poet. Every contest winner is automatically admitted into the college's English doctoral program; thus, Samantha will attend the college's English doctoral program.

What is a flaw in the argument's reasoning?
    a. It fails to define an important term.
    b. It appeals to an inappropriate authority.
    c. It overstates the evidence.
    d. It mistakes a necessary and sufficient condition.
    e. It relies on circular reasoning.

21. Thomas Edison is most commonly associated with inventing the electric light bulb, but that singular piece of trivia does not do justice to Edison's unrivaled contributions to the Industrial Revolution in the United States. Often called "The Wizard of Menlo Park", Edison applied cutting-edge business principles, like mass production, to the field of science for the first time, including creating the world's first industrial research laboratory. Edison also developed a power grid capable of generating and distributing power to homes and factories. A prolific inventor, Edison invented the phonograph and motion picture camera, and he held more than one thousand patents in the United States.

Which of the following best describes the conclusion set forth by the author?
    a. The Industrial Revolution in the United States would not have happened without Thomas Edison.
    b. Common knowledge does not do justice to the legacy of Thomas Edison.
    c. Thomas Edison was a prolific inventor.
    d. Thomas Edison is America's greatest inventor.
    e. Thomas Edison is one of the most important figures in American history.

22. Politician: Our country needs to adopt a much stronger stance on terrorism. We have witnessed carnage at the hands of terrorists, and therefore, we should impose harsher penalties on people who conspire to commit terrorist acts. Discovering who is plotting terrorist actions requires additional surveillance, so we should alter the balance between civil liberties and national security to favor the latter.

Police Chief: Although admittedly frightening, terrorism accounts for far less than one percent of violent criminal activity. The country would be much safer if we reallocated resources toward gun control. Over the last decade, terrorists have killed approximately one citizen per year, while more than 80 citizens are killed in firearm related incidents every single day. Although the right to bear arms is a fundamental protected freedom; we need to balance that right with protecting citizens.

The two authors would most likely agree on which one of the following statements?
    a. Gun control is an effective counter-terrorism strategy.
    b. Terrorism is a major problem.
    c. The country should reconsider citizens' rights to better protect Americans.
    d. Adjusting the balance between civil liberties and national security is necessary to prevent terrorism.
    e. The government should allocate more resources toward combatting terrorism.

23. The wild alligator population has declined tenfold over the last two decades, but the number of people killed by alligators has doubled over the same period.

Each of the following explains the apparent paradox EXCEPT:
   a. People have built homes near swampland where alligators once thrived.
   b. The nature tourism industry has exploded during the last two decades.
   c. Alligator meat has become an incredibly lucrative industry during the last two decades.
   d. Zoos have bred exponentially more alligators over the last two decades.
   e. The government passed a law legalizing alligator pet ownership two decades ago.

24. Activist: All drugs should be legalized. Despite the current crackdown, the black market has filled the supply, ensuring that people can obtain any drug at any time, if desired. The government currently incarcerates millions of nonviolent drug users at the cost of $50,000 per year per prisoner. This figure doesn't even take into account the financial burden placed on the police and judicial system. Legalizing drugs would not only reduce the cost of law enforcement, but the drugs could also be taxed to generate revenue.

Which one of the following, if true, most weakens the activist's argument?
   a. Legalizing drugs would increase the number of drug users.
   b. Legalizing drugs would raise government healthcare expenditures.
   c. Some drugs are more dangerous than others.
   d. Legalized drugs would be more potent than what currently exists on the black market.
   e. Legalizing drugs would make drug users more willing to enter rehabilitation.

25. A country's employment in the manufacturing industry has dramatically decreased over the last thirty years. During that same period, the country has led the world in developing automation. Therefore, automation is the reason behind the decreased unemployment in the manufacturing industry.

The author relies most upon which of the following assumptions?
   a. The manufacturing industry uses more automation than any other economic sector.
   b. The manufacturing industry is the only economic sector impacted by automation.
   c. The manufacturing industry is driving the automation.
   d. The manufacturing industry depends on automation to be competitive and profitable.
   e. The manufacturing industry uses automation.

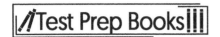

Section II: Analytical Reasoning

Time – 35 minutes

25 Questions

A high school debate team coach must pick five of eight students—George, Beatrice, Armando, Natasha, Pablo, Thomas, Sara, and William—to bring to the state finals to compete in accordance with the following conditions:

- Of the three students Beatrice, Armando, and Thomas, exactly two are chosen.
- If both George and Sara are selected, William is also selected.
- If Pablo is selected, Beatrice is not.
- If Natasha is chosen, neither Thomas nor Sara are selected.

1. Which of the following is a possible team selection?
    a. Armando, Thomas, Pablo, George, Sara
    b. Armando, Thomas, George, Natasha, William
    c. Armando, Thomas, George, Sara, Natasha
    d. Armando, Thomas, George, Sara, William
    e. Armando, Thomas, George, Beatrice, William

2. Which pair of students listed below cannot both be selected while still satisfying the conditions?
    a. Pablo and Armando
    b. Pablo and Natasha
    c. Beatrice and Thomas
    d. Pablo and Thomas
    e. Natasha and Beatrice

3. If Natasha is chosen, which two students do we know for sure are also selected?
    a. Beatrice and Armando
    b. Thomas and Armando
    c. George and Sara
    d. William and George
    e. Beatrice and William

4. If both Armando and Thomas are chosen for the team, which one of the following pair of students would both not be selected?
    a. George and Beatrice
    b. George and Natasha
    c. Pablo and Sara
    d. Beatrice and Pablo
    e. Beatrice and Natasha

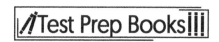

5. Which of the following must be true if neither Beatrice nor Sara is selected?
   a. Pablo is not selected
   b. Natasha will be selected
   c. The team must be Armando, Thomas, George, William, and Pablo
   d. Natasha and William are selected
   e. Armando is not selected

A teacher is handing back exams. She hands them back starting with the lowest grade and going to the highest grade. David is the first to receive his and he made a 62. The 4th person to receive their test back is Silvia and she made an 84. Javier gets his back and he made a 90. Lastly, Fiona receives hers and she made a 95. Kaleb, Sadie, Kris, and Denzel also got tests back. The following conditions are also apply:

- Javier scored lower than Sadie.
- Sadie scored higher than Denzel but lower than Kris.
- Only Fiona scored higher than Kris.
- Silvia scored higher than Kaleb and Denzel

6. What is the max number of students that could make a B (80-89)?
   a. 2
   b. 3
   c. 4
   d. 5
   e. 6

7. Which of the following is a possible score for Denzel?
   a. 92
   b. 88
   c. 86
   d. 84
   e. 78

8. Which of the following statements must be true?
   a. Silvia scored higher than Sadie.
   b. Denzel scored higher than Kaleb.
   c. Kris scored 92-94.
   d. Kaleb scored 72-83.
   e. Javier scored lower than Denzel.

9. How many students scored lower than Sadie?
   a. 2
   b. 3
   c. 4
   d. 5
   e. 6

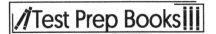

10. Which of the following is a possible solution for the order they got their exams back?
    a. David, Silvia, Kaleb, Denzel, Javier, Sadie, Kris, Fiona
    b. David, Kaleb, Silvia, Denzel, Javier, Sadie, Kris, Fiona
    c. David, Denzel, Silvia, Kaleb, Javier, Sadie, Kris, Fiona
    d. David, Denzel, Kaleb, Silvia, Javier, Kris, Sadie, Fiona
    e. David, Denzel, Kaleb, Silvia, Javier, Sadie, Kris, Fiona

Use the following problem to answer questions 11-15.

Holly is choosing movies for a marathon film festival. She must pick a total of six movies from among a group that includes three dramas—Fender Bender, Gold Rush, and Hollywood Front—three comedies—Mr. Funny Bone, Nearly Wed, and Orca Splash—and three action films—Westwood Hunt, Xander Falls, and Yellowstone Takeover. Two movies must be selected from each genre. The selected films must also satisfy the following conditions:

- Either Xander Falls or Yellowstone Takeover is played fifth.

- Mr. Funny Bone and Gold Rush cannot both be shown at the film festival.

- If Nearly Wed is played, then Orca Splash must be shown.

- If Xander Falls and Mr. Funny Bone are both played, then Xander Falls must be screened earlier in the lineup than Mr. Funny Bone.

- If Westwood Hunt and Hollywood Front are both shown, then Westwood Hunt is played immediately before Hollywood Front.

- Either Mr. Funny Bone or Orca Splash is shown first.

- Gold Rush and Hollywood Front cannot both be shown at the film festival.

11. Which one of the following could be a complete and accurate order of movies played, from first to sixth?
    a. Mr. Funny Bone, Fender Bender, Nearly Wed, Hollywood Front, Xander Falls, Yellowstone Takeover
    b. Orca Splash, Nearly Wed, Gold Rush, Xander Falls, Yellowstone Takeover, Hollywood Front
    c. Nearly Wed, Orca Splash, Yellowstone Takeover, Fender Bender, Xander Falls, Hollywood Front
    d. Orca Splash, Xander Falls, Mr. Funny Bone, Fender Bender, Yellowstone Takeover, Hollywood Front
    e. Mr. Funny Bone, Orca Splash, Hollywood Front, Westwood Hunt, Yellowstone Takeover, Fender Bender

12. If Mr. Funny Bone is shown first, then which one of the following could be true?
    a. Xander Falls is played third.
    b. Gold Rush is played sixth.
    c. Westwood Hunt is played third.
    d. Hollywood Front is played second.
    e. Nearly Wed is played fourth.

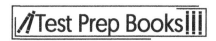

13. Which one of the following movies MUST Holly show at the film festival?
   a. Orca Splash
   b. Gold Rush
   c. Mr. Funny Bone
   d. Hollywood Front
   e. Westwood Hunt

14. If both Nearly Wed and Yellowstone Takeover are NOT shown, how many possible movie orders exist?
   a. One
   b. Two
   c. Three
   d. Four
   e. Five

15. If Mr. Funny Bone is shown second, then which one of the following movies CANNOT be played?
   a. Fender Bender
   b. Yellowstone Takeover
   c. Nearly Wed
   d. Westwood Hunt
   e. Hollywood Front

Use the following problem to answer questions 16-20.

A bakery shop owner bakes fresh treats every morning one at time before opening her doors at 6:00 AM. There are currently seven fresh goodies on her menu: breads, cookies, doughnuts, eclairs, muffins, pastries, and tarts. To ensure the baked goods are prepared in a logical order according to demand, preparation time, recipe yield, and oven time, the following conditions must be satisfied:

- If the muffins are made earlier than the doughnuts, then the breads must be made later than the tarts.

- The cookies are made second or sixth.

- Exactly two baked goods must be made between making the doughnuts and the cookies.

- If the muffins are made later in the morning than the doughnuts, then the breads must be made sometime before the tarts.

- The doughnuts are made earlier than the tarts or the pastries, but not both.

- The breads must be made immediately before or immediately after the cookies.

16. Which one of the following could be the order in which the treats are made from first to seventh?
   a. Breads, cookies, tarts, doughnuts, muffins, pastries, eclairs
   b. Muffins, eclairs, doughnuts, tarts, breads, cookies, pastries
   c. Pastries, eclairs, doughnuts, muffins, breads, cookies, tarts
   d. Eclairs, cookies, pastries, breads, doughnuts, muffins, tarts
   e. Tarts, cookies, breads, eclairs, doughnuts, pastries, muffins

17. Which one the following baked treats CANNOT be made fifth?
    a. Breads
    b. Pastries
    c. Tarts
    d. Muffins
    e. Eclairs

18. The exact baking order of all seven treats can be determined if which one of the following is known?
    a. The breads are made third, and the tarts are made sixth.
    b. The pastries are made first, and the cookies are made sixth.
    c. The muffins are made second, and the tarts are made fourth.
    d. The breads are made third, and the eclairs are made fourth.
    e. The pastries are made first, and the muffins are made sixth.

19. Which one of the following is a complete and accurate list of the possible slots in which the muffins could be made?
    a. First, fourth, sixth, seventh
    b. First, second, sixth, seventh
    c. First, second, third, fifth, seventh
    d. First, second, fifth, sixth, seventh
    e. First, second, fourth, sixth, seventh

20. Which one of the following could be a possible partial list of the order in which the treats are made?
    a. Breads, cookies, and muffins as first, second, and third, respectively
    b. Pastries, tarts, and doughnuts as first, second, and third, respectively
    c. Cookies, breads, and tarts as second, third, and fourth, respectively
    d. Muffins, doughnuts, and tarts as fourth, fifth, and sixth, respectively
    e. Breads, cookies, and muffins as fifth, sixth, and seventh, respectively

Use the following problem to answer questions 21-25.

A guitar collector has six guitars to showcase on a new three-tier shelf display case. Three of the six guitars are electric—a Fender, Gibson, and Harmony—and three are acoustic—a Jackson, Kustom, and Lyle. The three shelves of the display case are labeled #1, #2, and #3 from top to bottom, and any of the shelves can remain empty. The guitar collector's placement of his instruments must conform to the following conditions:

- The Kustom cannot be on Shelf #2.
- The Fender must be on the shelf immediately above the one that the Lyle is on.
- No single shelf can hold all three electric guitars.
- The Jackson and the Lyle cannot be on the same shelf.

21. If the Gibson and Harmony are on Shelf #2, which of the following must be true?
    a. The Lyle is on Shelf #2.
    b. The Kustom is on Shelf #1.
    c. The Jackson is on Shelf #3.
    d. The Gibson and the Jackson are on the same shelf.
    e. The Fender and the Kustom are on the same shelf.

22. If the Jackson is on Shelf #2, which of the following guitars must also be on Shelf #2?
    a. The Kustom
    b. The Fender
    c. The Gibson
    d. The Lyle
    e. The Harmony

23. If Shelf #3 has no acoustic guitars, which pair of guitars must be on the same shelf?
    a. The Fender and the Gibson
    b. The Lyle and the Harmony
    c. The Kustom and the Jackson
    d. The Lyle and the Gibson
    e. The Gibson and the Harmony

24. If Shelf #1 remains empty, which of the following must be FALSE?
    a. The Harmony and the Fender are on the same shelf.
    b. There are exactly three guitars on Shelf #2.
    c. Shelf #3 has exactly two guitars
    d. The Gibson and the Harmony are on the same shelf.
    e. The Gibson and the Kustom are on the same shelf.

25. If one of the shelves remains empty and the Lyle and the Gibson are on the same shelf, which of the following must be true?
    a. The two shelves that are used will be consecutive.
    b. The Kustom and the Lyle are on the same shelf.
    c. The Fender and the Kustom are on the same shelf.
    d. One of the shelves must hold four guitars.
    e. The Harmony is on Shelf #3, and the Jackson is on Shelf #2.

Section III: Logical Reasoning

Time – 35 minutes

24 Questions

1. Carter: Our hypothesis is that drivers in rural areas are guilty of more frequently texting while driving compared to urban drivers, so we need to make sure our demographics survey includes a question about the subject's town of residence's population size.

Olga: It's doubtful that most people know the exact population of their hometown, plus, we don't need specific population figures, so it makes more sense to ask subjects to identify the population range that their town of residence falls into.

Which of the following principles, if valid, best justifies Olga's position?
   a. Surveys that collect demographic information about participants should be as precise as possible if the information is needed for the research question.
   b. Subjects are less likely to answer survey questions accurately if they inquire about sensitive personal information.
   c. Surveys that collect demographic information about participants should be as detailed as possible to achieve the necessary information for the hypothesis.
   d. Subjects are more likely to answer survey questions accurately if they inquire about sensitive personal information.
   e. Surveys that collect demographic information about participants should be as generalized as possible to achieve the necessary information for the hypothesis.

2. Damien: Stores that have generous return policies have the most satisfied customers. Customer loyalty increases significantly in a company when the consumer is confident that he or she can return a product no matter what, especially if the product isn't defective but the customer still isn't satisfied.

Erin: Even if a company has to incur frequent losses from returned products, it behooves them to have a lenient return policy, because doing so positions them to take command of a greater share of the market because of their customer loyalty.

Which of the following best describes Erin's response to Damien's position?
   a. She provides an alternative explanation for the same situation described in Damien's stance.
   b. She identifies basic flaws in Damien's argument.
   c. She points out potential undesirable consequences of Damien's stance.
   d. She further elaborates on Damien's stance with additional supportive evidence.
   e. She provides a sensible rebuttal by demonstrating inconsistencies in Damien's stance.

3. Margaret came home after a long day of work to find her front door open and her waste basket knocked over with all of the contents strewn about the kitchen floor. She believes that her dog must

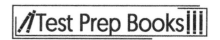

have knocked it over in search for some food scraps to eat, but this belief cannot be correct. Her husband took the dog with him to work all day.

Margaret's hypothesis requires which of the following assumptions?
    a. Margaret's husband brought the dog home on his lunch break.
    b. Margaret's house was broken in to.
    c. Margaret's husband accidently knocked it over on his way out the door this morning.
    d. Margaret has rats in her house.
    e. Margaret's husband left the door open that morning and a raccoon got in.

4. Mimi: The little coffee shop café by the library just closed. They said that not enough people were coming and that everyone was going to the big chain coffee shops. Small businesses can't survive in this town because everyone just goes to the big box stores and no one seems to care about shopping local. It's a waste for entrepreneurs to even try starting their own small businesses here; doing so is just asking to lose money!

Nancy: The coffee shop closed because the owner has small children that he took to school every morning so the shop didn't open until 10:00AM. Most coffee drinkers have already had a cup or two by then so they had to frequent the big chain café. There are plenty of thriving small businesses here. As long as the business model and hours are logical for the business, our townspeople definitely prefer to support local shops.

Which of the following best describes Nancy's response?
    a. Nancy partially agrees with Mimi but brings up a few good counter arguments.
    b. Nancy takes a stance opposite of Mimi's and provides some good points to back it up.
    c. Nancy completely ignores Mimi's thoughts.
    d. Nancy is in complete agreeance with Mimi.
    e. Nancy defends the small coffee shop owner.

5. Carol: The best choice for investment is real estate because the payout is huge. Even though the market can be a little unpredictable, it's the quickest way to turn a sizable profit.

Kenny: Real estate is way too risky and people get huge sums of money tied up into one house that sometimes they can't sell or the value depreciates precipitously. It's much wiser to invest in dependable things like utilities or bonds.

Based on the text above, which of the following can be assumed about Carol and Kenny's investment strategies?
    a. Carol is very risk averse.
    b. Kenny is willing to take risks only if the potential payout is huge.
    c. Neither of them thinks that real estate is worth the risk.
    d. Carol is more willing to take risks than Kenny.
    e. Kenny would invest in stocks before he would invest in real estate.

6. George: Parents should not give toddlers access to cellphones, tablets, or other screens because it is damaging to their eyes and brain. Parents just do it because they are lazy and don't want to get on the

floor and actually play with their child or teach them something. Increasingly younger kids are navigating and playing with phones and are missing out on books and real learning.

Karen: Not all screen time is bad; in fact, it's helpful for young kids to start tinkering with technology like smartphones because they will be using such devices their whole lives. Starting them young optimizes their skills; toddlers are like sponges! They learn so quickly and they *can* learn from the right apps on tablets and phones. There are many educational apps for babies and toddlers.

Which of the following best aligns with Karen's argument?
   a. Children of all ages should be allowed unlimited screen time.
   b. Toddlers should not be allowed any screen time.
   c. Children of all ages should be allowed 1-2 hours per day of screen time.
   d. Toddlers should be made to read at least 2 hours per day.
   e. Toddlers should just be left alone to decide for themselves.

7. Lucy, the skeleton of a female hominin species, was discovered in 1974 in Africa. Scientists think the skeleton is about 3.2 million years old. For six years, Lucy's remains were part of an exhibition called *Lucy's Legacy: The Hidden Treasures of Ethiopia*. However, there was much opposition to the exhibition for fear that Lucy's fossils would be damaged. It's a good thing that they started using casts instead; the preservation of these fossils should be the number one concern of excavators and scientists.

Which of the following would be used in opposition to the passage?
   a. Lucy's fossils, if they are kept in exhibition for too long, are certainly at risk for damage. Even if you can't see it with the naked eye, the constant handling of fossils will cause wear and tear that time could never recover.
   b. The Smithsonian Institution in Washington as well as the Cleveland Museum of Natural History both refused to exhibit Lucy's fossils. The latter says that the exchange of payment for a viewing of Lucy's bones is akin to prostitution and a shame to the scientific community.
   c. The exhibition of Lucy is an important step in raising an awareness of where humans originated and the studies thereof. Keeping the fossils isolated from the public will certainly preserve the remains; however, we might risk the deterrence of public knowledge.
   d. The controversy over the exhibition of Lucy's bones is irrelevant. Even if the bones are damaged, we have preserved the memory with scans, photographs, as well as accurate castings of the fossils. Scientists are making a huge deal over something that doesn't matter in the long run.
   e. Some scientists think that Lucy died from falling out of a tree, although they are not sure. There is also a tooth mark on top of a left pubic bone. What's even more curious is Lucy's age. Although she was considered "fully mature," Lucy only lived for about twelve years.

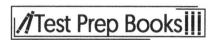

8. Dyson: The proposal paper to add solar panels to the new outdoor university seating in order to charge electronic devices includes a section at the end encouraging student participation by logging opinions online in relation to the proposal. This is a vital step in the proposal's content.

Myers: The proposal to add solar panels to the new outdoor seating does not necessarily need student participation at the end. Our audience is not the students, but the administration committee that approves space and funding for the project. We should instead appeal directly to the administrators to act in the name of progress and technology.

Which one of the following principles, if valid, most justifies Myers stance?
a. Appealing to students will in turn appeal to the proposal's committee. Students are the lifeblood of the university and it's critical that the committee determine whether or not students are on board.
b. Approval of space and funding are usually the most difficult obstacles to overcome in obtaining acceptance over a proposal's project. This is why the proposal must include a detailed budget along with plans on how to designate use of space.
c. Proposals should appeal to the project's recipients, or those who the project will directly affect. This way, the project will gain support from its followers.
d. Proposal audience should not be called upon to respond to an ethical or moral obligation; this is considered inappropriate and unprofessional in the art of proposal writing.
e. Proposals should appeal to the decision makers of the proposal, or those who will be reading the proposal in order to make a decision in favor or in opposition to the proposed project.

9. Hynson: Families of the deceased who sue hospitals for wrongful death due to misdiagnosis are searching for someone to blame. The best option for the family would be to get a second opinion while the deceased person was still alive. Relying 100% on a doctor's diagnosis is irresponsible.

Martinez: Wrongful death cases for misdiagnosis are set in place for accountability on physicians and their attention to their patients. A physician can only be accused of wrongful death if it is deemed that a misdiagnosis would not have been overlooked by a competent physician.

Martinez responds to Hynson's argument by
a. Comparing Hynson's argument to a flawed argument that has the same logical structure.
b. Disputing that Hynson's argument could be used to support a case that is inconsistent with the opinion of Hynson.
c. Providing a second interpretation for an event described in Hynson's argument.
d. Providing evidence that undermines one of the premises of Hynson's argument.
e. Arguing that the opinion supported in Hynson's argument could have disagreeable consequences.

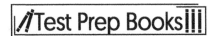 **Practice Test #3 | Section III: Logical Reasoning**

10. Gwin: Apparently the community playhouse is going out of business. This means that there is little to no cultural feeling in the town of Hillview. If you're planning on opening another playhouse in Hillview, I would think again.

Chambal: It's true that the playhouse is going out of business. However, its closing has nothing to do with the amount of culture in Hillview. All this means is that there is perfect opportunity for another playhouse to come to Hillview.

Based on the dialogue, which of the following statements do Gwin and Chambal most likely disagree over?
 a. The plays in Hillview were of inferior quality.
 b. It is possible to determine the cultural feeling in Hillview.
 c. It is a good idea for another playhouse to come to Hillview.
 d. Other cultural spaces have gone out of business in Hillview.
 e. Playhouses can close because of insufficient cultural feeling.

11. Haas: Our mission to bring quality foods to areas considered to be food deserts has failed. Our goal was to bring stores to all 415 areas considered to be food deserts. Out of 415 areas, our stores have only managed to be placed in 250 of them.

Burgess: But before we started our mission, there were no quality foods in any areas considered to be food deserts. I think that bringing quality foods to at least 250 of these areas is quite a success.

Haas and Burgess disagree over the truth of which one of the following?
 a. Leaving 165 food desert areas without quality foods at the end of the project counts as a failure to the mission.
 b. The stated goal of the mission was to bring stores to 415 areas considered to be food deserts.
 c. The mission must be considered a failure if any area considered to be a food desert does not have access to the quality food in their stores.
 d. Before the project began, there were no quality foods in any areas considered to be food deserts.
 e. There are 165 areas considered to be food deserts still do not have access to quality food.

212

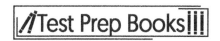

12. Editorial: It is the popular assumption that millennials are less altruistic than the generation that came before them. Company reports of top-down volunteer programs and suggested donations through work are less likely to be performed by millennials and more likely to be performed by the generation that preceded them. Millennials who are on board with company donation programs are rare.

Which of the following most accurately describes a flaw in the argument?

a. The argument fails to acknowledge corporate altruism, which is a responsibility that a corporation has to the environment and the impact it has on society. Corporate responsibility is just as important as individual responsibility, especially when it has so large an effect on the world.

b. The argument fails to consider altruistic millennial behavior outside of the corporate environment. It only mentions "top-down" volunteer programs and donations through a company. The argument does not take note of what causes millennials are contributing to in their own free time.

c. The argument assumes that corporate greed is the byproduct of the millennial attitude with no sufficient evidence backing this claim. The evidence presented has more to do with millennial behavior related to volunteering and less to do with direct corporate greed.

d. The argument confuses an assumption with evidence; that millennials being less altruistic is more of an abstract idea than a fact. The argument should be more forthcoming about its factual evidence and not confuse fact with a general assumption.

e. The argument assumes that for millenials to perform well they must be in competition with each other. This is not necessarily true, as there is evidence in the article that contradicts this notion.

13. Studies of enoki mushrooms show that the tall, white specimens grow by cultivation in a rich carbon dioxide environment. The wild mushrooms are a darker brown in color and grow on the sides of trees such as ash, persimmon and the Chinese Hackberry tree. Thus, mushrooms that are white in color must be grown in a carbon dioxide-rich environment.

The argument is most vulnerable to criticism on the grounds that it

a. commits the slippery slope fallacy, which states one event must inevitably follow from another event without questioning the inevitability of the event in question.

b. commits the *ad hominem* fallacy which attacks the arguer instead of the argument.

c. commits the wrong direction fallacy where cause and effect are reversed.

d. commits the red herring fallacy by distracting the audience from the topic at hand.

e. commits the *post hoc* fallacy, which mistakes correlation for causation.

14. In a recent experiment, researchers concluded that the phenomenon known as *runner's high* was caused by a biochemical reaction in the brain. Long-distance runners who ran long enough produced chemicals that have an opioid-like effect on mood. These runners not only felt euphoric after running, but they had a higher pain tolerance than the average person as well.

Which one of the following is most strongly supported by the information above?

a. The feeling of euphoria is almost always caused by the act of running.

b. Most biochemical reactions in the body come from strenuous exercise, such as running.

c. Long-distance runners have a higher pain tolerance than the average person.

d. Those who have runner's high will experience euphoria as well as a higher pain tolerance.

e. The average person will not experience feelings of euphoria unless they have runner's high.

15. Keaton is a better doctor than Bachman. A good doctor should act professional, have an empathetic attitude toward his or her patients, and demonstrate attentiveness to each specific case. One downside is that Keaton is constantly booked, so it's hard to get an appointment to see her, and it's also difficult for her to focus if she's had an especially busy day.

Which of the following, if true, most seriously weakens the argument?
   a. Bachman is professional, empathetic, and has more time than Keaton to see patients.
   b. Bachman gives to local charities to help sick children and Keaton does not.
   c. Keaton will have more time after the end of the year is over to see her patients.
   d. Keaton and Bachman work in the same hospital together and know each other.
   e. Keaton has been a doctor much longer than Bachman has been a doctor.

16. Ethicist: Utilitarianism argues that it is good and right to act in the best interests of all entities involved, and says the best action is that which serves the maximum number of those entities. For example, making vaccination of children a requirement is considered utilitarianism because _____.

Which of the following most logically completes the argument?
   a. it is seen as giving the parents complete control over the decisions they make for their children.
   b. it does more harm than good for the receivers of the vaccinations.
   c. it is an act administered by the government for the people.
   d. it is seen as an act of serving the majority of public good.
   e. is considered utilitarianism because there are more children than adults in the world.

17. Professor: This year, Texas A&M University has added to its faculty in the English department in order to escalate its rating in the World University Rankings by Subject. However, this obviously has not worked out too well for the department. The English department is still two rankings below its biggest rival, University of Texas.

Which of the following, if true, most seriously weakens the professor's conclusion?
   a. Texas A&M pays its faculty lower salaries than its competitor.
   b. Texas A&M is slightly older than University of Texas.
   c. Texas A&M used to be seven rankings behind University of Texas.
   d. The ranking system is biased which means the results are skewed.
   e. There has been a decrease in the department staff since the added faculty.

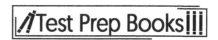

18. Most hospitals have treatment options for cancer patients. All hospitals are able to treat all kinds of burn victims as well as all kinds of Neurology disorders. Therefore, there must be some hospitals that treat both cancer and burn victims and some hospitals that treat both cancer and Neurology disorders.

The pattern of flawed reasoning in which of the following arguments is most parallel to that in the argument above?

a. Most insects are helpful to humans. Virtually every insect has an exoskeleton and is made up of three parts: a head, thorax, and abdomen. Therefore, if there are insects that are helpful to humans and have an exoskeleton, there must also be insects that are helpful to humans and have three parts.

b. Most certainly, most insects are helpful to humans, for almost all insects have an exoskeleton or three parts (a head, thorax, and abdomen), or both, and there are some insects that are helpful to humans and have exoskeletons and some that are helpful to humans and have three parts.

c. Most insects are helpful to humans. Nearly all insects have an exoskeleton and a body made up of three parts: a head, thorax, and abdomen. Therefore, unless there are some insects that are both helpful to humans and have an exoskeleton, there must be some insects that are both helpful to humans and are made up of three parts.

d. Most insects have an exoskeleton and three body parts: a head, thorax, and abdomen. Nearly all insects are helpful to humans. Therefore, since most insects are helpful to humans, there must be some insects that are both helpful to humans and have an exoskeleton and some insects that are helpful to humans and have a head, thorax, and abdomen.

e. All insects have an exoskeleton as well as a body that's composed of three parts: a head, thorax, and abdomen. Most insects are helpful to humans. Therefore, there must be some insects that are both helpful to humans and have an exoskeleton and some insects that are helpful to humans and have a head, thorax, and abdomen.

19. Lily: Admittedly, looking at poetics in translation should come from the bigger picture of accessibility to the reader. If the translator focuses on the literal linguistics of translation opposed to the content and emotion combined, the reader will not feel what is meant to be felt by the original poem or the translation. The translator has the obligation to rework the language into their own version of poetic feeling, even if the language is not translated in a word-by-word fashion.

Madison: But having the literal translation is the closest we as readers can get to the original meaning of the poem. If we put our own twist of experience and emotion on translation work, we will be writing our own poetry, and not that of the original author's. We would be doing a disfavor to the author by botching their truth. Literal translation is not entirely possible, but we should work to come as close as possible to the intended word or phrase expressed by the author.

Which one of the following most accurately expresses a point of disagreement between Lily and Madison?

a. Whether critics should use translation work that is closest to the poem's original meaning.

b. Whether a poem's cultivated feeling is more valuable than its literal meaning to its readers.

c. Whether a loose translation of a poem retains the same aesthetic quality of a literal translation.

d. Whether a translated poem can ever come as close to the truth as the original poem.

e. Whether translation work is a useful endeavor to the poetic canon.

20. Math teacher: In schools today, we no longer rely strictly on abstraction and form to teach our students math. Our students are embedded first with the knowledge that math is important for brain health; that is, studying math helps the brain remain active, recognize patterns, and develop creativity that undoubtedly helps all areas of brain function. Additionally, math is important for practical concepts such as counting change and figuring out percentages. However, even though abstract thought isn't the only thing taught anymore in math, _____.

The conclusion of the argument is most strongly supported if which one of the following completes the passage?

a. it's still one of the most important: having abstract thought means an ability to apply one formula to many situations, thus developing empathy and an understanding for other abstract concepts such as ethics, love, and beauty.

b. it's still one of the most important: learning practical concepts facilitates a better relationship with cooking, finances, and even exercise, thus creating a more well-rounded human being who is capable of taking care of themselves and the people around them.

c. it's not very important: abstract thought is really just a sounding board for too much thinking. Abstraction is the cause of useless arguments in ethics, love, and beauty, does not deserve the credit it's been given in the subject of mathematics.

d. the study of geometry is more important than the study of algebra because geometry deals with spatial relationships and is thus more inclusive in its practical uses than algebraic thinking.

e. the study of algebra is just the beginning of more difficult subjects for students. Modern technology is in great need of students who understand and can apply algebra to their work.

21. In fact, the state's water systems are directly related to the health of the aquifers. Aquifers are underground, porous rocks that store groundwater. This water can be brought up to the surface through natural springs or through pumping. In this state, many communities use the aquifers for drinking water. This is why it's so important that aquifers remain uncontaminated. Not only are they very difficult to fix after contamination, but many people rely on the purity of the water for their health and wellbeing.

Which of the following scenarios would the above statement most likely support?

a. Kyle is concerned with the economy of his community. He has a family of six and has decided that he'll support any legislation expanding job growth in his city.

b. Macy is writing a report on the danger of Florida sinkholes. Her father's old house had a sinkhole that opened up in 2010 and swallowed the living room. The sinkhole went all the way down into the main aquifer that supplied the community.

c. Gabriella is the CEO of a company that pumps groundwater out of the aquifers to provide to the public. She wants to educate the community on water conservation because she believes many people are unaware of the water scarcity perils we could face in the next century.

d. Nida is protesting a pipeline in North Dakota due to the high risk of contamination of the surrounding aquifers. The pipeline is meant to carry 570,000 barrels of oil a day.

e. Abram loves free diving and wants to convince his friends that the nearby springs are a perfect place to learn. Although the springs are not as vibrant as in his mother's day, Abram still believes that he and his friends can enjoy the beauty of the aquifers.

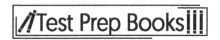

22. In 1998, archaeologists found a baby bird frozen in amber. Although the sample was not large enough to determine its flying habits at such a young age, scientists guessed that the three-day-old bird would have been able to fly from birth and might have been hunting at the time the tree sap fell onto the bird, preserving it. This proves how different this species of bird is from modern birds; modern birds depend on their parents for care for 2 to 3 weeks, while this ancient specimen was able to hunt right out of the nest.

The reasoning in the argument is most vulnerable to criticism because the argument
    a. overlooks the possibility that modern birds have also have hunting capability from a young age
    b. confuses the cause of death with the effects of death.
    c. takes an inconsistent stance regarding its premise and conclusion.
    d. draws its conclusion from data that cannot be proven true.
    e. does not consider the possibility that immediate flight was a risk to the species.

23. Jacqueline: I work one full-time job. With this job, I can make my own hours and work more if I needed to. However, I want to get a second job to change things up a bit. The second job would be part-time and I could work it on the weekends. Admittedly, I would be earning half the hourly wage with this part-time job and would do better to simply add more hours to my first job. Nonetheless, I still think I should get a second part-time job.

Which one of the following principles, if valid, most helps to justify Jacqueline's reasoning?
    a. It is better to stay with the full-time job and add more hours because it pays more.
    b. It is better to get a second part-time job, even if it pays less, for a mental change.
    c. It is better to get another full-time job because that would be the most amount of money Jacqueline would earn.
    d. It is better to get a second part-time job because working on weekends does not bother Jacqueline.
    e. It is better not to worry about making so much money; having freedom is the most important thing in life.

24. Psychologist: Substance abuse, in a sense, is both genetic and learned. Some families may have a predisposition to depression or anxiety, which is known to increase an individual's use of substances. Children who have parents who abused substances are four times more likely than the average person to abuse substances. The latter, however, is up for debate on whether this statistic is due to genetic predisposition or learned behavior.

Which of the following is most strongly supported by the statements above?
    a. The proof for the genetic factor in substance abuse lies in the fact that children with parents who abused substances are four times more likely to use substances themselves.
    b. Substance abuse is a learned behavior only; there is no "addictive" gene, and therefore we cannot consider the issue of substance abuse genetic in any way.
    c. The proof for the genetic factor in substance abuse lies in the fact that there may be indirect genes within families, such as depression or anxiety, that increase the potential use for substance abuse.
    d. The proof for the environmental factor in substance abuse lies in the fact that there may be indirect genes within families, such as depression or anxiety, that increase the potential use for substance abuse.
    e. The proof for the environmental factor in substance abuse lies in the fact that children with parents who abused substances are four times more likely to use substances themselves.

Section IV: Reading Comprehension

Time – 35 minutes

24 Questions

Questions 1 – 3 refer to the following paragraph.

The Brookside area is an older part of Kansas City, developed mainly in the 1920s and 30s, and is considered one of the nation's first "planned" communities with shops, restaurants, parks, and churches all within a quick walk. A stroll down any street reveals charming two-story Tudor and Colonial homes with smaller bungalows sprinkled throughout the beautiful tree-lined streets. It is common to see lemonade stands on the corners and baseball games in the numerous "pocket" parks tucked neatly behind rows of well-manicured houses. The Brookside shops on 63rd street between Wornall Road and Oak Street are a hub of commerce and entertainment where residents freely shop and dine with their pets (and children) in tow. This is also a common "hangout" spot for younger teenagers because it is easily accessible by bike for most. In short, it is an idyllic neighborhood just minutes from downtown Kansas City.

1. Which of the following states the main idea of this paragraph?
    a. The Brookside shops are a popular hangout for teenagers.
    b. There are a number of pocket parks in the Brookside neighborhood.
    c. Brookside is a great place to live.
    d. Brookside has a high crime rate.
    e. Brookside was developed as a "planned" community in the 1920s and 30s.

2. In what kind of publication might you read the above paragraph?
    a. Fictional novel
    b. Community profile
    c. Newspaper article
    d. Movie review
    e. Encyclopedia

3. According to this paragraph, which of the following is unique to this neighborhood?
    a. It is old.
    b. It is in Kansas City.
    c. It has shopping.
    d. It is one of the nation's first planned communities.
    e. It has Tudor and Colonial homes.

Questions 4 – 8 are based on the following two passages:

Passage A

Excerpt from *Preface to Lyrical Ballads* by William Wordsworth (1800)

From such verses the Poems in these volumes will be found distinguished at least by one mark of difference, that each of them has a worthy *purpose*. Not that I always began to write with a distinct purpose formerly conceived; but habits of meditation have, I trust, so prompted and regulated my feelings, that my descriptions of such objects as strongly excite those feelings, will be found to carry along with them a *purpose*. If this opinion be erroneous, I can have little right to the name of a Poet. For all good poetry is the spontaneous overflow of powerful feelings: and though this be true, Poems to which any value can be attached were never produced on any variety of subjects but by a man who, being possessed of more than usual organic sensibility, had also thought long and deeply. For our continued influxes of feeling are modified and directed by our thoughts, which are indeed the representatives of all our past feelings; and, as by contemplating the relation of these general representatives to each other, we discover what is really important to men, so, by the repetition and continuance of this act, our feelings will be connected with important subjects, till at length, if we be originally possessed of much sensibility, such habits of mind will be produced, that, by obeying blindly and mechanically the impulses of those habits, we shall describe objects, and utter sentiments, of such a nature, and in such connexion with each other, that the understanding of the Reader must necessarily be in some degree enlightened, and his affections strengthened and purified.

Passage B

Excerpt from "Tradition and the Individual Talent" by T.S. Eliot (1921)

If you compare several representative passages of the greatest poetry you see how great is the variety of types of combination, and also how completely any semi-ethical criterion of "sublimity" misses the mark. For it is not the "greatness," the intensity, of the emotions, the components, but the intensity of the artistic process, the pressure, so to speak, under which the fusion takes place, that counts. The episode of Paolo and Francesca employs a definite emotion, but the intensity of the poetry is something quite different from whatever intensity in the supposed experience it may give the impression of. It is no more intense, furthermore, than Canto XXVI, the voyage of Ulysses, which has not the direct dependence upon an emotion. Great variety is possible in the process of transmutation of emotion: the murder of Agamemnon, or the agony of Othello, gives an artistic effect apparently closer to a possible original than the scenes from Dante. In the *Agamemnon,* the artistic emotion approximates to the emotion of an actual spectator; in *Othello* to the emotion of the protagonist himself. But the difference between art and the event is always absolute; the combination which is the murder of Agamemnon is probably as complex as that which is the voyage of Ulysses. In either case there has been a fusion of elements. The ode of Keats contains a number of feelings which have nothing particular to do with the nightingale, but which the nightingale, partly, perhaps, because of its attractive name, and partly because of its reputation, served to bring together.

4. Which one of the following most accurately characterizes the relationship between the two passages?
   a. Passage A offers an explanation of the purpose of poetry, while passage B offers an explanation of the results of poetry.
   b. Passage A is concerned with the context of poetry involving nature, while passage B is concerned with the context of poetry involving urban life.
   c. Passage A focuses on lyric poetry, while passage B is concerned with epic poetry.
   d. Passage A argues that the source of great poetry comes from emotions within, while passage B argues that great poetry is based off the skill and expertise of the poet.
   e. Passage A deals with the ethical implications that poets have toward their readers, while passage B denies the poet's ethical obligations to the readers.

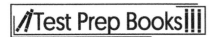

5. What does the author of passage B mean by the last sentence?

    a. The author is explaining that the feelings portrayed in Keats' ode are brought forth and signified by the symbolism of the nightingale used within the language of the poem.

    b. The author means that Keats' poetry is more valuable than epic verse because the feelings expressed in his poetry are backed by literary talent.

    c. The author means that the figure of the nightingale serves a myriad of purposes; here, for a symbolic use of a range of emotions such as grief, fear, and sorrow.

    d. The author is trying to argue that the reputation of the poet serves to bring about the feelings of the reader; or, that the ethos of the writing is closely related to the pathos in the audience.

    e. The author means to explain the etymology of the nightingale by mentioning its reputation and its attractive name, and what the etymology serves in relation to the meaning of the poem.

6. The author of passage A thinks which of the following about thoughts and feelings as they relate to poetry?

    a. That the thoughts of the poet are the primary source of inspiration, and that feeling is a secondary motivation for the poet. Once the poet gets their thoughts onto paper, the feelings of the poet will come after.

    b. That thoughts and feelings are one and the same thing; that they happen simultaneously, and that this merging creates the perfect condition to write a poem.

    c. That feelings from the past will accumulate into representations of thought. The poet is then responsible for putting these direct thoughts onto paper, creating a poem. Therefore, the original source of poetry is from the past feelings of the poet.

    d. That thoughts and feelings are overrated; namely, that critics of the past have put too much emphasis on thoughts and feelings as they relate to poetry.

    e. That if we contemplate thoughts and feelings side by side, we will recognize that poems are made up of the feelings, whereas prose is made up of the thoughts. This is the inherent difference between poetry and prose.

7. The authors of the passages differ in their explanations of great poetry in that the author of passage B

    a. argues that the intensity of the emotion felt while writing the poem counts for more than the effort put into a poem.

    b. argues that the effort put into a poem counts for more than the intensity of the emotion felt while writing the poem.

    c. argues that the purpose of poetry is for the reader to feel an emotional connection with the author.

    d. argues that good poetry is produced by poets who think long and deeply about their subjects before they write about it.

    e. argues that the difference between art and the event is always absolute.

8. The authors of the passages would be most likely to disagree over whether

    a. a painter uses oil colors or acrylic.

    b. an architect's success is based on quality or quantity of the building.

    c. what kind of structure a novelist uses for their work.

    d. a talented pianist should be able to read music or not.

    e. an apathetic sculptor can become successful.

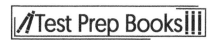

Questions 9 – 13 are based on the following passage:

Excerpt from "Self-Reliance" by Ralph Waldo Emerson (1841)

Society never advances. It recedes as fast on one side as it gains on the other. It undergoes continual changes; it is barbarous, it is civilized, it is Christianized, it is rich, it is scientific; but this change is not amelioration. For everything that is given, something is taken. Society acquires new arts, and loses old instincts. What a contrast between the well-clad, reading, writing, thinking American, with a watch, a pencil, and a bill of exchange in his pocket, and the naked New Zealander, whose property is a club, a spear, a mat, and an undivided twentieth of a shed to sleep under! But compare the health of the two men, and you shall see that the white man has lost his aboriginal strength. If the traveller tell us truly, strike the savage with a broad axe, and in a day or two the flesh shall unite and heal as if you struck the blow into soft pitch, and the same blow shall send the white to his grave.

The civilized man has built a coach, but has lost the use of his feet. He is supported on crutches, but lacks so much support of muscle. He has a fine Geneva watch, but he fails of the skill to tell the hour by the sun. A Greenwich nautical almanac he has, and so being sure of the information when he wants it, the man in the street does not know a star in the sky. The solstice he does not observe; the equinox he knows as little; and the whole bright calendar of the year is without a dial in his mind. His note-books impair his memory; his libraries overload his wit; the insurance-office increases the number of accidents; and it may be a question whether machinery does not encumber; whether we have not lost by refinement some energy, by a Christianity entrenched in establishments and forms, some vigor of wild virtue. For every Stoic was a Stoic; but in Christendom where is the Christian?

There is no more deviation in the moral standard than in the standard of height or bulk. No greater men are now than ever were. A singular equality may be observed between the great men of the first and of the last ages; nor can all the science, art, religion, and philosophy of the nineteenth century avail to educate greater men than Plutarch's heroes, three or four and twenty centuries ago. Not in time is the race progressive. Phocion, Socrates, Anaxagoras, Diogenes, are great men, but they leave no class. He who is really of their class will not be called by their name, but will be his own man, and, in his turn, the founder of a sect. The arts and inventions of each period are only its costume, and do not invigorate men. The harm of the improved machinery may compensate its good. Hudson and Behring accomplished so much in their fishing-boats, as to astonish Parry and Franklin, whose equipment exhausted the resources of science and art. Galileo, with an opera-glass, discovered a more splendid series of celestial phenomena than any one since. Columbus found the New World in an undecked boat. It is curious to see the periodical disuse and perishing of means and machinery, which were introduced with loud laudation a few years or centuries before. The great genius returns to essential man. We reckoned the improvements of the art of war among the triumphs of science, and yet Napoleon conquered Europe by the bivouac, which consisted of falling back on naked valor, and disencumbering it of all aids. The Emperor held it impossible to make a perfect army, says Las Casas, "without abolishing our arms, magazines, commissaries, and carriages, until, in imitation of the Roman custom, the soldier should receive his supply of corn, grind it in his hand-mill, and bake his bread himself."

9. Which of the following most accurately expresses the main point of the passage?
   a. The passage is a problem-solution structure. It means to convince the reader that civilized society has never made meaningful advancements, and then proposes a solution to the reader based on the creeds of Christianity.
   b. The passage is a critique of Christianity. The author examines the Christian who does missionary work in uncivilized areas and questions the viability of their motives.
   c. The passage is a critique of society, and explores the notion that an "advancement" of the human race is not possible—that a perceived strength gives way to another weakness.
   d. The passage is an exploration of man's relation to nature. The first paragraph is an abstract evaluation of this relationship, while the second paragraph serves to bring concrete examples to the reader.
   e. The passage is a critique of academia. The author analyzes the education system and points out the ineffectiveness of its value by giving examples of human deficiencies.

10. With which one of the following statements would the author be most likely to agree?
    a. The illusion of the civilized person is that they are both mentally and physically better off than the uncivilized person.
    b. The uncivilized person is far more progressed than the civilized person due to their closeness with nature.
    c. The advancement of society is a natural flow of the universe and does not owe its success to that of human beings.
    d. The Stoic and Christian are both valuable to society in that they seek the truth and aim to do good no matter what the consequences.
    e. Transportation has come a long way in civilization, but there are many improvements that can be made.

11. What is the purpose of the beginning of the second paragraph?
    a. The author presents us with a synecdoche that implies the importance of transportation.
    b. The author attempts to stir up the reader's empathy by sharing brief stories about the daily struggles of disabled persons.
    c. The author gives a short description of the civilized man and what his day-to-day life looks like.
    d. A series of mini allegories are listed in order to show the reader the paradox of the civilized man—that civilization necessitates a certain kind of ignorance.
    e. The author begins a narrative of a man who has adopted civilization then casts it off for inner enlightenment. This is an attempt to convince the reader to do the same.

12. It can be inferred from the discussion of Plutarch's heroes in the third paragraph that
    a. because we've experienced technological growth as a society, we have greater men than Plutarch's heroes.
    b. simply because we've experienced technological growth as a society does not mean that we have greater men than Plutarch's heroes.
    c. because we haven't experienced technological growth as a society, there are no greater men than Plutarch's heroes.
    d. because we haven't experienced technological growth as a society, there are greater men than Plutarch's heroes.
    e. the author is distrustful of the dates of when Plutarch's heroes lived and seeks to create a timeline of them.

13. The information in the last paragraph most helps to answer which of the following questions?
   a. Who are some of the heroes of classical history and what are their contributions to society?
   b. What are some stories of the inventions of machinery and how do they aid in human exploration?
   c. What are some examples that prove that the moral fiber of a society is due to its scientific developments?
   d. What are some examples that prove that the moral fiber of a society is not due to its scientific developments?
   e. Which period of time was considered the most advanced and why?

Questions 14 – 18 are based on the following passage:

An excerpt from *Ice-Caves of France and Switzerland* by Rev. G.F. Browne, M.A. (1865)

In the summer of 1861, I found myself, with some members of my family, in a small rustic *pension* in the village of Arzier, one of the highest villages of the pleasant slope by which the Jura passes down to the Lake of Geneva. The son of the house was an intelligent man, with a good knowledge of the natural curiosities which abound in that remarkable range of hills, and under his guidance we saw many strange things. More than once, he spoke of the existence of a *glacière* at no great distance, and talked of taking us to see it; but we were skeptical on the subject, imagining that *glacière* was his patois for *glacier*, and knowing that anything of the glacier kind was out of the question. At last, however, on a hot day in August, we set off with him, armed, at his request, with candles; and, after two or three hours of pine forests, and grass glades, and imaginary paths up rocky ranges of hill towards the summits of the Jura, we came to a deep natural pit, down the side of which we scrambled. At the bottom, after penetrating a few yards into a chasm in the rock, we discovered a small low cave, perfectly dark, with a flooring of ice, and a pillar of the same material in the form of a headless woman, one of whose shoulders we eventually carried off, to regale our parched friends at Arzier. We lighted up the cave with candles, and sat crouched on the ice drinking our wine, finding water, which served the double purpose of icing and diluting the wine, in small basins in the floor of ice, formed apparently by drops falling from the roof of the cave.

A few days after, our guide and companion took us to an ice-cavern on a larger scale, which, we were told, supplies Geneva with ice when the ordinary stores of that town fail; and the next year my sisters went to yet another, where, however, they did not reach the ice, as the ladder necessary for the final drop was not forthcoming.

In the course of the last year or two, I have mentioned these glacières now and then in England, and no one has seemed to know anything about them; so I determined, in the spring of 1864, to spend a part of the summer in examining the three we had already seen or heard of, and discovering, if possible, the existence of similar caves.

14. Which one of the following most accurately expresses the structure of the passage?
    a. The narrator employs a cause and effect structure throughout the passage. The narrator begins with the suggested cause of how ice caves have formed in France, with the conclusion stating several effects that arise out of ice cave formation.
    b. The narrator begins with raising an issue about the availability of ice caves. Then, the narrator draws upon a childhood experience, ending with a proposed solution.
    c. The narrator begins with a story to provoke pathos within the reader. Then, the narrator tries to convince the reader, at the passage's conclusion, of the existence of these ice caves in France and Switzerland.
    d. The narrator employs logos throughout the structure of the narrative, which is told in chronological order. The logos serves to convince the reader of the facts of the passage, and thus raises the credibility of the author.
    e. The narrator begins with a story to catch the reader's attention, slowly showing the narrator's dedication to the story. The passage ends with a foreshadowing of how the narrator plans to discover more about the given subject.

15. According to the passage, the narrator's sisters
    a. worked in Geneva in order to supply the town with ice from the ice caves.
    b. went to an ice cave, but did not have a ladder to get to the platform of ice.
    c. failed to get ice to the town of Geneva when they needed it most.
    d. went to Geneva but did not go to an ice cave because they did not have a ladder.
    e. went to an ice cave, but the ladder dropped to the bottom of the ice and they could no longer use it.

16. What is the meaning of the word *patois* in the following sentence?

    but we were skeptical on the subject, imagining that *glacière* was his patois for *glacier*, and knowing that anything of the glacier kind was out of the question.

    a. Penchant
    b. Despondency
    c. Vernacular
    d. Representation
    e. Repletion

17. Which one of the following would the author be most likely to agree with?
    a. Ice caves are mesmerizing natural features that are not explored enough by people.
    b. People should be required to pay to get into ice caves in order to begin preserving them.
    c. A good business idea would be to turn ice caves into chilled wine cellars.
    d. Ice caves are beautiful features, yet they are too dangerous for us to explore.
    e. Geneva is the best place in the world to find the most beautiful ice caves.

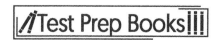

18. Which one of the following most accurately expresses the author's purpose in writing the passage?
    a. The author set out to write the passage in order to convince the reader that the discovery and exploration of ice caves should be something everyone experiences at least once in their life.
    b. The author set out to write the passage in order to enlighten the reader on the perils of the glaciers in France and Switzerland; that humankind is slowly destroying them with advancing technology and that we should do something to save them.
    c. The author set out to write the passage in order to give a detailed account of the narrator's first time in an ice cave and the subsequent events that led to the narrator's desire for further exploration.
    d. The author set out to write an informative essay wherein other scientists would be able to build upon the discoveries of the ice caves of France and Switzerland and use the author's research for future ventures.
    e. The author set out to write a review of Geneva's consumer economy and came to find that ice caves were an important part of that economy. The author's interest is piqued by the end of the passage, and the author dedicates himself to finding out more about the caves.

Questions 19 – 24 are based on the following passage:

Excerpt from chapters 1 of *Art*, by Clive Bell, called "The Aesthetic Hypothesis" (1914)

. . . The starting-point for all systems of aesthetics must be the personal experience of a peculiar emotion. The objects that provoke this emotion we call works of art. All sensitive people agree that there is a peculiar emotion provoked by works of art. I do not mean, of course, that all works provoke the same emotion. On the contrary, every work produces a different emotion. But all these emotions are recognizably the same in kind—so far, at any rate, the best opinion is on my side. That there is a particular kind of emotion provoked by works of visual art, and that this emotion is provoked by every kind of visual art, by pictures, sculptures, buildings, pots, carvings, textiles, etc., is not disputed, I think, by any one capable of feeling it. This emotion is called the aesthetic emotion; and if we can discover some quality common and peculiar to all the objects that provoke it, we shall have solved what I take to be the central problem of aesthetics. We shall have discovered the essential quality in a work of art, the quality that distinguishes works of art from all other classes of objects.

For either all works of visual art have some common quality, or when we speak of "works of art" we gibber. Every one speaks of "art," making a mental classification by which he distinguishes the class "works of art" from all other classes. What is the justification of this classification? What is the quality common and peculiar to all members of this class? Whatever it be, no doubt it is often found in company with other qualities; but they are adventitious—it is essential. There must be some one quality without which a work of art cannot exist; possessing which, in the least degree, no work is altogether worthless. What is this quality? What quality is shared by all objects that provoke our aesthetic emotions? What quality is common to Sta. Sophia and the windows at Chartres, Mexican sculpture, a Persian bowl, Chinese carpets, Giotto's frescoes at Padua, and the masterpieces of Poussin, Piero della Francesca, and Cézanne? Only one answer seems possible—significant form. In each, lines and colors combined in a particular way, certain forms and relations of forms, stir our aesthetic emotions. These relations and combinations of lines and colors, these aesthetically moving forms, I call "Significant Form"; and "Significant Form" is the one quality common to all works of visual art.

19. Which one of the following most accurately expresses the main point of the passage?
    a. The property of emotion is extremely valuable to a work of art, because it is that same property that enables a work of art to be called a "work of art." The works of art we see are direct representations of our own emotions.
    b. The region in which a work of art is created (i.e. Mexico, Persia, China) is critical in determining the value and quality of that work of art. This is called "Significant Form," wherein the historical properties of a work of art are as important as its immediate effects.
    c. The study of lines and color is essential in becoming a critic of art. Those who do not have formal training will not recognize the subtleties with which art comes together. Although an emotional intelligence is important, formal training is absolutely essential.
    d. The concept known as "Significant Form," where lines and colors combine with each other in a certain way, is the one quality all works of art have in common. In order to be considered in the class of "art," objects must have this aesthetic quality about them.
    e. It is futile to try and discern the essential quality of a work of art. Great men have made it their life's work to explore this question, but the result is always the same: the qualities that make objects a work of art remain unknown to human beings.

20. The primary function of the second paragraph is to
    a. Offer additional evidence for the conclusion reached in the first paragraph.
    b. Draw a conclusion from the points raised in the first paragraph.
    c. Present an argument that weakens the argument made in the first paragraph.
    d. Identify assumptions relied upon by a type of analysis referred to in the first paragraph.
    e. Reject a possible response to the argument made in the first paragraph.

21. The information in the passage most helps to answer which one of the following questions?
    a. What is the one quality common to all works of art with the ability to provoke Significant Form?
    b. What is one quality that artists have to possess in order to produce great works of art?
    c. What is an essential quality that the aesthetic works of China, Persia, and Mexico have in common?
    d. When is aesthetic emotion deemed the most important in the creative process?
    e. What is the one quality common to all works of art with the ability to provoke aesthetic emotion?

22. What is a repetitive persuasive device the author uses throughout the second paragraph?
    a. Metaphorical language
    b. Rhetorical questions
    c. Allusion
    d. Parallelism
    e. Juxtaposition

23. What does the author most likely mean by the phrase "we gibber" at the beginning of paragraph 2?
    a. We tremble
    b. We ramble
    c. We talk foolishly
    d. We are inarticulate
    e. We stutter

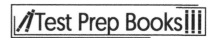

24. Which of the following would the author most likely agree with?

a. In every visual work of art that we consider to be of value, there must be some semblance of significant form—whether it is painting, sculpture, architecture, or pottery.

b. The concept of significant form is not apparent in every type of great visual art—architecture has its own rules of aesthetics that determine whether or not the quality is high.

c. The aesthetic emotion of a work of art is the feeling that precedes the process of creation. This is the feeling produced by the artist before and during the work of art.

d. The justification of a work of art lies in the way people speak about art. This creates an interactive existence between artist and viewer, wherein value is created between the two participants.

e. One of our single aims as human beings is to find what it is that makes a work of art a work of art. The great paradox lies in our impossibility of doing so.

Answer Explanations

Section I: Logical Reasoning

1. C: The last sentence functions as the professor's conclusion. The professor believes that politicians should only be held to the strict letter of the law. The law in this case—the anti-corruption statute—only holds liable those politicians who trade political favors for personal financial gain. According to the argument, only the local construction company made any personal financial gain, so the state governor did not violate the anti-corruption statue under a strict interpretation. Thus, Choice *C* must be the correct answer. Choices *A* and *D* are outside the scope of the argument. Choice *B* is incorrect since the state governor did not violate the strict letter of the law. Choice *E* appears to accurately describe the situation, but it does not follow the professor's reasoning.

2. E: The author is clearly in favor of zoos. According to the passage, zoos strengthen people's relationship with nature and save endangered species. As such, the author would strongly agree that wild animals should sometimes be held in captivity. Thus, Choice *E* is the correct answer. Choice *D* goes too far; the author expresses support for nature, generally, and there is nothing that describes keeping all animals in captivity. Choice *C* is the second-best answer choice, considering the author's clear support for zoos, but there is considerably more evidence in support of Choice *E*. Choices *A* and *B* chase the red herring in the last sentence. Although the author supports zoos, there is no support for owning tigers or wild animals as pets.

3. B: The conclusion is that the updated food guide (the depiction of the plate) has been wildly successful, because citizens have lost a significant amount of weight. The correct answer will attribute the weight loss to the updated recommendations. Choice *B* states that eating more lean proteins and vegetables, which were boosted in the updated guidelines, contribute to weight loss. Thus, Choice *B* is the correct answer. Choices *A* and *D* are irrelevant, because heart disease and the authorship of the two pictorial guidelines are not related to weight loss. Choice *C* is incorrect because the layout of the pyramid and the plate are not related to weight loss and the plate does not use vertical layers. Choice *E* contradicts the conclusion by offering an alternative cause of the weight loss.

4. A: The argument provides several reasons why Arnold is likely to win the national championship. The previous five winners of the West Coast regional contest went on to win the national championship, and Arnold is this year's winner. The trainer's confidence in Arnold further bolsters the argument since the trainer has worked with past champions. However, the conclusion states that Arnold *will* win the national championship. This goes too far, confusing a probability with a certainty. Thus, Choice *A* is the correct answer. Choice *B* does not appear in the argument. Choice *C* is incorrect. The only necessary condition in the argument is the requirement of winning a regional contest to compete in the national championship, but it is not asserted as a sufficient condition. Choices *D* and *E* are also incorrect since the trainer is an appropriate authority and the small sample size is reasonable in this context.

5. E: The argument provides an if-then statement and draws a conclusion based on its contrapositive. The contrapositive of the argument's if-then statement is: if John is not attending business school, then John is attending medical school. Thus, the argument's conclusion is valid since it correctly follows the contrapositive. Choice *E* correctly mirrors the argument's use of the contrapositive to draw a valid conclusion. Thus, Choice *E* is the correct answer. Choice *A* does not follow this logic; instead, it draws a conclusion based on one piece of supporting evidence. Choices *B* and *D* look promising, but they draw a conclusion based on the converse of the if-then statement, rather than the contrapositive.

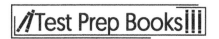

Consequently, both choices draw a false conclusion since a converse is always illogical. Choice *C* can be translated into an if-then statement—if an individual is a scientist, then the individual holds a graduate degree—and bases the conclusion directly off that statement, unlike the argument.

6. A: The argument concludes that there is no downside to journalists using anonymous sources. The correct answer will be a dependent assumption, so the argument would be significantly undermined if it were not true. If no journalists worked for national newspapers, then no journalists would be required to corroborate their sources, upending the entire argument. Thus, Choice *A* is the correct answer. Choice *B* is irrelevant, and Choices *C* and *D* are unsupported by the argument. The journalist would agree with Choice *E*, but it is not a dependent assumption, so it cannot be the correct answer.

7. C: The movie director and studio head disagree about creative control over movies. The movie director believes that an auteur should be fully empowered, while the studio head argues that the studio's team should play a role in the process. Choice *C* correctly describes this dispute over creative control. The studio head would vehemently disagree with Choice *A*, but it is not clear whether the movie director prioritizes critical acclaim over box office success. The movie director even refers to box office success in the same phrase as critical acclaim. Choice *B* is a fairly strong answer, but like Choice *A*, it is unclear how the movie director feels about that issue. The movie director could believe that an auteur understands audiences' preferences better than test screenings or other studio insights. Choice *D* is incorrect. The studio head mentions incorporating feedback through informal discussion, so he does not believe that "notes" are *always* the best way to communicate feedback. Choice *E* is the second-best answer choice. The studio head would firmly disagree that test screenings are a waste of money, while the movie director would likely agree; however, Choice *C* better describes the *main* point at issue—creative control.

8. A: The discrepancy is that the city continues to receive federal funding every year, which requires raising the high school literacy rate, but the city remains the most illiterate city in the country. Choice *A* resolves the apparent discrepancy by introducing a new factor—the arrival of illiterate immigrants, which is causing the illiteracy rate to remain high despite increasing high school literacy rates. Choices *B*, *C*, and *D* are irrelevant since they do not address the discrepancy. Choice *E* actually augments the paradox because if the national literacy rate is falling, then it is would seem likely that the city would have outperformed at least one other city by this point.

9. B: The argument is describing a crisis in the water supply. More importantly, it calls for citizens to take action by lobbying the government and reducing their household's biological footprint. The conclusion emphasizes the need for citizens to actively respond to mitigate the crisis. Thus, Choice *B* is the correct answer. Although the argument either references or agrees with all of the other answer choices, these choices are not the primary purpose, which is to spur activism.

10. D: The passage provides several if-then statements followed by a descriptive statement about the number of Purple Party politicians in office. An attempt at criminal justice reform, let alone instituting the reform, will not happen during this legislative session since it requires 60 Purple Party politicians. The second if-then statement concludes that the government will go bankrupt without reform. Thus, Choice *D* is the correct answer. Choice *A* is outside the scope of the passage; furthermore, it does not follow logically since 60 Purple Party politicians is only a necessary condition. Choice *B* seems like a strong answer choice on its face, but it follows the inverse of the first if-then statement, so it is does not need to be true. Choices *C* and *E* are unsupported by the passage.

11. E: The psychologist's conclusion is that ADHD drugs should be banned, despite their efficacy with ADHD symptoms, based on the risk of prescribing the drugs to the wrong people. Choice *E* best describes the underlying proposition that risk prevention should take precedence over efficacy. Choice *A* is too broad, applying the principle to all drugs. The psychologist would likely agree with Choice *B*, but it is not the proposition that the reasoning follows. The argument does not mention popular wisdom or doctors' financial incentives, so Choices *C* and *D* cannot be correct, respectively.

12. C: The argument asserts that Kekistan is the most moral country in the world. However, the argument fails to provide much justification for why Kekistan is moral. In particular, the author's second sentence suffers from circular reasoning, asserting that Kekistan's actions are moral due to the country's inherent morality. Thus, Choice *C* is the correct answer. The argument attempts to make a logical argument, not an emotional one, so Choice *A* is incorrect. Choice *B* is a strong answer choice since the argument finishes with a metaphor that is unsupported; however, the circular reasoning is why the metaphor is unsupported. Choice *D* is another strong answer choice since the argument does not reasonably define morality, but the circular reasoning is an attempted definition of morality provided by the author. Consequently, the circular reasoning is the more serious mistake. Choice *E* is incorrect, because no false dichotomy is drawn.

13. D: The first sentence provides a definition of corruption. The second sentence gives two different examples of how governments can be corrupt, illustrating how corruption is inherent in modern government. The third sentence speculates that humanity is the cause of corruption, so corruption will never be eliminated. The third sentence is speculative, because it assumes that no form of government could be devised that eliminates corruption. Thus, Choice *D* is the correct answer. The other answer choices include either a bright-line test or generalization, and neither of these appear in the argument.

14. A: The argument is based on the notion that the age of 21 is a pivotal moment for brain development. The correct answer will undermine that age's importance. Choice *A* claims that the brain does not fully develop until reaching the age of 24, so according to the argument's own logic, the drinking age should be increased, rather than remain the same. Thus, Choice *A* is the correct answer. Choice *B* does not weaken the argument, because it follows logically. More alcohol-related brain damage in people older than 21 years of age would be expected since they are the only ones legally permitted to drink. Choice *C* is incorrect since the argument does not remove the possibility of alcohol-related brain injuries at a later age. Choice *D* strengthens the argument, and Choice *E* is irrelevant.

15. C: The correct answer will be something that can be directly inferred from the closed world of the passage. The passage states that only electors vote for the president, and political parties nominate electors according to their own methods. As such, it can be properly inferred that the Electoral College is not a direct election. Thus, Choice *C* is the correct answer. The other answers are factually correct, but they cannot be inferred from the language contained in the passage.

16. D: The argument's conclusion is that deregulation strengthens the financial sector—the backbone of a healthy economy. The correct answer will directly address the conclusion. According to Choice *D*, no heavily regulated financial sector has ever been strong. Thus, it is the correct answer. Choice *A* is the next best answer, since deregulation allows capital to flow more freely, which facilitates business growth and decreases unemployment. However, it is more attenuated than Choice *D*. Choices *B* and *E* are irrelevant as to how deregulation impacts the economy. Choice *C* is either also irrelevant, or it weakens the argument, since more competition could be seen as a positive development.

17. B: The argument concludes that soccer is the most popular sport in the world, as evidenced by the World Cup's record-breaking viewership, due to its minimal economic cost. Negating the dependent assumption will undermine that reasoning. If nobody who plays the game is a soccer fan, then minimal economic cost cannot be the reason behind its popularity. Thus, Choice *B* is the correct answer. Choice *A* is unsupported by the argument and irrelevant to its reasoning. The author would almost certainly agree with Choices *C* and *E*, but the argument does not depend on either being true. Choice *D* is the second-best answer choice; however, it is weaker than Choice *B* since it is too broad, claiming economic cost is the *most* important factor in determining *every* sport's popularity.

18. C: The factory in question employs more than two thousand people, and according to the passage's third sentence, only widget factories employ more than one thousand employees. Thus, the factory must be a widget factory, and Choice *C* is correct. Although the factory is privately owned, the second clause of the second sentence states that nearly all widget factories are publicly owned; therefore, some widget factories could be privately owned. Choices *A* and *B* *could* be correct since the factory is a widget factory, and no widget factory is located in the Western Time Zone. However, neither answer choice *must* be true. Choice *D* misinterprets the meaning of the third sentence. Choice *E* is unsupported by the argument.

19. E: The passage states that for a tech start-up to survive, it must have more than one million dollars in initial investments, a compelling product, and it must release that product within twelve months of development. Based on the blind test, Jason has developed a compelling product, but he only has two hundred thousand dollars in initial investments. Furthermore, the product needs to hit the market within twelve months of its development, so time is of the essence. Choice *E* is the best answer choice, because Jason needs a larger initial investment to meet the threshold for survival. The other answer choices do not directly relate to a requirement for a start-up's survival.

20. D: The argument concludes that Samantha will be attending the college's English doctorate program, since winning the poetry contest awarded her admission. The argument is confusing a necessary and sufficient condition. Admission into a graduate program is a necessary condition to attend a program, but admission alone is not sufficient to mean a candidate is actually attending the program. Thus, Choice *D* is the correct answer. The author does not fail to define an important term or overstate any evidence, so Choices *A* and *C* are incorrect, respectively. Choice *B* is also incorrect. The only authority cited is Samantha's English professor, and that is an appropriate appeal, considering the professor's professional expertise and knowledge. The third sentence appears to be circular reasoning, but after close examination, it makes sense logically. Being taught by a talented poet would increase a student's gift for poetry; therefore, Choice *E* is incorrect.

21. B: The conclusion is that Thomas Edison's genius surpasses the popular association with inventing the electric light bulb. As evidence, the argument cites Edison's unprecedented application of business principles, development of an advanced electric grid, and other historic inventions. Choice *B* best describes this sentiment. The other answer choices are either premises or statements that the author would agree with, but they fail to include how common knowledge undervalues Edison's legacy.

22. C: The politician and police chief strongly disagree about terrorism. The politician believes that terrorists are unleashing carnage, and therefore, the country should pass harsher laws that prioritize national security over civil liberties. In contrast, the chief of police believes that gun violence is a bigger threat than terrorism, so the country should reconsider the balance between the right to bear arms and protecting citizens. Although the two disagree about what is the bigger threat, both would agree with rebalancing citizens' rights to better protect Americans. Thus, Choice *C* is the correct answer. The politician would likely disagree with Choice A, while the police chief would likely disagree with Choices B, D, and E.

23. D: The correct answer will fail to explain why alligator attacks are increasing when their population is decreasing. Choice A explains the apparent paradox, since the construction of homes near swampland would increase the number of encounters between humans and alligators. Choice B would also increase the number of encounters between humans and alligators, even if the alligator population was declining. Similarly, Choice C would explain the increased attacks since hunting would also increase those encounters. Choice E would explain why attacks from alligators are increasing, despite the declining wild population, since the law allows people to own them as pets. Unlike the other answer choices, the breeding of alligators in zoos does not explain why the number of attacks have increased. Thus, Choice D is the correct answer.

24. B: The activist's conclusion is that all drugs should be legalized, and all of the premises involve saving money. If legalizing drugs did not save the government money, then the reasoning would be severely harmed. Choice B asserts that legalizing drugs would raise government healthcare expenditures. This undermines the activist's argument that legalizing drugs will save money. Thus, Choice B is the correct answer. Choice A looks appealing, but the activist does not mention reducing drug use as a reason to legalize drugs. The number of drug users could increase, and the activist's argument would be the exact same—government savings justify legalization. Choices C and D are irrelevant. Choice E strengthens the argument by adding an alternative reason—other than just financial savings—to justify legalization.

25. E: The conclusion that automation caused unemployment in the manufacturing industry is based on the correlation between that decline and increased automation. The dependent assumption will tighten the correlation, and like all dependent assumptions, if it were negated, the reasoning would fall apart. If the manufacturing industry does not use automation, then it cannot be the cause of unemployment in the manufacturing industry. Thus, Choice E is the correct answer. Choices A, B, and D are irrelevant since they do not address automation's impact on unemployment. Choice C merely restates the conclusion; it is not a dependent assumption.

Section II: Analytical Reasoning

1. D: Choice D does not violate any of the conditions. Exactly two of the Thomas, Armando, and Beatrice trio (Thomas and Armando) are selected, so the first condition is satisfied. Both George and Sara are selected and so is William, so the second condition is satisfied. Natasha and Pablo are not in this lineup, so the third and fourth condition are not relevant. The other answer choices all contain at least one incompatibility. In Choice A, with the selected group, William would also need to be chosen to satisfy the second condition, but the team is already maxed out at five members, making this incorrect. Choices B and C both contain Thomas and Natasha, who are incompatible according to condition four. Lastly, Choice E violates the first condition since we can't have all three students Armando, Thomas, and Beatrice; we can only have two.

2. B: Pablo and Armando cannot both be selected because it would violate conditions one and three. If Pablo is chosen, then Beatrice is not (rule 3), which means that Thomas and Armando are according to the first rule (since two of the three students: Armando, Thomas, and Beatrice are). But if Natasha is selected, according to the fourth condition, neither Thomas nor Sara are chosen. We need Thomas if Pablo is chosen so Pablo and Natasha are an incompatible pair. The other four choices cannot be proven to break the provided rules so they cannot be definitively eliminated.

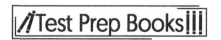

3. A: This question is actually quite simple because conditions around selecting Natasha are spelled out in the fourth provided: if Natasha is chosen, neither Thomas nor Sara are selected. Therefore, we can immediately rule out Choices *B* and *C*, because these options each contain one of those debate members. This fourth condition also helps us directly find the correct answer, using condition one. We know Thomas is not chosen if Natasha is and the first condition tells us that two of the three students out of Beatrice, Armando, and Thomas are chosen. If Thomas is not, then the other two are, making Choice *A* the correct option. There is not enough information to prove Choices *D* or *E*.

4. E: This question asks test takers to consider the scenario where both Armando and Thomas are chosen to represent the team and then, if so, determine which of the provided pair of students could, consequently, not be selected. The first stated condition in the problem asserts that of Armando, Thomas, and Beatrice, only two are chosen. Since this question is having us imagine that both Armando and Thomas are chosen, we know Beatrice is not. This tells us that we are looking for an answer choice that includes Beatrice, so that eliminates Choices *B* and *C*. The last provided condition stipulates that if Natasha is selected, neither Thomas nor Sara are chosen, which means that Natasha and Thomas cannot both be picked. Here, since we know that Thomas *is* selected, we can eliminate the possibility that Natasha is chosen and therefore, she joins Beatrice to form the pair that can't be selected, which makes the correct answer *E*.

5. C: There is nothing in the conditions that keeps Pablo from being selected, so Choice *A* doesn't have to be true. There is nothing in the conditions that would force Natasha to be selected, so Choice *B* also doesn't have to be true. The same can be said for Choices *D* and *E*. In Choice *C* if Beatrice isn't selected then that means that Armando and Thomas had to be. This leaves 3 spots to fill and 4 people. We can rule out Natasha since she can't be with Thomas. This means that the team must be Armando, Thomas, George, William, and Pablo.

6. B: There can't be more than 3 students who scored a B on the exam. The information provided says that Silvia scored an 84. It also says that she scored higher than Kaleb and Denzel. From this it can be determined that Kaleb and Denzel scored between a 62 and an 84. This means that they could have made a B. Javier scored a 90 and Sadie scored higher than him. Also Kris scored higher than Sadie, and Fiona made a 95. This means that only Silvia, Kaleb, and Denzel could score make a B.

7. E: Based on the information given, Denzel lower than Silvia, but scored higher than David. David scored a 62 and Silvia scored an 84. This means that Denzel had to score somewhere in between. This makes Choice *E* the only possible answer.

8. C: Choice *A* is not true because it is given that Javier scored lower than Sadie and he scored a 90. This means Sadie scored higher than a 90 and scored higher than Silvia. Choice *B* could be true but doesn't have to be true. The only thing that can be determined is that both Denzel and Chris scored higher than David, but lower than Silvia. Their relationship to each other can't be determined. Choice *D* is false because could have scored as low as a 63. It is only known that he scored higher than David's 62. Choice *E* is false because it is known that Javier scored a 90 and Denzel scored lower than Silvia's 84. This leaves only Choice *C* to be true. Kris scored lower than Fiona's 95, but higher than everyone else, including Sadie who scored higher than Javier.

9. D: It can be determined that Sadie scored higher than Javier but lower than Kris. Kris scored the 2nd best behind Fiona. No one else scored higher than Javier. This means that only Kris and Fiona scored higher than Sadie. This leaves the other 5 students scoring lower than her. So, Choice *D* is the correct answer.

10. E: The student's exams were handed back from lowest grade to highest grade. It is stated that David was first, Silvia was 4th, and Fiona was last. From this information, choices *A*, *B*, and *C* can all be eliminated as Silvia is not listed as 4th. Choice *D* can be eliminated because it is stated that only Fiona scored higher than Kris. This leaves choice *E*, which has the students listed in a possible correct solution.

11. D: The best approach for this problem is to systematically evaluate each answer choice against the provided conditions and eliminate those answers that violate a rule. We know there are two films chosen per genre. Combining this stipulation with the other stated conditions allows several conclusions to be made. Since the drama movies Gold Rush and Hollywood Front are mutually exclusive according to the last rule, the other drama film—Fender Bender—must be shown in all cases. For the comedies, if Nearly Wed is shown, then so is Orca Splash. Mr. Funny Bone and Nearly Wed cannot both be shown, since this would violate the third condition, and therefore, Orca Splash *must* be played. For action films, according to the first rule, we know that either Xander Falls or Yellowstone Takeover must be played fifth. Choice *A* is incorrect because it contains Newly Wed but not Orca Splash, so it violates the third condition. It also is an incompatible order according to the fourth condition because Xander Falls must be played before Mr. Funny Bone when both of those movies are screened. Choice *B* violates the last rule because it includes both Gold Rush and Hollywood Front. Choice *C* violates the sixth condition because neither Orca Splash nor Mr. Funny Bone is first. Choice *E* violates the fifth condition, because Westwood Hunt must be shown immediately before Hollywood Front if both are shown. Choice *D* does not violate any conditions so it is a plausible order.

12. C: After plugging in the new information given in this question, a few points are discovered. According to the fourth condition, when Mr. Funny Bone is first, Xander Falls cannot be shown because it would have to be played prior to Mr. Funny Bone (and that wouldn't be possible when Mr. Funny Bone is first). Therefore, Choice *A* is incorrect. Ruling out Xander Falls is also a helpful piece of information because it means the other two action films—Yellowstone Takeover and Westwood Hunt—have to be shown. Additionally, according to the first rule, since Xander Falls is out, Yellowstone Takeover must be screened fifth. According to the second condition, when Mr. Funny Bone is played, Gold Rush is not shown, so Choice *B* is incorrect, and the two dramas must be Fender Bender and Hollywood Front. According to the fifth condition, Westwood Hunt must immediately precede Hollywood Front when both films are selected. Choice *D* is not possible because Hollywood Front cannot be second because if Mr. Funny Bone is shown first. The earliest it could be played in the lineup is third. This is because Westwood Hunt would need to be shown before it. Finally, Choice *E* is incorrect because Nearly Wed cannot be in the same lineup as Mr. Funny Bone because according to the third condition, when Nearly Wed is played, so is Orca Splash. Thus, two comedies are already selected, which poses an incompatibility. Choice *C* works because Westwood Hunt can be played either second or third without violating any of the conditions.

13. A: Some of the information needed to answer this question has been previously discovered through analyzing the prior two questions. For example, the previous question revealed that it is not necessary to have Gold Rush in the lineup, so Choice *B* can be eliminated. For the other answer choices, the possible permutations should be amalgamated and tested. Hollywood Front does not appear in the following valid lineup: Orca Splash, Nearly Wed, Fender Bender, Gold Rush, Xander Falls, and then Yellowstone Takeover. This means that Choice *D* is incorrect. Choices *C* and *E* can be eliminated because it is possible to have a lineup that omits both Mr. Funny Bone and Westwood Hunt while still adhering to the conditions. This would include, in order, Orca Splash, Fender Bender, Hollywood Front, Nearly

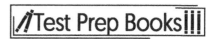

Wed, Yellowstone Takeover, and Xander Falls. It is not possible to combine movies in accordance to the conditions without including Orca Splash, so Choice *A* is the only correct choice.

14. B: Because Nearly Wed is not shown, Mr. Funny Bone and Orca Splash have to be. Again, because Mr. Funny Bone is shown, Gold Rush is not or it would violate the second condition. Thus, Fender Bender and Hollywood Front have to be shown. If Yellowstone Takeover is not played, then Xander Falls and Westwood Hunt must be. According to the fourth rule, because Mr. Funny Bone and Xander Falls are both shown, Xander Falls has to be shown prior to Mr. Funny Bone, and since Xander Falls or Yellowstone Takeover must be fifth (but Yellowstone Takeover is out), Xander Falls must be fifth, and Mr. Funny Bone must then be sixth. Lastly, the fifth rule states that if Westwood Hunt and Hollywood Front are both shown, Westwood Hunt must be shown right before Hollywood Front. This information leaves two possible permutations: 1. Orca Splash, Fender Bender, Westwood Hunt, Hollywood Front, Xander Falls, and Mr. Funny Bone or 2. Orca Splash, Westwood Hunt, Hollywood Front, Fender Bender, Xander Falls, and Mr. Funny Bone.

15. C: As found in the second question, Mr. Funny Bone has critical relationships with several other movie options. Choices *A* and *B* can be eliminated because with the second condition, if Mr. Funny Bone is played, Gold Rush is out. We need two dramas so both Fender Bender and Hollywood Front must be shown. Choice *C* is correct because if Mr. Funny Bone is played second, Orca Splash must be played first according to the sixth condition. This means that Newly Wed can't be shown since both comedy slots are already accounted for. Now we know that Orca Splash is first and Mr. Funny Bone is second, so in accordance with the fourth condition, Xander Falls cannot be shown. This is because Xander Falls would have to be shown before Mr. Funny Bone (if they are to both be played) and the first two slots are already taken. That means that Westwood Hunt and Yellowstone Takeover must be played since we need two action films and Xander Falls is out. Therefore, Choices *D* and *E* are invalid.

16. C: This question was best tackled by considering each answer choice and systematically running through each condition with that choice, to identify any incompatibilities that would render the answer invalid. The first condition is somewhat complicated, so in the interest of saving time on the exam, it's best to skip it initially. The second condition appears to be the simplest, so it's a good place to start: cookies must be made second or sixth. The sixth condition says that the breads are made either directly before or after the cookies. The third condition ties into the second one because it informs us that it's either doughnuts, then two unknowns, and then cookies, or cookies, two unknowns, and then doughnuts (D __ __ C or C __ __ D). Therefore, doughnuts must be made third or fifth. The first and fourth rules are difficult to consider in isolation so it's better to consider them in the context of each question. As discussed, the third condition states that the order slots for the cookies and doughnuts must be separated by two other baked goods, so you can eliminate Choice *A*. Choice *B* is incorrect because according to the fifth condition, doughnuts cannot be made before both the pastries and the tarts. The sixth condition dictates that the breads must be made right before or right after the cookies, so Choice *D* is incorrect. Choice *E* can be eliminated because it contradicts the fourth rule by placing the tarts before the breads in the lineup. Choice *C* is correct because it is a viable order.

17. D: Choice *A* can be eliminated off the bat because the prior question discovered that breads could be made fifth. Choice *B* can be eliminated because pastries can be a viable choice for the fifth slot. If pastries are made fifth, eclairs must be made third, cookies must be sixth, and bread has to be last. This means that muffins must be made before doughnuts since the breads are made after the tarts. Therefore, muffins must be made first or second and eclairs must be made fourth. The fifth condition dictates that tarts cannot be fourth, but must be first or second, so a possible order with pastries occupying the fifth slot is muffins, tarts, doughnuts, eclairs, pastries, cookies, then breads. Choice *C* can

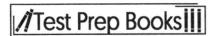

be ruled out by using the same logic as that for Choice *B*. A viable option with tarts as the fifth treat is: pastries, muffins, doughnuts, eclairs, tarts, cookies, then breads. Choice *E* places eclairs fifth. The conditions given do not place many restraints on eclairs, so this is a possible position, and therefore, an incorrect choice. If eclairs are made fifth, doughnuts cannot be fifth. As determined in the previous question, doughnuts must be fifth or third and if we are assuming eclairs are fifth, doughnuts are, by default, third. That means cookies are sixth (because of the second condition) and breads are seventh (because of the last condition). Muffins can now not be made after doughnuts because breads are last and this would otherwise violate the fourth condition. Therefore, muffins must be made first or second and either tarts or pastries would have to be fourth. So, there are multiple possibilities for the order with eclairs as fifth but one is: muffins, pastries, doughnuts, tarts, eclairs, cookies, and breads. Choice *D* is the correct answer because muffins cannot be made fifth because then cookies would be sixth and breads would be last. However, this would put doughnuts before muffins. This is only permissible (according to the fourth condition) when breads are made before tarts, which cannot happen if breads are made last.

18. E: This is a tricky question because it requires the test taker to essentially try working through each answer choice to determine if there are multiple permutations that are possible, which would then render that choice incorrect. Choice *A* is invalid because breads and tarts can be made third and sixth, respectively, with two plausible orders: eclairs, cookies, breads, pastries, doughnuts, tarts, and muffins or pastries, cookies, breads, eclairs, doughnuts, tarts, and muffins. Choice *B* is also incorrect. If pastries are made first and cookies are made sixth, there are several viable orders: pastries, muffins, doughnuts, eclairs, tarts, cookies, and breads; pastries, muffins, tarts, eclairs, cookies, and breads; and pastries, eclairs, doughnuts, muffins, breads, cookies, and tarts. Choice *C* is incorrect because it would also not provide sufficient information to definitively solve the puzzle. If muffins are made second and tarts are fourth, then doughnuts must be third and pastries must be first. Cookies must be sixth, but the breads can be fifth or seventh, and eclairs can also be fifth or seventh, which mean there are two choices and thus, this is an incorrect answer. If breads are made third and eclairs are fourth, then cookies must be made second and pastries have to be made first. This means doughnuts have to be made fifth, but muffins can then be made sixth or seventh and so can tarts. Therefore, Choice *D* is incorrect. Lastly, if muffins are made sixth and pastries are made first, then cookies must be made second (according to the second rule), the breads have to be made third (according to the last condition), and doughnuts must be fifth, according to the third rule. Because doughnuts are made fifth and pastries are first, tarts have to be made seventh, according to the fourth and fifth conditions. This leaves the fourth slot open, which can only be filled with eclairs. Therefore, there is only one possible lineup, so this is the correct answer.

19. E: Before individually trying to work through the potential slots in which muffins could be made, it's prudent to compare the answer choices for similarities and differences as a time-saving technique. For example, all choices include muffins as first and seventh, so these can be assumed to be true and therefore, it's unnecessary to work through the details for how these positions are viable. Choice *A* is the only one that is missing "second" as a potential spot, so it can also be considered an outlier and an unlikely option, tabled for later if necessary. Four of the five choices also include muffins as the sixth treat made, so that slot can also be temporarily ignored. The information garnered in the prior questions can also be applied to the answer choices. For example, in the second question of this set, it was found that muffins cannot be made fifth, so Choices *C* and *D* are incorrect. That means that the difference between the two remaining likely choices (Choices *B* and *E*) is whether the muffins can be made fourth. In the first question of the set, it was found that muffins could be fourth (pastries, eclairs, doughnuts, muffins, breads, cookies, tarts), so Choice *B* is missing that option and therefore, is incomplete and incorrect. That leaves Choice *E* as the correct choice.

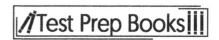

20. C: This question is again best solved by trying to apply each condition against each answer choice. Although only a partial order is mandated, it is necessary to deduce the entire order in several cases to fully evaluate the conditions. If breads, cookies, and muffins fill the first, second, and third slots respectively, then muffins are made before doughnuts. In accordance with the first rule, when muffins are made before doughnuts, breads must be made after tarts, which would not be the case. This means that the partial order presented in Choice *A* is not possible. A triad of pastries, tarts, and doughnuts violates the sixth condition because both pastries and tarts would precede doughnuts. Therefore, Choice *B* is incorrect. Choice *C* is correct. If cookies, breads, and tarts fill the second, third, and fourth slots respectively, then doughnuts must be made fifth. According to the fourth rule, since tarts are made after breads, muffins must be made after doughnuts, and rule five dictates that pastries must be made after doughnuts, so eclairs must be made first. Therefore, this is a plausible option because the lineup could be eclairs, cookies, breads, tarts, doughnuts, and then either pastries and then muffins, or muffins and then pastries. Choice *D* is also invalid. If muffins, doughnuts, and tarts are made fourth, fifth, and sixth respectively, then muffins are made before doughnuts. This necessitates that breads are supposed to be made after the tarts according to the first rule, but breads cannot be made seventh because they have to be just before or after cookies (according to the last condition), which would be second. Lastly, the order in Choice *E* is also not possible. When breads, cookies, and muffins fill the fifth, sixth, and seventh slots, muffins are made after doughnuts, which, according to the fourth conditions, would mean that breads have to be made before tarts, which would be impossible since the only available slot left for tarts would be before breads.

21. A: We know that no shelf can have all three of the electric guitars. The second condition states that the Fender is located on the shelf directly above the one that the Lyle is on. Therefore, there are two possibilities: The Fender could be displayed on Shelf #1 and the Lyle would then be on Shelf #2, or the Fender could be displayed on Shelf #2 and the Lyle would then be on Shelf #3. In accordance with the fourth condition, the Jackson and the Lyle cannot occupy the same shelf, so in the first option (when the Lyle is on Shelf #2), the Jackson cannot be on Shelf #2 and in the second option, the Jackson cannot be on Shelf #3. The Kustom can't be on Shelf #2 in either Fender/Lyle option in accordance to the first rule. In this question, because the Gibson and Harmony are on Shelf #2 and we know that not all three electric guitars can inhabit the same shelf, we know we are working with the first of the two options (the Fender on Shelf #1 and the Lyle on Shelf #2) because the Fender cannot also be on Shelf #2. This means that the Fender would be on Shelf #1 and the Gibson, Lyle, and Harmony would be on Shelf #2. Therefore, Choice *A* is correct.

22. B: This question has a simple solution. We know that the Jackson and Lyle cannot be on the same shelf. This means that the Lyle has to be on shelf 1 or 3. If the Lyle is on shelf 1 then it can't satisfy the stipulation that the Fender must be directly above it. This means that the Lyle would have to be on shelf 3 in this scenario and that the Fender would have to be on shelf 2. This makes *B* the correct answer.

23. C: Again, in this problem, the first option for the Fender/Lyle pair must be used (the Fender on Shelf #1 and the Lyle on Shelf #2) because in the second option, there would be an acoustic guitar on Shelf #3, and we were given that there are no acoustic guitars on Shelf #3. In the Fender on Shelf #1 and the Lyle on Shelf #2 option, neither the Jackson nor the Kustom can be displayed on Shelf #2. The Jackson and the Kustom are acoustic guitars, so they cannot be on Shelf #3. These two guitars are also not permitted on Shelf #2 because according to the first condition, the Kustom cannot be on Shelf #2 and the fourth rule states that the Jackson cannot be on the same shelf as the Lyle, and the Lyle has already been placed on Shelf #2. Therefore, the Jackson and the Kustom are both on the same shelf: Shelf #1.

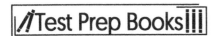

24. C: In this question, we are looking for the one choice that is not true. Again, we need to use our two options for the Fender/Lyle duo; only the second option is possible in this case, because the in the first option, the Fender must be displayed on Shelf #1, but this question specifically adds the condition that Shelf #1 must remain empty. That relegates us to use the option where the Fender is on Shelf #2 and the Lyle is on Shelf #3. Next, we need to figure out where the other guitars can or cannot go. In the Fender/Lyle positioning selected, the Jackson cannot go on Shelf #3 because the Lyle is there, and obviously, it can't go on Shelf #1, so it has to go on Shelf #2. According to the first rule, the Kustom cannot be on Shelf #2, and it can't be on Shelf #1 in this problem, so it must be on Shelf #3. The Gibson and Harmony are trickier to place. According to the third rule, they cannot go on Shelf #2 because the Fender is already there. They could potentially go together on Shelf #3 or get split up with either occupying Shelf #2 and the other on Shelf #3. At this point in the analysis, it probably makes sense to evaluate each answer choice systematically to see if any of them are definitely impossible. Choice A has the Harmony and Fender on the same shelf. As just mentioned, this is possible when we split up the Gibson and Harmony and put one on Shelf #2 (the Harmony, in this case, because that's where the Fender is) and one on Shelf #3. Therefore, Choice A is a viable option. In Choice B, exactly three guitars are on the same shelf—an arrangement we know is permissible as just demonstrated in Choice A (where Shelf #2 had the Fender, Harmony, and Jackson and Shelf #3 had the Gibson, Lyle, and Kustom). Choice C only permits two guitars on Shelf #3. The Lyle and the Kustom must be on Shelf #3, so that means no other guitars would be allowed there. This would force the Gibson and the Harmony on to Shelf #2 with the Fender, which violates the third condition because it puts all three electric guitars on one shelf. Therefore, Choice C is not workable and thus, it is the correct answer. It is still helpful to check the remaining two choices. Choice D has the Gibson and Harmony on the same shelf. This is possible, as discussed, as long as they are both on Shelf #3 and not Shelf #2. It was already determined that the Kustom must be on Shelf #3. The Gibson is also allowed on Shelf #3, with or without accompaniment of the Harmony, so Choice E is also valid.

25. A: This one is actually somewhat simple. Due to the fact that the Fender must be directly above the Lyle, we know that the two shelves used must be consecutive. Shelf 2 can't be left open. The other four answer choices have the ability to be true or false. For choice B, the Kustom could be on Shelf #1 or Shelf #3, and the Lyle could be on Shelf #2 or Shelf #3. The same concept holds true for Choice C. It is possible for one of the shelves to end up holding four guitars, but it is also possible to come up with a scenario where each of the two shelves hold three guitars. This means Choice D doesn't have to be true. The Harmony has no restrictions on where it must be placed. So, it could end up on any of the 3 shelves as long as it isn't with the other two electric guitars. So, Choice E is incorrect.

Section III: Logical Reasoning

1. E: Olga argues that most people would not know the exact population of their hometown. She also argues that it wouldn't be necessary to collect that information. Instead, she says that the question should be generalized to ask what range their hometown falls in to. Choices A and C are wrong because they say the exact opposite of this. Choices B and D are wrong because this isn't referring to any sensitive information.

2. D: She has the same stance as Damien on return policies. She just continues to elaborate on why stores should have generous return policies. Choices B, C, and E are all wrong because they mention Erin disagreeing with Damien, and this isn't the case. Choice A is close but doesn't describe exactly what Erin is saying, so it is wrong too.

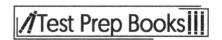

3. A: While any of these scenarios could potentially be true, the only one that supports Margaret's thoughts about her dog knocking it over is choice *A*. All of the other choices would support a different hypothesis.

4. B: Nancy takes a stance that is opposite of Mimi. She argues that the little coffee shop wasn't shut down due to the big chain coffee shop. She says that it was due to the owner not making good business decisions by not opening until 10 am. She even goes on to say that there are plenty of other thriving small businesses in the town and that people there love to support local business when they can.

5. D: Based on what each of them said it can be assumed that Carol is willing to take more risks with her investments. She is will to invest in the riskier real estate while Kenny isn't. Choice *A* is wrong because she is not the one who is risk averse. Kenny is not willing to take the risk on real estate even though the payout can be sizable. This makes Choice *B* wrong. Carol thinks that real estate is worth the risk, which makes Choice *C* wrong. Finally, Kenny mentions that he would invest in utilities or bonds over real estate but mentions nothing about stocks, which are considered riskier than bonds or utilities.

6. C: This would seem to most closely align with Karen's stance because she states that "Not all screen time is bad." She then goes on to explain why she feels that way. From this we can assume that she would agree with a reasonable amount of screen time per day, like 1-2 hours. Choices *A* and *B* are incorrect because they argue both extremes of the spectrum. Choice *D* is wrong because it is talking about reading. Finally, Choice *E* is wrong because neither of them say that toddlers should be left alone.

7. C: The best answer is Choice *C*. This choice shows a viable argument of the passage, that there is a downside to keeping Lucy's fossils isolated and out of public viewing. Choice *A* agrees with the passage in saying that the fossils are at risk for damage. Choice *B* gives information about the refusal to exhibit the fossils, but does not argue in opposition of the argument that it is good that casts were used instead. Choice *D* forces a neutral/uncaring position and does not take an opposing stance. Choice *E* gives information on Lucy's age and how she possibly died, but does not take a stance in opposition of the argument.

8. E: The best answer is Choice *E*. This choice backs the argument that the proper audience to appeal to would be the decision makers of the proposal. Choice *A* is incorrect. This choice most justifies the opinion of Dyson. Choice *B* is incorrect because it is irrelevant to the argument of who the argument's audience is. Choice *C* is another choice that backs the statement of Dyson. The students would be who the proposal directly affects, and Myers disagrees that the proposal should appeal directly to them. Finally, Myers thinks that the proposal *should* appeal to the administrators' sense of ethical obligation, so Choice *D* is incorrect.

9. D: The best answer is Choice *D*. Martinez provides the evidence that "a physician can only be accused of wrongful death if it is deemed that a misdiagnosis would not have been overlooked by a competent physician." This undermines Hynson's statement that families "who sue hospitals for wrongful death due to misdiagnosis are searching for someone to blame." If physicians are sued for wrongful death because they are incompetent, it discredits Hynson's argument that physicians are sued because the families want someone to blame.

10. C: Gwin and Chambal disagree over whether it is a good idea for another playhouse to come to Hillview. Choice *A* does not come up in the argument, whether or not the plays were inferior, so it is incorrect. They would most likely agree with Choice *B*; both apparently think it is *possible to determine* the cultural feeling in Hillview; they just disagree over what that cultural feeling is. Choice *D* is incorrect. There is no talk of any other cultural spaces in Hillview. Finally, Choice *E* is incorrect. The two don't disagree over whether or not playhouses can close due to insufficient cultural feeling, but over whether the playhouse in Hillview closed due to insufficient cultural feeling.

11. A: Choice *A* is the best answer. Choice *B* is incorrect. Haas states the goal of the project, and Burgess does not disagree over that goal. Choice *C* is also incorrect. We are not sure if Haas would think leaving any area without quality food would be a failure. We only know that he thinks leaving 165 areas without food deserts is considered a failure. Choice *D* is incorrect. The two would agree that there were no quality foods in any areas considered to be food deserts before the project began. Finally, Choice *E* is incorrect. Both would agree that 165 areas still do not have access to quality food.

12. B: Choice *B* is the best answer. The passage fails to consider millennial behavior outside of the corporate environment, and is limiting altruism to that within corporate life. Choices *A*, *C*, *D*, and *E* are inconsistent with the article's statements and do not describe flaws in the argument.

13. E: Choice *E* is the best answer. The argument commits the *post hoc* fallacy, which mistakes correlation for causation. The argument states that the plants must be white in color because they have been grown in a CO2-rich environment, but the argument doesn't take into consideration that the mushrooms could be white for other reasons, such as a lack of sun.

14. D: Those who have runner's high will experience euphoria as well as a higher pain tolerance. Choice *A* is incorrect. The argument does not say that euphoria is almost always caused by the act of running. Choice *B* is incorrect. The argument contends that biochemical reactions can be caused by strenuous exercise, but it does not necessarily say that "most" reactions are caused by exercise. Choice *C* is incorrect. The argument doesn't state that long-distance runners have a higher pain tolerance than the average person, but that those who experience runner's high will have a higher pain tolerance than the average person. Finally, Choice *E* is incorrect. The average person could experience euphoria in other ways than having a runner's high.

15. A: The argument is that Keaton is a better doctor than Bachman. We are then given the criteria of a good doctor: professional, empathetic, and attentive. We know that Keaton excels in two of these areas. Choice *A* tells us that Bachman excels in all three of these areas. Therefore, Choice *A* most seriously weakens the argument that Keaton is a better doctor than Bachman.

16. D: Making vaccination of children a requirement is considered utilitarianism because it is seen as an act of serving the majority of public good. Utilitarianism is an ethics system concerned with what's best for a majority. Utilitarianism ethics says that an action is morally right if the consequences lead to happiness, which is considered absence of pain. Utilitarianism's moral principles are always seen through the consequences of an action.

17. C: Texas A&M used to be seven rankings behind University of Texas. The argument is based on the conclusion that adding the faculty has not worked. Choice *C* proves that adding the faculty *has* worked. Choices *A* does not weaken the argument. If anything, it serves to uphold the argument that things generally aren't going too well for the English department at Texas A&M. Choice *B* is irrelevant. The fact that Texas A&M is older than University of Texas does not weaken or strengthen the argument in any way. Choice *D* is close. However, this would weaken the argument's premise, not its conclusion. Choice *E* is incorrect; this would not weaken the argument, because the department's staff doesn't have anything to do with the argument in question.

18. E: This line of reasoning follows the original argument exactly. The only difference is the order of information. However, the argument is still the same. Choice *A* is incorrect because after the word

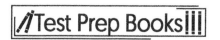

"therefore" the argument has a necessary condition in order for there to be insects that are helpful to humans and have three parts that doesn't exist in the original argument. Choice *B* is incorrect because the first part of the argument has the word "for" in it, which means that it logically follows that since most insects are helpful to humans then all insects have an exoskeleton and three parts, which is not true in the originally flawed argument. Choice *C* is incorrect because it adds the word "unless" to the conclusion which changes the meaning. Choice *D* is incorrect because the premise of the argument contradicts the conclusion, which does not happen in the original argument.

19. B: Whether a poem's cultivated feeling is more valuable than its literal meaning to readers. Choice *A* is incorrect because neither of the speakers mention anything about critics or what they should use. Choice *C* is incorrect because the aesthetics of a literal translation and a loose translation are not being compared—for all we know, Madison might agree that a loose translation's aesthetics is just as intact as a literal translation's. However, Madison thinks that the literal meaning is closer to the truth and thus more valuable than the cultivated feeling of the translation. Choice *D* is incorrect; the argument isn't setting up the original poem against the translation, but a literal translation against a loose translation. Choice *E* is incorrect because the value of translation work itself never comes into question.

20. A: it's still one of the most important: having abstract thought means an ability to apply one formula to many situations, thus developing empathy and an understanding for other abstract concepts such as ethics, love, and beauty. Choice *B* is incorrect because it expands on "practical concepts" rather than abstract thought, and abstract thought is the last-mentioned term in the sentence. Choice *C* is incorrect because the transition doesn't logically flow from the statement before. If we wanted to say that abstract thinking "isn't very important," the sentence would need to begin like this: "Not only is abstract thought *not* the only thing taught anymore in math . . . " instead of "But even though abstract thought isn't the only thing taught anymore in math . . . " Choices *D* and *E* are both incorrect. They are a stretch to connect to the sentence before it because they both discuss either geometry and algebra or algebra and technology, thus going off-topic.

21. D: Nida is protesting a pipeline in North Dakota due to the high risk of contamination of the surrounding aquifers. The pipeline is meant to carry 570,000 barrels of oil a day. Choice *A* is incorrect. Kyle would not use the above statement to support expanding job legislation. The statement is about health of the aquifers. Choice *B* is incorrect because, although the situation mentions aquifers, the main point of this answer is the danger of sinkholes. Choice *C* is incorrect, although it's close to a relevant scenario. Gabriella would be looking more toward how to conserve water, however, and the statement is more about the contamination of aquifers. Finally, Choice *E* is incorrect. Abram knows the springs aren't as clean and fresh as in previous generations, but this doesn't seem to bother him much, as he is content with the current state of the springs.

22. D: The argument draws its conclusion from data that cannot be proven true. This is the strongest criticism because the argument that this species of bird was different from modern birds was derived from the guess that it might have been able to fly from birth. Choice *A* is incorrect, as this is not true. Choice *B* is incorrect because there is no cause and effect relationship in the argument. Choice *C* is incorrect because there is no inconsistency from premise to conclusion, only a statement that the data cannot actually be proved true. Choice *E* is incorrect because if the possibility were true, it would most weaken the argument, but it's not known if immediate flight was a risk to the species.

23. B: It is better to get a second part-time job, even if it pays less, for a mental change. Although Jacqueline has some doubts throughout her reasoning, she eventually decides that she should get a second part-time job. Choice *A* is incorrect, although Jacqueline does consider this line of reasoning in

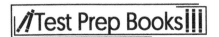

her argument. Choice *C* is incorrect; the thought of getting another full-time job never crosses Jacqueline's mind. Choice *D* is incorrect; although half of it is true, we don't know for sure that working on the weekends does not bother Jacqueline—she simply says she would be willing to do it. Choice *E* is incorrect because, although Jacqueline mentions having freedom, her reasoning does not conclude that having it is the most important thing in life.

24. C: The proof for the genetic factor in substance abuse lies in the fact that there may be indirect genes within families, such as depression or anxiety, that increase the potential use for substance abuse. Choices *A* and *E* are incorrect because it says in the statement that this sentiment is "up for debate." Choice *B* is incorrect; this statement would not be supported by the argument because the argument gives no indication that substance abuse is a learned behavior only. Choice *D* is incorrect because this is the opposite sentiment of what the passage states. The passage thinks the proof for genetic factors in substance abuse lies in the fact that depression and anxiety are characteristics of higher potential use of substance abuse. The arguer believes these are usually genetic factors, not environmental factors.

Section IV: Reading Comprehension

1. C: All the details in this paragraph suggest that Brookside is a great place to live, plus the last sentence states that it is an *idyllic neighborhood*, meaning it is perfect, happy, and blissful. Choices *A*, *B*, and *E* are incorrect because although they do contain specific details from the paragraph that support the main idea, they are not the main idea. Choice *D* is incorrect because there is no reference in the paragraph to the crime rate in Brookside.

2. B: A passage like this one would likely appear in some sort of community profile, highlighting the benefits of living or working there. Choice *A* is incorrect because nothing in this passage suggests that it is fictional. It reads as, if anything, non-fiction. Choice *C* is incorrect because it does not report anything particularly newsworthy, and Choice *D* is incorrect because it has absolutely nothing to do with a movie review. Choice *E* is incorrect because it does not seem like the type of information found in an encyclopedia, nor carry an encyclopedic tone or style.

3. D: In the first sentence, it states very clearly that the Brookside neighborhood is *one of the nation's first planned communities*. This makes it unique as many other neighborhoods are old, exist in Kansas City, have shopping areas, and have Tudor and Colonial homes. For these reasons, all the other answer choices are incorrect.

4. D: Passage A argues that the source of great poetry comes from emotions within, while passage B argues that great poetry is based off the skill and expertise of the poet. Choice *A* is incorrect; both passages attempt to explain how great poetry is created, not its aim or its results. The "purpose" passage A talks about are the author's individual poems, but the main idea of the passage is contained in the middle, starting with "For all good poetry." Choice *B* is incorrect; neither passages make any mention of nature or urban life. Choice *C* is incorrect; passage B does use epic poetry for most of its examples, but it is not solely concerned with epic poetry. It recalls Keats' "Ode to a Nightingale" at the very end. This is not the best answer choice. Finally, Choice *E* is incorrect; no mention of the ethics of the poet is involved in either passage, besides a brief mention of criterion in the beginning of passage B.

5. A: The author is explaining that the feelings portrayed in Keats' ode are brought forth and signified by the symbolism of the nightingale used within the language of the poem. Eliot is relating it back to the original point of the passage: that great poetry doesn't simply come from powerful emotion, but that it is that emotion coupled with the literary devices of the poet that makes great poetry. Some of the other choices have similar wording to the last sentence, but they are not the best answer choice.

6. C: That feelings from the past will accumulate into representations of thought. The poet is then responsible for putting these direct thoughts onto paper, creating a poem. Therefore, the original source of poetry is from the past feelings of the poet. This is explained by the author beginning with the sentence "For our continued influxes of feeling . . . " The author is very clear about feelings from the past accumulating into representations of thought, so all the other answer choices are incorrect.

7. B: The author of passage B argues that the effort put into a poem counts for more than the intensity of the emotion felt while writing the poem. Choice *A* is the opposite of what passage B argues. Choices *C* and *D* are more closely related to the ideas of passage A. Finally, Choice *E* comes directly from passage B. However, this isn't an explanation on how the authors differ in their views of poetry.

8. E: An apathetic sculptor can become successful. The main disagreement between the two passages is whether or not the creator's emotion is manifest in the work of art. The author of passage A would disagree that an apathetic sculptor could become successful. The author of passage B would say that if the sculptor is talented and the process of creating is intensive, the sculptor could become successful.

9. C: The passage is a critique of society, and explores the notion than an "advancement" of the human race is not possible—that a perceived strength gives way to another weakness. Choices *A* and *B* are incorrect. The author mentions Christianity as an example of the main point, and not the main point itself. Choice *D* is incorrect; the passage is not a critique of man's relationship with nature. Finally, Choice *E* is incorrect. The author mentions almanacs and libraries for the purpose of describing the civilized man, not to evaluate education.

10. A: The illusion of the civilized person is that they are both mentally and physically better off than the uncivilized person. The author would agree with this statement because the main critique of the passage is that society, even the civilized man in society, does not advance. Thus, Choices *B* and *C* are incorrect. Choice *D* is incorrect; we have no way of knowing the author's evaluation of the Stoic or the Christian. Finally, Choice *E* is incorrect; the author mentions transportation, but we do not have sufficient information to know if the author would agree with this statement.

11. D: A series of mini allegories are listed in order to show the reader the paradox of the civilized man—that civilization necessitates a certain kind of ignorance. The other answer choices have similar language to this section of the passage, but they are not the best answers. Choice *D* sets this section in the correct context of the passage.

12. B: The author thinks that simply because we've experienced technological growth as a society does not mean that we have greater men than Plutarch's heroes. The author does not think society capable of advancement—especially in a morally superior kind of way. However, he does acknowledge the growth in technology that society has experienced. Even so, the author does not believe that this growth has encouraged our superiority over past generations.

13. D: What are some examples that prove that the moral fiber of a society is not due to its scientific developments? The last paragraph most closely answers this question. Choice *A* is incorrect; though the paragraph mentions some classical heroes, it does not mention them for long nor does it speak much about their contributions to society. Choice *B* is incorrect. The paragraph explains more of how individuals explored and conquered the world *without* the use of machinery. Choice *C* is incorrect; this is

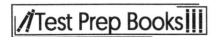

the opposite of what the paragraph is explaining. Finally, Choice *E* is incorrect. The paragraph does not designate a more advanced time period within history.

14. E: The narrator begins with a story to catch the reader's attention, slowly showing the narrator's dedication to the story. The passage ends with a foreshadowing of how the narrator plans to discover more about the given subject. Choice *A* is incorrect; there is no exploration of the cause of ice caves or the effects of ice caves. Choice *B* is incorrect; there is no problem/solution structure in the passage. Choice *C* is incorrect; the narrator does begin with a story. However, the narrator does not try to persuade the reader of anything at the conclusion of the passage. Choice *D* is incorrect; the narrator may employ logos throughout the story, but this isn't the best answer. The passage also uses pathos and ethos as well, so this answer choice is incomplete. Choice *E* is the best answer.

15. B: The narrator's sisters went to an ice cave, but did not have a ladder to get to the platform of ice. It explains this in the second paragraph: "the next year my sisters went to yet another, where, however, they did not reach the ice, as the ladder necessary for the final drop was not forthcoming." "Not forthcoming" here means not available. Thus, Choice *B* is correct.

16. C: The meaning of the word *patois* is *vernacular*, Choice *C*. Choice *A*, *penchant*, means fondness. Choice *B*, *despondency*, means depression or grief. Choice *D*, representation, is close to the correct answer. The words exchanged are representations of each other. However, it is not the *best* choice here. Choice *E*, repletion, means satiation or indulgence. The narrator is talking about the man's vernacular in this sentence.

17. A: The best answer here is Choice *A*—ice caves are mesmerizing natural features that are not explored enough by people. Choice *B* is incorrect. The author mentions nothing about requiring people to pay in order to get into ice caves for their preservation. Choice *C* is incorrect. Although the author mentions that they chilled wine in the cellar, we have no way of knowing if this would be the author's idea of a good business plan. Choice *D* is incorrect. The author expresses the opposite sentiment here, that ice caves *should* be explored. Finally, Choice *E* is incorrect. The author has not yet explored enough caves to make this assertion.

18. C: The author set out to write the passage in order to give a detailed account of the narrator's first time in an ice cave and the subsequent events that led to the narrator's desire for further exploration. Choice *A* is incorrect; this might be something the author would agree with, but it is not the main purpose in writing the passage. Choice *B* is incorrect. The author mentions nothing of the ice caves being in peril from advanced technology. Choice *D* is incorrect because the passage does not resemble a scientific article. Finally, Choice *E* is incorrect because, although the author mentions that a large cavern supplies a Geneva town with ice, the main purpose of the passage has nothing to do with economy.

19. D: The concept known as "Significant Form," where lines and colors combine with each other in a certain way, is the one quality all works of art have in common. In order to be considered in the class of "art," objects must have this aesthetic quality about them. The passage mentions emotion in relation to a work of art, but emotion is not considered the essential quality of a work of art. Thus, Choice *A* is incorrect. Choice *B* is incorrect. The region of the work of art's formation is not considered in this passage. Choice *C* is incorrect. The passage is not about how to become an art critic, although the value of lines and color is talked about. Finally, Choice *E* is incorrect. The passage designates the essential quality of a work of art, and does not dismiss it.

20. B: Draw a conclusion from the points raised in the first paragraph. The conclusion of the passage in the second paragraph is that "Significant Form" is the essential property all works of art have in

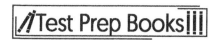

common. The first paragraph ponders on the effects of works of art and brings up points that would lead us to a conclusion of the cause of the works of art, which is Significant Form. The other answer choices do not represent this, and thus are incorrect.

21. E: What is the one quality common to all works of art with the ability to provoke aesthetic emotion? The passage best answers this question. Choice *A* is incorrect; the topic of significant form would be the answer to the question asked, and not the initial question. Choice *B* is incorrect. The passage is not concerned with a quality within the artist, but with a quality within the work of art. Choice *C* is incorrect. The passage is not concerned with these particular places, but with a few specific examples of art from these places. Finally, Choice *D* is incorrect. The passage does not seek to explain the creative process.

22. B: Rhetorical questions. The author poses a series of rhetorical questions in the second paragraph as a way to present the conclusion: that significant form is the "quality common and peculiar to all members of this class." Choice *A*, metaphorical language, is absent in the second paragraph. Choice *C*, allusion, is an indirect passing reference, so this is incorrect. Choice *D*, parallelism, is a technique used wherein authors repeat the same beginning phrase of sentences. Choice *E*, juxtaposition, is two things placed together with a contrasting effect.

23. C: We talk foolishly. All of the answer choices are synonyms for the word "gibber." However, the author means that when we speak of "works of art," we are using that phrase too generously, as if any object were a "work of art," so therefore we are showing that we are ignorant, or foolish, over what a work of art actually is.

24. A: In every visual work of art that we consider to be of value, there must be some semblance of significant form—whether it is painting, sculpture, architecture, or pottery. Choice *B* is incorrect. The author concludes the concept of significant form *is* apparent in every type of great visual art. Choice *C* is incorrect. The aesthetic emotion does not precede the process of creation. Choice *D* is incorrect. The author does not say that a justification of a work of art lies in the way people speak about it. Finally, Choice *E* is incorrect. What makes a work of art a work of art, according to the author, is *significant form*.

Dear LSAT Test Taker,

We would like to start by thanking you for purchasing this study guide for your LSAT exam. We hope that we exceeded your expectations.

Our goal in creating this study guide was to cover all of the topics that you will see on the test. We also strove to make our practice questions as similar as possible to what you will encounter on test day. With that being said, if you found something that you feel was not up to your standards, please send us an email and let us know.

We have study guides in a wide variety of fields. If you're interested in one, try searching for it on Amazon or send us an email.

Thanks Again and Happy Testing!
Product Development Team
info@studyguideteam.com

FREE Test Taking Tips Video/DVD Offer

To better serve you, we created videos covering test taking tips that we want to give you for FREE. **These videos cover world-class tips that will help you succeed on your test.**

We just ask that you send us feedback about this product. Please let us know what you thought about it—whether good, bad, or indifferent.

To get your **FREE videos**, you can use the QR code below or email freevideos@studyguideteam.com with "Free Videos" in the subject line and the following information in the body of the email:

    a. The title of your product

    b. Your product rating on a scale of 1-5, with 5 being the highest

    c. Your feedback about the product

If you have any questions or concerns, please don't hesitate to contact us at info@studyguideteam.com.

Thank you!

Made in the USA
Coppell, TX
20 September 2022

83375906R00142